Alexei Mukhin

PHARAOH

Translated by Anastasia Naumenkova

ISBN: 978-1-7327687-1-0

Many people imagine their own Putin.
They discourse with the President in absentia,
and become seriously offended when
Putin does not conform to their vision of him...
Alexei Mukhin

CONTENTS

FROM PUBLISHER

Address to the academic community on the publication of "Pharaoh"

Dear Friends and Colleagues,

The discord between the United States and Russia, which has been destabilizing the livelihood of the world community, has in our opinion reached a critically alarming phase. Time has come to intercede the endless political conflict.

We are sure that the best way to extinguish the conflict is to help sides to better understand each other. As a result, the trustees of the Arts & Science Achievement Foundation, a non-profit organization founded in 1996, have decided to commence the publication of the literary series "People Who Changed the World". The series will be published from 2018 in both the United States and Russia. We will try to give people chance to see the other side objectively, putting aside the propaganda and conjectures that fill mass media these days.

Here we present for your consideration the first book of this new project – "Pharaoh" – written by the Russian historian and political scientist Alexei Mukhin.

"Pharaoh" provides not only the author's version of the evolution of the strong influence of Vladimir Putin on the Russian society, not only the genesis of his political growth and popularity, but also a microscopic analysis of those characteristics of the Russian president that are as greatly disfavored by his western partners as they are adored by the Russian public.

The author has attempted to answer the multitude of "why" questions while maintaining objectivity and, in our opinion, impartiality. He has presented the Russian understanding of those issues and problems that deeply concern those who study the interaction of the two great powers – Russia and the USA.

We hope that this work will be perceived by the academic community of the USA, Canada and Great Britain as a starting point for a great discussion with Russian experts.

The founders and trustees of the Arts & Science Achievement Foundation wish to express their deep gratitude to authors, experts, politicians and students, who devote themselves to the study of the Russian-American relations and request the submissions of manuscripts pertinent to the theme of the literary series "People Who Have Changed Our World" for publication in Russian on the territory of Russia.

Arts & Science Achievement Foundation - http://en.asafound.org/

INTRODUCTION

Even if Vladimir Putin were to disappear for some reason from the Russian political field, a lot would continue to be done in his name. Since the moment of his proclamation as the country's *"national leader"*, **Putin has transformed into a "folk hero"** along the lines of *Ilya Muromets*, the Russian epic legendary warrior, or *Aleksander Peresvet*, the warrior-monk who defeated the Tibetan champion warrior Chelubey in the inaugural Battle of Kulikovo against the Golden Horde's Khan Mamay in 1380, but fell in the contest.

It is interesting that **the image of a warrior-monk is exploited by Putin quite often**. That is why there is practically no information about his new marriage in the information field. Putin himself has declared that he is **"married to Russia"**.

Putin's practice of judo is a powerful factor towards enhancing his image in the eyes of the Russian population: the people intuitively perceive their President as a *protector*. The efforts of the Kremlin's political strategists are designed to deepen this impression.

The question *Who is Mr. Putin?* that was asked as early as the late 1990's and early 2000's, remains unanswered. Perhaps, it will remain unanswered for at least another ten to fifteen years.

Most likely, Vladimir Putin is a **political idealist and a philosophical pragmatist** who believes in his messianic mission to restore Russia's national sovereignty, which the country has been losing rampantly since the beginning of the 1990's. The key to restoring this sovereignty currently lies within the framework of the **Eurasian project**, which is turning into an analogue of the European Union in the post-Soviet space[1].

---

[1] Justification for the Eurasian Integration. Edited by A.A. Mukhin. Moscow: Algoritm, 2015, 223 pages.

The greater Eurasian project arose on the heels of the activation and dissemination of another Putin's project called the **"Russian world"**[2] . This ideologeme was used by the Kremlin to identify the Russian population "scattered" after the collapse of the Soviet Union throughout the post-Soviet republics and further abroad – in western, southern and eastern countries. The identification was to be followed by mobilization of the whole "Russian world" on the basis of the Russian cultural code mediated by the Russian language.

The current project of Eurasianism carries the inception of an **ideology**, a special form of worldview, which may serve for a significant portion of the Russian population as a method of defining their national identity at this new stage of historical development.

When conceptually defining Eurasianism, we should note that it is **a systematic view regarding the historically united territories of Europe and Asia that implies their balanced development**[3]. The timeliness of the new form of integration in the post-Soviet space is evident to the participants in the process. The collapse of the Soviet Union, committed forcibly and against the will of its population, had split up its economic infrastructure. This led to the disruption of the industrial and technological links between the regions and the overall downfall in the economies of the former Soviet republics.

Subsequent actions of the NATO countries only worsened the situation in and around Russia (e.g., the entry of the former Warsaw Pact countries into the Atlantic alliance, the construction of the joint European missile shield, supposedly to defend against Iranian missiles, etc.). As a result, with the objective of self-protection, the presidents of Russia and Kazakhstan (joined later by the president of Belarus) initiated the process

---

[2] According to the general concept, the "Russian world" should unite all those people, to whom the Russian language and culture are dear. On June 21, 2007, Putin signed a Decree on the creation of the Russian World Fund. The Fund's main goal is to promote and develop the cultural heritage of Russia, the study and popularization of the Russian language in the country and in the world. Vladimir Putin signed a Decree on creation of the Russian World Fund. President of Russia, 21.06.2007. http://kremlin.ru/events/president/news/40799

[3] This system of views emerged in the works of several historians of the 20th century (from Georgy Florovsky to Lev Gumilyov), but it did not become a part of the academic knowledge and, of course, was not included in the Soviet classical historiography.

of economic integration in the form of the Customs Union, raised the level of national security of these states in the form of the Collective Security Treaty Organization, and announced the modernization of the Russian Armed Forces. It was the latter factor, which, in our view, provoked the large-scale crisis in Ukraine, starting with the late 2013 coup d'état in Kiev.

Nevertheless, **political integration in the post-Soviet space proved to be difficult:** the leadership of other republics of the former USSR eyed the growth of Russia's influence in the post-Soviet space with considerable concern, fearing a full or partial loss of sovereignty. Nevertheless, the guarantees from Putin, which the leaders of the republics received and continue to receive, do not allow them to formalize their fears into real political claims.

The Western community, in the face of then Secretary of State Hillary Clinton and the German Chancellor Angela Merkel, reacted with similar anxiety to the attempts to organize the integration process on the former Soviet territory in the form of the Customs Union, as well as other processes within the framework of *the Eurasian project*. This, however, provided an additional supporting argument for the process initiators; as is well known, territorial integration proceeds faster under external pressure.

Vladimir Putin, who stood at the very center of these unfolding events, was consequently predictably "disciplined": the G8, the union of the self-proclaimed politically leading countries, turned into the G7 – Russia was expelled from the "Big Eight", which essentially *left the country with full latitude to* form its own regional center of influence. Another thing became obvious: the G7 countries inadvertently limited their influence on the economic and political processes in the Eurasian space and simultaneously stimulated the development of the G20 format[4].

Attempts to expel Russia (particularly Putin) from the latter format as well[5] exposed the existence of strong opposition to the initiatives of the

---

[4] As the global crisis unfolded, it was the G20 that became the leading official format for coordinating interstate relationships, testing and smoothing emerging conflicts. These twenty countries account for 90% of world GDP, 80% of the world trade and two thirds of the world's population. Initially, it was established as a working group (officially called the Group of Twenty Finance Ministers and Central Bank Governors) to hold negotiations between the seven developed countries with the developing countries on economic and financial problems arising from the crisis.

[5] Russia was expelled from the G8, is the G20 – next? Moskovsky Komsomolets.

U.S. and its G7 partners. In essence, **by trying to reduce Russia's influence the United States created their own problem out of thin air.** As a self-defense against this aggressive behavior, various countries began to develop their own financial transnational institutions as a counterweight to the International Monetary Fund (IMF) and the World Bank, and to duplicate the functions of the international institutions of the United Nations (UN) that had been weakened as a result of U.S. policy.

The international community began to regard Russia, among many things, as a country that can say "no" to the U.S., which is striving to maintain dominance over other countries. In fact, **Washington has achieved the opposite effect by its actions, having forged a rather strong counter-opposition** in the form of various regional alliances. In addition to Russia, these countries include Iran and Turkey. Complex but special relationship are being established between Putin and the leaders of both these countries, as well as China.

Russia's relationship with Europe is also developing in a complicated manner. Despite the attempts of the European media to present Russia as a mostly Asiatic country, the European community nevertheless recognizes it as its main partner with a European identity. This is no wonder, since geographically the Russian part of Europe is comparable in size with both the eastern and western parts of Europe. The division of Europe into the Western Europe and Eastern Europe with no regard for the European part of Russia, which stretches all the way to the Urals, was artificially imposed by the political geography of the 20th century. This "division" was intended to exclude Russia from the group of European countries. However, Russia's entrance into the Council of Europe *de facto* confirmed its status as a European country.

The rapid expansion under Putin of cooperation first with the European countries and then with the countries of Asia is a consequence of not only the intense cultural exchange between them, but also of objective trends of the global economy.

Russia's main trade and economic partner, the European Union, which is losing national sovereignty due to the increasing U.S. military presence

---

26.03.2014.   http://www.mk.ru/politics/article/2014/03/26/1003781-rossiyu-isklyuchili-iz-bolshoy-vosmerki-na-ocheredi-quotdvadtsatkaquot.html

in the European countries, currently exhibits slow rates of economic growth, strives to diversify its suppliers of energy resources, and actively invests in energy conservation and the search for alternative sources.

On the other hand, China has already become the world's largest energy consumer. In the short term, China's demand for energy resources will most likely increase, particularly in light of the *New Silk Road* project. It should be noted that under "peacetime" conditions **the nature of Russia's trade and economic pivot towards the eastern countries would be much slower and circumspect.** Yet by expanding the cooperation with Asian countries, the Russian leadership in the face of Putin is solving several strategic tasks at once.

First, Russia's economic security is being strengthened through the diversification of economic ties.

Second, the expansion will propel the development of the Russian Far East, whose natural resources, according to strategic documents, should form the basis for implementing highly profitable projects and creating vast new production facilities to produce and process high-tech products.

Third, by virtue of their relatively close geographic position, Russia and China share similar geopolitical challenges. For example, China is interested in providing security in the relatively troubled Xinjiang Uygur Autonomous Region, while one of the security priorities for Russia is to ensure stability in the countries of the Central Asian region, whose destabilization can negatively impact the security of its own borders.

Fourth, cooperation with Asian countries in high-tech industries is mitigating the consequences of the U.S. attempts to isolate Russia technologically. After Western countries imposed restrictions on the sale of high-tech products to Russia, some Russian companies that previously actively purchased these products found themselves on the brink of collapse. Expanding cooperation with Asian countries, primarily with China, which has achieved serious success in technological development, provided an immediate solution prior to the import substitution policy. Drawing further on these successes will allow Russia to avert the threat of deepening technological inferiority.

Fifth, the alliance of the actively developing BRICS countries (Brazil, Russia, India, China and South Africa) serves as a special factor and at the same time a mechanism for expanding the Russian-Chinese cooperation.

Nevertheless, in order to meaningfully cooperate with China, **Russia needs to boost its own industrial and trade potential.** Efforts in this direction are being made already. Thus, after implementing procedures for establishing economic cooperation and creating free trade zones (the EurAsEC and the Customs Union), Russia, Kazakhstan and Belarus turned towards gradual **comprehensive integration.** This trend is quite timely, as the expansion of China to the markets of Kazakhstan, for example, had acquired such an impressive scale as to cause concerns among the Kazakh leadership.

The main tasks facing the countries implementing the project of Eurasian integration are, of course, the **development of an effective regulatory framework** and the creation of **international legal standing.** Naturally, activities within the framework of the Eurasian project must meet the national interests of the member countries; the principle of respect for partners should be dominant. The partner countries will have to boost the industrial, technological, trade, scientific and cultural bases in order to be competitive against the countries united in other integration projects (the European Union, NATO, etc.).

A further step in this process is the formation of Eurasian elite groups, capable of acting jointly on the international arena and overcoming various forms of disunity, including religious ones. This is not about **rebuilding the USSR – the world has changed.** But it is quite realistic to generate fundamentally new political entities on an economic basis on the situs of the former Soviet Union, as Putin has repeatedly said[6]. Moreover, their

---

[6] Characterizing the integration processes of the Eurasian Economic Union (EEU), Putin said, "Our common market has worked as a kind of safety airbag, in spitshape." Putin: The integration processes of the EEU have worked as a safety airbag. Vzglyad. 14.04.2017 https://vz.ru/news/2017/4/14/866315.html

"When working out the Strategy for the Economic Development of Russia, we, of course, take account of the trends that take place in the world, and intend to use the global technology shifts, the formation of new markets, the integration and cooperation opportunities in the interests of our own development." A plenary session of the St.-Petersburg International Economic Forum. 17.06.2016. https://www.forumspb.com/ru/2017/sections/22/materials/196/news/550

emergence is not inhibited, but rather stimulated by the aggressive behavior of some Western leaders (and whole countries) towards Russia.

At the same time, the cult of the "aggressive" Russia, implanted in Western countries with the help of the media, undoubtedly causes serious concern among the Russians and in the Kremlin. Russia perceives itself as a part of the world community, and **"self-isolation" is far from its society's plans**. Putin himself regularly insists that "self-isolation" is absolutely out of the question[7].

The defensive mechanisms of the Soviet period were revived when Barack Obama uttered the phrase "Cold War"[8]: long-buried ideological weapons were extracted from the depths of the citizens' post-Soviet consciousness and began to work as in the good old days.

In reality, it can be argued that Western leaders who, in their rash endeavors, attempted to subordinate the Russian leadership at all costs, *"show them their place"*, actually **forced Russia entirely into mobilization mode**, which back in his day helped Stalin and his team to elevate the USSR into a world leader.

At the present stage, this level of economic, social and political mobilization could not be achieved on the basis of, so to speak, internal resources – the political system had started getting "tired" of Putin. Yet all attempts to discredit him personally in the eyes of the Russian people turned him into a real national leader, comparable in stature with Joseph Stalin.

---

[7] "We will never go along the road of self-isolation, xenophobia, suspiciousness, searching for enemies. These are signs of weakness, but we are strong and self-confident. Our goal is to obtain as many equal partners as possible, both in the West and in the East. We shall expand our presence in those areas where integration processes are now gaining momentum, where politics and economy are not mixed together, but on the contrary, where barriers to trade, technology and investments exchange, and free movement of people are removed." Vladimir Putin determined the Russia's priorities in external and internal politics for the coming year. Channel One. 4.12.2014 http://www.1tv.ru/news/2014-12-04/30388-vladimir_putin_oboznachil_prioritety_rossii_vo_vneshney_i_vnutrenney_politik e_na_god_vpered

[8] According to Obama, Russia's approach to international relations brought back "the antagonistic spirit, which, as I see it, existed during the "Cold War". You must be skeptical of those who wield big power." Gazeta.ru. 19.01.2017. https://www.gazeta.ru/politics/2017/01/19_a_10481981.shtml#page1

CHAPTER 1

RUSSIA AND THE USA – THE UNDERLYING REASONS FOR ENGAGEMENT AT THE CURRENT STAGE

Russia and the United States are too similar to peacefully coexist: the former has its imperial past, the latter – its imperial present. **The messianic perception of reality**, the higher calling, the attempts to change the course of history – both their own and that of other countries – based on idiosyncratic ideas about justice and values, the cultivation of great politicians – all these factors prevent Russia and the United States from remaining neutral with respect to each other for even a short frame of time[9].

After the so-called "Munich speech" delivered by the Russian president in February 2007[10], it was **George W. Bush**, not Vladimir Putin, who

---

[9] "I believe in American exceptionalism with every fiber of my being. But what makes us exceptional is not our ability to flout international norms and the rule of law; it's our willingness to affirm them through our actions," Obama stated addressing the graduates of the West Point Military Academy. What is the peace that Obama shows to the world? Rossiyskaya Gazeta. 18.06.2014. https://rg.ru/2014/06/18/obama.html

From Obama's speech to the U.S. Congress: "When it comes to every important international issue, people of the world do not look to Beijing or Moscow to lead – they call us." "The United States is the most powerful nation on Earth." The U.S. "spends more on its military than the next eight nations combined." Therefore, "no nation dares to attack us or our allies because they know that's the path to ruin." There is an urgent need for new leadership. Vzglyad. 13.01.2016. https://vz.ru/world/2016/1/13/788303.html

[10] Speech and discussion at the Munich Conference on security policy issues. President of Russia. 10.02.2007. http://kremlin.ru/events/president/transcripts/24034

launched a new round of confrontation between the two great nations. The posture of Bush, followed by **Barack Obama**, formed the starting point for constructing a new system of relations with Putin personally, which in itself **led to the global confrontation between the two powers**.

Many in Russia believe that Putin successfully used the developing situation – specifically **both American presidents' mistakes** – to lead the country out of the *"deadly embrace"* of the United States, in which it had been held since the time of Boris Yeltsin and the G8, **and thereby restored Russia's status sovereignty**.

Mistakes that change the world

One of the foremost recent trends is a global external information attack on President Putin in particular, and on Russia in general. The opponents of the current Russian regime, however, have been unpleasantly surprised to discover that, rather than destroying his political position, these attacks have only mobilized the Russian population around the President. A similar process had already taken place in the 1930's and 1940's, when Stalin's opponents hoped that the population of the Soviet Union would "surrender" him to Hitler after the so-called *"Great Terror"*[11], with which western historians, prone to exaggeration, are fond of regaling the impressionable public. At the current stage, like in the 20th century, it appears that efforts to simulate conditions to provoke an internal crisis in Russia from the outside have played a *cruel joke* on the simulators – as in the past, their efforts have had the exact opposite effect.

The external factor for the new wave of mobilization became *the enemy image* that emerged gradually, as Washington's rhetoric towards Russia and Putin personally took on an increasingly rigid tone. When sensing danger, people tend to defend themselves, uniting around a strong leader.

The examples of Muammar al-Gaddafi, Saddam Hussein, Bashar al-Assad, most often cited in connection with the "demonization" of Putin,

---

[11] A book by an Anglo-American historian Robert Conquest, The Great Terror: Stalin's Purge of the Thirties, was published in 1968. It was dedicated to the study of the reasons, internal logic and scale of the terror organized by Stalin in the 1930s.

are, of course, an element of the global game played by Russia and those countries opposing the G7. An impression has been created that Gaddafi and Hussein were killed merely to set *a precedent of the illegal removal of a legitimate leader of a sovereign state*, that is, with the goal of **exerting psychological pressure** on the other participants in the processes, including Putin personally.

It must be noted that the Kremlin, since the Stalin times, has always regarded these types of challenges very seriously. The Russian society, impressed by the *act of demonstrative liquidation of Gaddafi*, immediately reacted by consolidating around the supreme authority, having once again confirmed that the Russian public, as well its elite, contrary to expectations, have not yet turned into individual consumers willing to change their rulers under pressure from the outside just to maintain their socio-economic status. This is evidenced by **the unprecedently high level of support for Putin by the population in 2014-2017 and the continued loyalty of the elites** under the conditions of the maximum pressure on him by Washington and Brussels.

Since 2012, Vladimir Putin openly exploits the image of an *enlightened conservative – Russian nationalist*, which, as practice shows, has proved to be very advantageous against the backdrop of politicians of different countries, who waste themselves on social and political posturing. Herein indeed lies the second secret of Putin's popularity in his own country and abroad.

As part of the project to discredit Putin, foreign media have gradually popularized the "imperialist" theme of the restoration of the USSR. In reality, Putin believes that it makes sense to create an entirely different kind of state, one that builds partner relationships with its neighbors[12]. Today he maintains this point of view and expresses it publicly. Unfortunately, it is that very notion that provokes pervasive irritation

---

[12] "In general, we have very good relations with our neighbors. We regard Turkey as our friend, the Turkish people as friendly people, with whom we will certainly build the most good-neighborly relations. [...] Taking into account our own interests, we, of course, will develop relations with all our partners, including our neighbors.." The Direct Line with the President: the Crimea – Sakhalin – Moscow. Rossiyskaya Gazeta, 14.04.2016. https://rg.ru/2016/04/14/putin-u-nas-dobrye-otnosheniia-s-podavliaiushchim-bolshinstvom-stran-mira.html

among globalists who instead insist on erasing the Russian national identity and relegating it to a category of folklore.

In general, the withdrawal of Russia from the G8 format clearly benefitted the country and, in fact, rather than alter its *"anti-Western power status"*, has allowed Russia **to build new systems of interstate relations and to strengthen the old ones**. We should note that, in addition to the assets freeze, the notorious sanctions banned U.S. legal entities and individuals from conducting any transactions with the listed officials.

The Russian **political, financial, and other institutions emerged out of the psychological shock rather quickly and stressed in every way that their state was stable or even improving**. For instance, the net profit of Bank Rossiya, which was one of the first subjected to the sanctions, increased in January-April 2014 by 30% compared to the same period of the previous year, amounting to 1.9 billion rubles[13]. In addition, it is known today that Bank Rossiya has started operating in Crimea and Sevastopol.

In essence, by responding to the emerging challenges as the head of state, Putin stimulated the provision of preferences within Russia to the institutions subjected to sanctions from the outside, thereby strengthening the prerequisites for the growth of the national economy and the development of the national infrastructure. As a result, many representatives of Russian business began to invest, forcibly or willingly, exclusively inside Russia.

At the same time, German companies, including the chemical concern BASF, the Siemens group, Volkswagen, Adidas and DeutscheBank, unequivocally expressed their opposition to broader economic sanctions against their Russian partners. It is notable that at the beginning of the "sanctions war" there were about 6,200 German companies in Russia – more than all the other European countries combined. After a while they were forced to gradually give up their positions and de facto adopted the sanctions as a reality. Germany's trade with Russia could be called relatively modest – 76 billion euros in 2013 (at its peak). Yet, while Russia consumed only 3% of German exports, Germany met 30% of its oil and gas

---

[13] The net profit of Bank Rossiya grew by 30% for the four quarters of 2014. TASS, 12.05.2014. http://tass.ru/ekonomika/1179461

needs from Russia[14]. Accordingly, the loss of access to Russian energy products hurt the German economy first and foremost.

American companies, which had much less at stake in Russia, similarly expressed their concerns regarding the sanctions to Barack Obama's Administration, the initiator of the anti-Russian activity, but in private – officially they were compelled to comply with the orders of the U.S. ministries.

Incidentally, during the period from 2014 to 2017, the interest of Western investment funds in, for example, Russian real estate grew significantly. Large funds have contemplated investments in commercial facilities in Moscow (including the Deka Group, which includes Deka Bank and a number of subsidiaries, investing in securities and real estate, as well as the American fund Tishman122Speyer). The fact is that the average yield in Europe, acceptable to investors, is 5-6% per annum, whereas similar investments in Russia yield 9-11% per annum[15]. Considering all the negative political and macroeconomic trends, real estate in Russia generates a much higher yield than that in Europe. Of course, Western funds try not to attract attention to such investments, for obvious reasons.

Tools of influence: Brussels–Beijing

Despite demonstratively high "morale", **Russia, in particular Putin's team, has rather cautiously weighed the prospects of a long-term competitive confrontation with the United States**. The Kremlin understands that the main instruments of influence of the U.S. on global processes are its military machine and the so-called "dollar system".

The systemic principle of currency competition provokes the dominant forces – primarily the U.S. – to **exploit many tools of influence, including those that are unjust from the point of view of international law**: from financial emissions to direct political and even military pressure.

---

[14] Business class for the Chancellor. Rossiyskaya Gazeta, 5.05.2014. https://rg.ru/2014/05/05/sankcii.html

[15] Western investment funds invest in Russian real estate secretly. Izvestia, 8.05.2014. https://iz.ru/news/570488

Critics of the existing U.S. economy-oriented system often say that in recent years, **it has essentially functioned as a classical "financial pyramid"**, forcing users to permanently expand their foreign exchange reserves in U.S. dollars.

The basis of the international trade economy after the Second World War has been in energy resources, especially oil. Most likely, oil will continue to provide a vital basis for development in the 21st century[16]. Nevertheless, it is becoming evident that the future global world order needs a much broader energy agenda. The latter involves the intensive development of the **gas industry** and **alternative energy sources**.

That is why the United States, trying to restore its global domination, is searching for **cheap sources of energy** around the world. Those persons or countries that hinder – or may potentially hinder – the U.S. from achieving this goal become *"victims of political circumstances"* with amazing and threatening regularity.

Under complex global conditions, the United States plans to become a leader in the formation of the gas market infrastructure, just as it had previously formed the oil market together with Saudi Arabia. However, this initiative comes into direct conflict with the aspirations of the Russian leadership, which advocates de-monopolization of decision-making in this sphere.

In order to establish new rules and infrastructure in the global energy market, **Washington plans to involve the mechanisms of the G20, emerging here as a rival to Russia and China**. That is why Russia has become the main target in this poignant struggle, which today is called the *"sanctions war"*, but is, in fact, an instrument of unfair and illegal competition, as both Russia and the United States are members of the World Trade Organization (WTO), both subject to its rules.

The success of the new American geopolitical strategy will be assured if the U.S. manages to establish its new rules in the gas market and to provide new transport routes for gas supply, ousting rivals in the face of Russia and Iran (as well as several other countries) as the main source of the world's energy reserves.

---

[16] BP Statistical Review of World Energy 2017.

At this interim stage, the U.S. perceives a key objective in easing the dependence of Europe on Russian gas. The so-called "Ukrainian crisis" was inspired, inter alia, to solve **the artificial "*problem of energy dependence*"** of the European Union on Russia. The informational support and theoretical justification of this thesis was initially developed as early as the middle 2000's, in the wake of the artificially organized "gas wars" between Russia and Ukraine[17].

Additionally, Washington is already working to fuel the growth of gas consumption in China. This is achieved through the involvement of Beijing in the international initiatives in the field of ecology and climate conservation – today the Chinese economy depends on coal, which has an excessively high level of environmental hazard. Incidentally, China was also the country where the "color revolution" model was employed (Hong Kong, September 2014).

It should be noted that the United States has prepared very well for large-scale investments in the gas transportation infrastructure in Asia, where Russia has its interests, too. Moreover, given the difficult geopolitical situation, the U.S. plans to develop this infrastructure in such a way as to avert the possibility that China could seize control over it – **Beijing should only act as a gas consumer with ever-growing needs**.

For this purpose, United States plans to locate a number of key elements of the gas infrastructure on the territory of India and in the countries of South and South-East Asia. At the same time, it is predicted that Washington will intercept any prospects of Beijing obtaining gas from Central Asia.

Putin's implacability in geopolitical issues, as well as his active endeavors in building the Russo-Chinese bilateral relations, have played their own role in NATO having gone through a kind of political reincarnation, albeit to date **absent clear prospects for financial development** and plagued by global controversies among the alliance member countries.

NATO's prospect for success - by maintaining attractiveness for member countries - had historically rested upon the bloc's apparent ability

---

[17] "Gas" conflicts between Russia and Ukraine. RIA Novosti, 29.10.2013. https://ria.ru/spravka/20131029/973397544.html

to fight without losses, due to its huge technological superiority, and primarily, its prevalence for various high-precision weaponry.

However, operations in Iraq and Libya, which had no anti-aircraft defense systems, along with the rejection of a global missile strike against Syria (which, on the contrary, had both the air defense and other types of weapons) led some experts to believe that **NATO "is capable of fighting" only with those countries, which cannot deliver manpower losses to the alliance**[18]. Poland and the Baltic states must have assessed adequately the fact that NATO did not render direct military assistance to either Georgia in 2008 or Ukraine in 2014.

As a result, the American part of the alliance's leadership was compelled to resort to certain distortions of reality in order to create the appearance of NATO's relevance for external observers. China served as the first deflector of attention[19], early on appearing on the pages of official U.S. documents as the *"number one threat"*. However, after the consequent strong political and economic rapprochement between China and Russia, **the public's attention was diverted to Russia and Putin** as the main "threat factor" for the "world order". It is enough to analyze, in particular, the speech of Barack Obama at the UN General Assembly on September 24, 2014[20].

---

[18] Jonathan Marcus, the BBC's diplomatic correspondent, commented: "For well over a decade, the Americans and their allies have largely given up traditional land wars. Yes, they participated in operations in Iraq and Afghanistan. But let's be honest, the rivals they dealt with there were much weaker from the point of view of technical equipment. They got air superiority practically without any effort, and many of the technical means of the Western armies (the same drones) were used in ideal conditions". The Russian military machine is capable of defying NATO - an expert. BBC, 08/11/2016. http://www.bbc.com/ukrainian/ukraine_in_russian/2016/08/160811_ru_s_russia_army_nato

[19] Obama's advisor took Trump's position: China was called a greater threat to the United States than Russia. Russian News Agency, 25.12.2016. http://новости-россии.ru-an.info/новости/советник-обамы-стал-на-позицию-трампа-китай-назван-большей-угрозой-для-сша-чем-россия/

[20] In July 2017, the Speaker of the Verkhovna Rada of Ukraine, Andrei Parubiy, at a meeting with UN Secretary-General Antonio Guterres, called for depriving Russia of the veto right in the UN Security Council. Obama's speech at the UN General Assembly: "furore" and "quintessence". Voice of America, 25.09.2014. https://www.golos-ameriki.ru/a/vv-obama-speech/2462097.html

As far as the issue of geopolitical competition between Russia and the United States is concerned, **Putin still has to organize a pool of countries that will form an alliance** ready to say – at least in principle – "no" to the U.S. and their methods of suppressing opposition. Formation of such a geopolitical climate is a key strategy for Russia seeking to prevent situations that have become commonplace at the UN General Assemblies.

Recent events have made it especially clear that when the Warsaw bloc disintegrated and the USSR disappeared as a state, the United States and its allies initiated a serious game aimed at lowering the prestige of international institutions. Observers of international processes have reached an opinion that, **in this new reality, the United Nations simply exists to legitimize the United States' "right of force"**. This is why attempts have recently been made to **abolish the institution of the veto power in the Security Council as an excessive function, which should either be cancelled or at least curtailed**. Another option that has been put forward is to limit specifically Russia's use of its veto power. The latter initiative is regularly advocated by some satellite countries of the United States, especially Ukraine[21].

It is likely that the restoration of the multi-polar equilibrium within the UN (not necessarily under Russia's leadership) will improve the situation and lead to the restoration of the balance of power.

Among the risks that can lead to the rejection of the unconditional dominance of the U.S. dollar as a symbol of the consumption agenda advanced by the U.S. is the **stagnancy and inefficiency of the current global resource distribution system**. These lead to the hypertrophied strengthening of some market participants (China and other Asian countries as an "industrial base") and to the artificial weakening of others (Russia, as a "raw material base", along with the countries of the Middle East, Africa and Latin America). It is clear why Putin and other participants of the processes regularly call for the revision of the rules of the game in this sector of the economic field[22], thereby utterly irritating those who want to preserve the existing order.

---

[21] Parubiy demanded to deprive Russia of the right of veto in the UN Security Council. Lenta.ru, 9.07.2017. https://lenta.ru/news/2017/07/09/opyat/
[22] BRICS and the West. Belarus Today, 12.04.2012. https://www.sb.by/articles/briks-i-zapad.html

The risks also include the deliberate weakening of international institutions by the U.S. in order to solve its domain specific problems (the dilemma of the United States and the UN). This weakening has led to the imbalance of the institutions designed to solve interstate conflicts within the framework established by the international law.

As a result, many countries have lost the ability to negotiate with their opponents. The U.S. took advantage and imposed itself as an "arbitrator", thereby supplementing the existing institutions. The crises first in Georgia in 2008 and then in Ukraine in 2013 serve as examples of such "arbitration".

The myth of omnipotence of the United States and its armed forces is undermined by the aggregate military power of China, Russia and the countries adjoining them, which can soon surpass (or have already surpassed) the power of the NATO countries. It was this fact[23] that has caused serious fear and even hysteria among the U.S. population, traditionally accustomed to the sense of security and complete impunity for the actions of their military machine in many countries across the globe, which are now commonly called "hot spots".

The slow but steady creation of the so-called *"gas OPEC"* in alliance with the countries of the Middle East, especially Iran and Qatar[24], which bypasses the U.S., poses another risk for the systems supporting the dollar dependence of the global economy.

Perhaps the main mistake committed by the U.S. in recent history has been the regular threat of imposition of "sanctions" against Europe. At the same time, it should be noted that a large number of factors continue to contribute to the maintenance of U.S. dominance in the European Union in the near future.

This dominance is guaranteed by the U.S. military power and war as a mechanism for maintaining the old financial order. Since 2007 in general, and since 2014 in particular, Russia has been under serious military

---

[23] The hidden dragon: why the Pentagon is afraid of China's military power. RIA Novosti, 9.06.2017. https://ria.ru/world/20170609/1496131576.html. Should the USA be afraid of the Russian-Chinese relations? Inosmi.ru, 1.02.2016.
http://inosmi.ru/politic/20160201/235234027.html
[24] Who will join the "gas cartel". Rossiyskaya Gazeta, 11.11.2008. https://rg.ru/2008/11/11/gaz.html

pressure of the U.S. The United States justifies the introduction of more and more "sanctions" by the alleged military presence of Russia in the South-East of Ukraine. **This brings a strong imbalance to the world system, which already suffers from not tension, but rather a real overload.**

Consequences that cannot be avoided

The arguments often used by liberal experts, that the Russian cluster of the global economy is not significant, are confuted by the following fact: along with Russia, the United States exerts pressure on Iran and China. The total number of countries that have been subjected to U.S. "sanctions" is estimated at several dozen. **This brings the macroeconomic situation to a fundamentally different level.**

At first glance, the actions of the United States form a very simple scheme aimed at "isolating" the Russian economy. However, it is obvious that Barack Obama, when he announced his policy of political isolation of Russia, did not entirely act out of his own common sense. His motivation was emotionally charged and displayed his personal animosity towards Putin. It is rumored that this animosity emerged after the Russian president was late for the meeting with his American counterpart, which is quite typical of him. It was then that Obama became angry, and had since treated Putin with extreme bias, suspecting him of disrespect.

The pressure exerted by the United States is adversely affecting the EU countries, which also joined the so-called "anti-Russian sectoral sanctions" despite the obvious risks. Being a global partner of Russia, Brussels, contrary to the opinion of the business community of the EU member states, literally "pushes" the idea that the notorious energy dependence of the European market on Russian suppliers is, in fact, an "*unacceptable burden*"[25].

---

[25] A useless struggle. Europe could not stop purchasing Russian oil and gas. Life.ru, 6.02.2017 https://life.ru/t/экономика/968884/biespolieznaia_borba_ievropa_nie_smoghla_ otkazatsia_ot_rossiiskikh_niefti_i_ghaza

As a result, **the position of the European Union has weakened**, today and for the foreseeable future. This is executed specifically in order to further subordinate the economy of European countries to American influence, including by means of the Transatlantic Trade and Investment Partnership. Although U.S. President Donald Trump has announced the "freeze" of the negotiations on this document, the situation may change in the future.

Realization of the idea of Europe's "energy dependence" on Russia, the authorship of which is attributed to Washington, can indeed seriously choke Russia on the European market. This is largely the goal of the current political processes initiated by the U.S. in Ukraine at the end of 2013.

It should be noted that **the information war against Russia and Vladimir Putin is already being waged on a global scale**, including in the post-Soviet space, with attempts to engage Russian partners and allies. Thus, one of Russia's closest partners, President of Kazakhstan Nursultan Nazarbayev, decided to draw attention to himself at the most "sensitive moment" of the confrontation by expressing displeasure[26] with both Russia, on the one hand, and the United States with Europe, on the other hand, for having entered the "sanction war" without consulting him.

The stand taken by Nazarbayev appeared somewhat dubious, as the "sanctions measures" against Russia were to have a positive effect on the economy of Kazakhstan and Belarus: Russia's partners in the Customs Union had obtained all the advantages of the re-export of the banned goods to Russia, albeit not quite legally.

Moreover, Western companies that were apprehensive of investing into Russia, but interested in maintaining their positions in its market segment, had instead invested into Kazakhstan or Belarus, set up production there, and then entered the Russian market without customs duties and restrictions.

---

[26] "Kazakhstan is deeply disappointed with the fact that some countries are cloning today the worst legacy of the last century – lack of restraint, justification of coercive approaches to conflict settlement. This creates dangerous precedents for the rest of the world, in fact encourages forms of bias in resolving interstate disputes," said Nazarbayev. Nazarbayev condemned economic sanctions. Today.kz, 23.05.2014. http://today.kz/news/kazakhstan/2014-05-23/511841-nazarbaev-osudil-ekonomicheskie-sankcii/

This example illustrates the very difficult situation, in which the leadership of Russia found itself, compelled to react to both the "sanctions" and the behavior of its Customs Union partners.

Vladimir Putin and his team are playing a deep multi-level game on numerous levels. They exercise a special model of behavior that allows, on the one hand, to avoid causing serious damage to the European economy in the expectation of a long-term partnership in the future, and, on the other hand, to arouse strong indignation of those market participants in the EU who are interested in cooperation with Russia. In addition, the Russian authorities have announced the following policies as priority areas:

1. "Import substitution", implying the support of Russian producers (notably within the framework of the norms of the World Trade Organization and the Customs Union);

2. "Nationalization of elites" (including state officials and deputies), meaning the withdrawal of the Russian establishment from under the influence of the Western community and the transfer of their funds and assets to the Russian jurisdiction, to the possible extent;

3. Legal efforts to use the protective mechanisms of the WTO, the United Nations, etc., in order to counter the illegal methods of competition, which the U.S. uses and compels other countries to use (the European Union, Japan, for example).

The passive behavior of the European Union leaves it disassociated from the transformation processes taking place in the Eurasian space, which today is the "battlefield", where Russia and Putin are in fact the dominant force. Nonetheless, the European Commission is extremely concerned about **the possibility of non-deliveries of Russian energy resources as a result of the position of the Ukrainian leadership.**

Formally disassociated is also the United States, as it planned, if not to take the Ukraine's gas transportation system onto the books and launch a U.S.-controlled privatization process, then at least to buy up the Ukrainian assets as cheaply as possible. This is another model of a "hybrid" (information) war – **remote impact on the situation under the guise of external "neutrality" of the interested countries**. This allows the interested countries to obtain the opportunity to manipulate the conflicting parties, while shifting onto them full responsibility.

Analyzing the specifics of the ongoing information war, in which the United States, the European Union and Russia take part – through Ukraine, it can be stated it has **reached a breaking point**.

Waves of the sanctions against Russia, initiated by the United States and initially supported by Europe, were introduced after a preliminary informational rationale, which *had an emotional effect*, but has remained unverified. At first, it was the exaggerated alleged reluctance of Russia to admit Ukraine to the association with the European Union (in essence – with NATO), then it was the mysterious circumstances of the MH17 disaster, and later the alleged "Russian invasion" of Ukraine was defined as the reason for imposing the sanctions.

In all these cases, the U.S. and Ukraine used *Hollywood special effects*, appealing more to the audience's emotions, rather than to reasonable arguments. As a result, the United States created **a virtual picture of events**, so large-scale that it was simply impossible to maintain it in a "working condition". Constructing both models, the U.S. used, figuratively speaking, *cheap scenery*, which began to crumble immediately after setting. That is why the United States so forcefully tried to impose the sanctions repression of Russia on Europe and other countries.

In the long run, the USA is likely to achieve a reverse effect: any country, that does not approve of the activities of the United States, was once hurt by their impact or fears this impact in the future, can become Russia's partner. These can be **countries in Latin America, North Africa, Asia and even in Europe.**

China, one of the main creditors of the United States, is already becoming such a partner for Russia. Even the European Commission has refused to take more radical measures to influence Russia. For example, it has abandoned the idea of disconnecting Russia from the *SWIFT system*. Moreover, there are countries that formally joined the sanctions, but, in fact, are expanding their cooperation with Russia in other areas (e.g., Japan).

The EU committed a key mistake when it **announced that Russia was no longer its partner.** This statement caused very strong repudiation at the level of both the EU civil society and its business community[27]. Thus, Brussels placed itself on one *"chessboard"* with the United States and has to play separately from the chess pieces of the national economies, which form the EU's economic content. It is quite likely that to complete the blueprint of the new world financial and economic order, the EU itself would need to be reformatted.

In this regard, **the Eurasian project, which is now being implemented by Putin, may well form part of a larger union**, with which both Europe and the United States will have to reckon in the political field. Basically, just as in the beginning of the 20th century, after the Russian Revolution of 1917 left it under sanctions war conditions, it is the adversarial position of the Western countries and their allies that may serve as the impetus for the global integration project on the site of the collapsed USSR.

In the Western countries, it is widely believed that Putin is a product of the Soviet system, an alum of the legendary USSR State Security Committee (KGB). However, our Western partners should remember the fact that the formation of his personality took place not only in the Soviet Union, but also within the western realities and the post-Soviet "wild west" 1990's.

Resume. *The Russian public has regarded the attempt of the Western establishment to exert pressure on the leadership of Russia seriously, but not in the way expected by the initiators of this pressure.*

As a result, the supreme leader Putin, regardless of the post he has occupied for the last 18 years (president or prime minister), obtained at his disposal consolidated social groups ready to support him personally in the most difficult political and economic conditions.

---

[27] "We want to see real action. That means that the peace plan alone is not enough. If it is observed, then we might discuss the lifting of the sanctions. But first we would like to make it clear: what has happened in eastern Ukraine and, I hope, will soon come to an end, is a violation of the territorial integrity of Ukraine and the cooperation of Russia with the so-called separatists is something we do not accept. The way to a dialogue remains open. We will continue to conduct these negotiations, but first the twelve items of the peace plan must be fulfilled," Angela Merkel stated. Thus, the position of the Chancellor has bifurcated – they support the sanctions, but are ready to accept Russia back as a partner at any point.

Moreover, the idea of proclaiming him the "national leader", very risky at first glance from the point of view of political strategy, had worked with unexpected success, perhaps even for those who invented it.

An axiom exists in Russia: if the West considers any Russian politician "a friend" and accepts him, such a politician causes suspicion, and thereafter the discontent of the populace. There are many examples, from Boris Yeltsin to Boris Nemtsov. On the contrary, if the "collective" West begins to criticize a Russian politician, the public pays him special attention, and then invariably begins to trust and support him.

When Vladimir Putin was close friends with U.S. President George W. Bush, the degree of criticism against him inside the country was quite high, but when he delivered his Munich speech in 2007, his authority in the country unequivocally increased, and Russian people began to forgive many of his mistakes.

CHAPTER 2.
THE PSYCHOLOGICAL PORTRAIT OF VLADIMIR PUTIN: RELATING HIS PAST TO HIS PRESENT

The destiny of Vladimir Putin has not been predetermined, it is still not determined...

The psychological portrait of one of the most influential politicians in the world requires constant revision, of course, as conditions around him change, events are reassessed and his behavior adjusts to the circumstances.

The most important thing that happened to Vladimir Putin over the 17 years at the helm of the country is that **he found the inner strength to change and psychologically adapt to new challenges and threats.**

The foundation of Putin's personality, as he has admitted, lies in the streets of Leningrad, the city that survived the horror of the blockade and raised a harsh generation of the "children of war" who were "immunized" against warfare and confrontation. The future president of Russia spent his childhood and adolescence in an environment ruled by a very specific street code, defined within a tight-knit residential community. In then-Leningrad, the rough streets formed its residents' values, which remained in their subconscious for the rest of their lives.

The "Leningrad period" of Putin's life was formative for his persona, inculcating both strong qualities and flaws that have helped and hindered his progress in becoming the person that he is today.

Putin's **strengths and weaknesses, as well as responsive changes in his character**, indicate the development of a strong personality: his rigorous political life has not interfered with his study of the English language, works of leading philosophers, hockey or even the piano. Unlike most of his colleagues and even friends, Putin displays a steady personal growth year after year.

Putin's private life belongs still in the special domain of the Russian Federal Guard Service (the FSO) and is practically unknown to the general public. Information about his private life circulates only at the level of rumors. It was only in 2016, during a press conference, that the President himself broke his vow of silence on this topic and admitted that he "loves and is loved"[28]. Later he confided that he has grandchildren from the children of his first marriage – to the legendary American film director Oliver Stone, who was shooting a film about the Russian president.

Thanks to certain "information leaks" by the media unfriendly to Putin, we can only assume that Putin has remarried; reportedly, the ceremony was performed in accordance with the Russian Orthodox rites. These media also report that his new wife is Alina Kabaeva, a former Olympic medalist in gymnastics, who now holds a top position at the Independent Media Group. Accounts that Alina Maratovna, as she is respectfully called within Putin's circle, converted to Orthodox Christianity appeared years ago, but again only on the level of rumors.

Putin's first wife remarried, as well, reportedly with the caring support of the President, and her new marriage is said to be a happy one. Her new husband is an entrepreneur Artur Ocheretny[29].

The secrecy of Putin's life, though not absolute, provides a measure of assurance for his personal tranquility and, accordingly, for the impossibility of using this factor to influence his decisions. Attempts to disturb this order have always resulted in a harsh response by Russia's intelligence agencies.

---

[28] Putin relayed this conversation with one of his friends: "One friend of mine from Europe asked me not so long ago, "So do you have love?" I said, "In what sense?" "Do you love anyone?" "Yes." "And does someone love you?" Apparently, he thought that I became a brute. I answered yes. "Well thank God!" Vladimir Putin admitted that he loved and was loved. Komsomolskaya Pravda, 18.12.2014. https://www.kp.ru/daily/26322.4/3202678/

[29] Lyudmila Putina is married. Delovoi Peterburg. 25.01.2016 https://www.dp.ru/a/2016/01/25/Ljudmila_Putina_vishla_zamuzh

Who is Mister Putin?

Since 1999, foreigners have been wondering "Who is Mister Putin?" It seems that the time has come to provide a comprehensive answer[30].

Vladimir Putin is **singular psychological type**[31]. Unyielding to outside influence, he has formulated for himself **a set of values**, which have undergone significant revisions at several points in his life – in 1996, 1999 and 2012.

Thus, during the so-called "St. Petersburg period" (1991-1996), the former KGB officer Putin underwent the process of reappraisal, the transition from a particular mentality formed during his service in foreign intelligence, to a different – civil – mentality informed by a period of liberal changes in society[32] and the total collapse of the Soviet ideology.

At that time, Putin could be characterized as a **typical "guardian"**, for whom his first patron Anatoly Sobchak was the embodiment of a new Russia, *weak and in need of protection*. Putin then widely exploited the image of a **"samurai"**: his practice of judo, a Japanese martial art, provided him with the necessary material.

The "service" to Sobchak required Putin to demand all team members to resign in 1996, after the Sobchak's defeat in the election of the mayor of St. Petersburg, as had been previously agreed amongst them. The fact that not all of them followed this demand caused Putin significant emotional stress, which he relieved by taking care of his disgraced chief Sobchak until the latter's death, despite the apparent unpopularity of the former mayor of St.-Petersburg among Boris Yeltsin's setting. In the future, this almost impaired Putin's Moscow career.

---

[30] See also A.A.Mukhin "A special folder" of Vladimir Putin. Results of the first presidential term and relations with large owners. Moscow, 2004.

[31] The material is evaluative in nature and is based on the author's personal observations and research.

[32] In the Leningrad State University, at the beginning of his fifth year of study, Vladimir Putin was recruited by the employees of the State Security Committee (KGB). He was sent to the Moscow School of the KGB after graduation from the University. In his own words, Putin agreed to work for the KGB immediately and without hesitation, for patriotic reasons. One of his friends recalled that Putin tried to initiate his own recruitment in his young days, but it did not work – the Committee was suspicious towards those who initiated it themselves.

During this "St. Petersburg period", Vladimir Putin took the path of the development of **religious self-determination**. At the same time, a new spiritual search began – the search of the **mystic Putin**.

It has been said that among the unofficial advisors to the president of the Russian Federation, there have been consultants specializing in esoteric practices. Then again, such extrasensory experts reportedly worked in the environment of Boris Yeltsin, as well. Moreover, these "experts" of the first Russian president were former employees of the KGB or state security agents.

The first period of Putin's "Moscow career" (1997-1999) was experimental: the future President tried his hand as a federal official, tasked with bringing order to the state of federal property (as Head of the Foreign Property Office) and its civil servants (as Director of the Federal Security Service). Putin performed this work, as reported by his contemporaries, with **responsibility and thoroughness**.

Nevertheless, **Putin's rapid moves from one post to another** (Secretary of the Security Council, Director of the FSB and Prime Minister by 1999) did not enable him to display his new emotional and psychological qualities at that stage. The offer to become president of Russia, made on behalf of Boris Yeltsin, reportedly with the direct participation of Valentin Yumashev and Tatyana Dyachenko, and the victory in the election of March 2000 **disturbed the balance of Putin's mind for a while**. Later Putin mentioned several times that he had tried to convince Yeltsin that he was not ready for the heavy burden of succession. (The latest such admission was made during a meeting with students at the Sirius educational center in Sochi in July 2017.)

2001-2002 witnessed the formation of a new "emotional type" and spiritual qualities of Putin: the loyalty and the sense of duty to Boris Yeltsin's family were gradually replaced with a different posture – **the foundation of his own team and formulation of methods for ruling the country**. The formation of a new image of power at this early stage was clearly **a collective act**, in which Sergei Ivanov, Viktor Ivanov, Dmitry Kozak and several other members of the President's inner circle participated.

By 2006-2007, Putin began to display pronounced **messianic traits** (the desire to "*save Russia*", which, in his opinion, Boris Yeltsin possibly wished but failed to do), and – together with his colleagues and associates – developed **his own concept of a social state** based on **hyper-responsibility for the destiny of the country**.

The messianic traits easily combined in his conscience with **sensitivity to personal offenses and fears about the safety of his family and close friends**. It were these feelings, which probably did not permit him to withdraw from power even for a short period in 2008-2012, forcing him to further the election of Dmitry Medvedev as president of Russia as a temporary ruler, who, in turn, appointed Putin as Prime Minister.

As a result, the so-called "ruling tandem" was formed, characterized by a strict system of control by one party (Putin) over the other (Medvedev). The concept of the "ruling tandem" clearly demonstrated that Putin, having even overcome his bygone self-consciousness, **would not allow the situation around him to go out of control even for a short while**.

According to witnesses, a serious reappraisal of values again took place in the mind of Vladimir Putin by 2012 – the literal **"consecration" of his own role as a ruler of Russia**. At the same time, Putin addressed the issue of **developing personal qualities** through **self-improvement**. This became evident through his music playing, study of Sufism, participation in hockey and resumption of his judo practice.

If earlier he considered the options of a self-styled collegial governance of the country (with the help of his associates), it now became clear that he no longer sees them as absolute partners and prefers to receive their undivided loyalty.

Putin seems to have become very disappointed with the activities of the Russian Orthodox Church Patriarch Kirill, who succeeded Alexy II. If the latter enjoyed a very warm and special relationship with Putin, Kirill clearly did not generate similar feelings. The reason lay in the continuing attempts of Kirill to create a "symphony" of secular and spiritual power based on the example of Byzantium. These aspirations "repelled" the President from the Patriarch once and for all.

As previously mentioned, **Vladimir Putin's mystical leanings** were used, according to sources, by the West (Vatican) and the Jewish communities. Masonic circles spread rumors that Putin is a freemason of the 32nd degree of an American lodge. This information, of course, deserves to remain on the conscience of its sources. The initiation is said to have taken place when Putin went to the United States to see his old friend George W. Bush and visited the ranch of his American counterpart. Surprisingly, Mikhail Gorbachev had been subjected to the same "story", as he was allegedly "initiated" at an official reception during a visit to the UK (the famous 40-minute absence of Gorbachev, noted by other members of the delegation). Boris Yeltsin has such a "story", too: he was supposedly initiated as a Knight of the Order of Malta. It is said there is even a photo of him in full regalia...

In any case, today the country has determinately formed the largest group of influence – Putin's team, or rather, **a group of persons identified with the Kremlin, which has assumed the functions of protecting the interests of the state**.

For obvious reasons, Putin personally is the symbol and the sacral leader of this group, whose personal life is now ritually devoted to the **service to Russia**. Even the president's divorce from his wife Lyudmila, which for a while led to a considerable drop in Putin's political rating in the regions, was used to strengthen his personal power over time: **as if he now had only one woman – Russia – and would never abandon her.**

It is likely that **Putin partially encouraged the mythologizing of his persona**, for political, strategic and security reasons. That is why we have tried to reveal more or less reliable information about the early stages of his political career that may be useful in forming an estimate of the President.

It should also be borne in mind that, as was mentioned, between 2000 and 2013, **significant changes occurred in the consciousness of Putin**. Moreover, the President has initiated the process of permanent self-change in accordance with the views, to which he now adheres.

Defining characteristics at different stages of personality development

As is known from numerous interviews, Vladimir Putin's favorite color is dark blue, his favorite time of the year is summer, he usually wakes up early and likes to take a bath in the morning. He likes plain food; among meat dishes he prefers lamb; likes eating soups. He appreciates oriental cuisine (sushi, sashimi), and especially spicy meat with potatoes. He likes fruit – melons, watermelons, apples, oranges, pineapples, grapes. He likes drinking the finest green tea. He does drink alcohol, but not very often, preferring white wine and beer (for example, visiting Germany, he preferred beer, while in Austria he drank red wine). Of non-alcoholic beverages, he likes milk. Lately, at official events, he has been seen with a small glass of vodka. During trips, he always tries to taste national (local) dishes and drinks.

Apparently, Vladimir Putin was greatly influenced by his father. Notably, the fellow countrymen of Putin Sr. had an uncomplimentary opinion of him: in his youth, he *"gave the girls no peace"*, was an *"impious man and mischief-maker"*[33]. The same traits in varying degrees appeared later in the character of Vladimir Putin Jr., despite the fact that he was a late child, who had a very warm and trusting relationship with his mother.

Putin loved his mother very much (sensitivity), but there always remained the need for the father, as well (strictness and masculinity).

Some sources say that Putin is left-handed because he wears his watch on the right hand. If this is true, he is a "latent" lefty. Perhaps, he was retrained at an intelligence school, and at least now he is ambidextrous.

Eyewitnesses claim that as a child, Vladimir Putin was a communicative boy, liked company (according to his neighbors, he never came to dacha alone, always with friends), but was nevertheless shy and quiet. **He was markedly polite with his elders**: for long time, he brought his parents their pension money personally, even while serving at the St. Petersburg Mayor's Office as a high-ranking official.

Respect for the elders and authoritative people is another pronounced trait of Vladimir Putin, which will be covered in more detail below.

As a teenager (during his school years), according to the data from his pupil's mark book[34], Putin was pugnacious, active, a trouble-maker, – generally speaking, was *a normal urban guy.*

---

[33] Versia, 15-21.02.2000.
[34] Komsomolskaya Pravda, 12.03.2001.

His educational progress up until the 7th grade was decidedly average, but then there was a leap – at that moment he became very interested in the German language. During that period, his **sense of responsibility** began to form – a defining trait of his character, which manifested itself later during his presidency.

Vladimir Putin did not excel at exact sciences – he had only a C mark in physics, chemistry, algebra and geometry in his certificate. Teachers recall that Putin was more inclined to the humanities[35]. As was already mentioned, he especially liked German and Russian History. In addition, Putin **willingly held political briefing hours**, reading newspaper reports about current events in the world. According to witness recollections, he typically "*defended Russians and Russia*" in these endeavors.

According to his schoolmates, Putin was moderately introverted, but friendly, **liked to argue**, even with the teachers.

KGB colleagues remember Putin as a competent careerist. They were impressed by his "*well-tuned*" eyes, which allegedly did not allow his interlocutors to lie. Later, psychologists describing this virtue called Putin an **"investigator"** who liked and knew how to interrogate, to lead in conversation, and to reason his position effectively.

Vladimir Putin's colleagues in Dresden and Leipzig remember him as "*a typical representative of the Russian red aristocracy, who was proud of the fact that his ancestors had participated in the October Revolution*", as well as an ascetic who hated alcohol[36]. He left a strong impression on the participants of one reception organized by the Stasi when he poured his glass of vodka into a flowerpot, instead of drinking it.

One employee of the Stasi characterized him most pithily and correctly, in our opinion: "*He was always very cautious and self-controlled. He worked behind the scenes, without attracting attention. People simply did not notice him. He is very smart. He is silent but very effective.*"[37]

Vladimir Putin rationalized his departure from the KGB in 1991 by the disappointment that he felt during the collapse of the Soviet Union and the state security bodies. According to him, he felt that the country no longer

---

[35] Komsomolskaya Pravda, 12.01.2000.
[36] Versia, №2, 2000.
[37] Kommersant, №4, 2000.

needed him. His genuine surprise at the fact that – as a *"promising officer"* – he was so easily let go upon his resignation, masks a deeply wounded pride.

Putin's version of the disappointment in the service is indirectly confirmed by the fact that the East German station officers of the KGB were, practically speaking, abandoned and left to fend for themselves. That was why in that period **KGB officers by and large left the service for business**. Putin was no exception: **his participation in business projects has always been large-scale**, though not always public.

During the period of his work in the St. Petersburg Mayor's office, colleagues remembered Putin as by now a relaxed, cheerful and sociable person. Women at the Mayor's office considered him **an attractive man**.

Interestingly, it was during this period that Vladimir Putin attained the nickname **"gray cardinal"**. He did not like to be in the limelight, although reportedly few of the issues at the Mayor's office were resolved without his direct involvement. This practice helped his chief Anatoly Sobchak to avoid many scandals, as the mayor could not refuse the "good people" and was constantly surrounded by all sorts of opportunists and charlatans. In this regard, Sobchak considered Vladimir Putin reliable and indispensable.

From an interview with Anatoly Sobchak given three days before his death:

– Is Putin a riddle to you, too?

– This riddle was invented by the mass media, speculating about the sensational growth of Putin's popularity. In fact, it is easy to explain. First, Putin clearly and distinctly explains what he is going to do. Second, he keeps his promises. Third, people see in him their reflection. And, fourth, he does not belong to any party, but represents the state.

El Pais. "Putin will push the Family and oligarchs into a corner". Translated by Fyodor Kotrelev. Quoted as a publication in the newspaper Kommersant, 22.02.2000.

Present-day traits of Putin's character

A defining feature of Putin's image is his **competence**: *competence* first as a consequence of his service in the *"competent authority"* (as Soviet citizens often referred jarringly to the KGB), and then as a consequence of outstanding analytical skills, demonstrated in St. Petersburg and in Moscow. It should be noted, however, that publicly Putin's erudition had been displayed in narrowly defined spheres.

Another important trait of Putin's character is **caution**, which in turn further assures his interlocutor in his great competence. In our opinion, it is actually *"super-caution"*, which can also be a negative trait.

Analysis of Vladimir Putin's activity in various leadership positions leads to the conclusion that he **is inclined to solve problems mainly through negotiation and the creation of a system of agreements**. However, in case of force majeure, Putin **is capable of disregarding the surrounding noise and moving deliberately towards the target**.

Putin's ability to take unpopular decisions impressed the people of Russia, especially during the presidential election. This was often exploited during his campaigns.

Vladimir Putin is, of course, **an intellectual, prone to logical thinking with a minimum of external manifestations of emotion**. Incidentally, it was logic and restraint that has helped Putin to get out of most critical situations. At the same time, he is also capable of playing on people's emotions. For example, in one of his most successful PR-actions his words about terrorists who *"must be rubbed out in the outhouse"*[38] were meant to extract that very emotional reaction of the audience that actually occurred.

Putin is always **polite, precise, and, in spite of that, a little bit sardonic**: his rigidity is always concealed behind a joke. By the way, Putin is known

---

[38] The phrase was pronounced by Putin in 1999, in connection with the bombing of Grozny. He said, "Russian planes are delivering and will be delivering strikes in Chechnya exclusively at the terrorists' bases, and this will continue wherever terrorists are. We will chase terrorists everywhere. If in an airport, then in the airport. So if we find them in the toilet, excuse me, we'll pummel them in the head. And that's it, case closed". Putin later regretted the promise to "pummel them in the head". Lenta.ru, 15.06.2011. https://lenta.ru/news/2011/07/15/vsortire/

to be weary of any efforts to sharply reduce the distance in relations with him.

Putin regards people's experiences under extreme conditions (in Chechnya during the conflict in the 1990's, in other *"flash points"*, in service at a border zone, etc.) as a particular "mark of quality". Accordingly, security officers, military personnel, border guards, policemen and employees of other security bodies are held in high esteem.

Putin is certainly a **reserved** person. Like most reserved people, he is **suggestible**, but this suggestibility is resistant to direct pressure. In response to any attempt to put pressure on him, Putin will invariably adopt a temporary solution that is typically the opposite of that sought by his opponent.

At the same time, Putin is **boyishly open to everything new and unknown**. In particular, he was once – to the dismay of his personal guards, the Presidential Security Service of Russia – thrilled to fly a fighter plane Su-25UB in the copilot's seat, and to then enthusiastically share his impressions[39]. Besides that, he has descended to the bottom of Lake Baikal on a bathyscaphe. Incidentally, this trait – Putin's ability to genuinely delight in life in all its manifestations – always leaves a strong impression on the public and serves as an additional factor of his popularity in the country.

Putin likes holidays and trips abroad; it is his special passion. He has admitted that he began to celebrate Christmas with friends back in Eastern Germany, long before it became an official holiday in Russia.

Putin is very attentive to his interlocutors, able to listen and to consider their arguments. He is **personable and punctual in keeping his promises**, and he **possesses a tenacious visual memory**.

Preferring not to make rash decisions, he **always tries to stick to his word** (this was especially illustrated by the situation with Mikhail Khodorkovsky, who ended up in prison, despite international pressure on the Kremlin, and was later pardoned). However, he apparently does not believe other people's words of honor, and always carefully studies the motivation of his interlocutors. In the case with Khodorkovsky, this

---

[39] Putin extinguished two forest fires in an amphibian plane. RIA Novosti, 10.08.2010. https://ria.ru/hs_mm/20100810/263796841.html

instinct did not fail him: after being pardoned and going abroad, the latter took up politics – despite a promise to the contrary – and became one of the most virulent political opponents of the Russian president.

According to some reports, Putin's favorite question during the preparation of documents on various issues is *"Is this legal?"*. This feature allowed him to avoid many questionable situations, which often befell his colleagues in the St. Petersburg Mayor's office.

An interesting quality attributed to Putin is his almost **maniacal loyalty to his former bosses, despite a certain degree of obstinacy**. As was already mentioned, as Sobchak's subordinate, he "covered" him very thoroughly and accurately. As a subordinate to Pavel Borodin, the Head of the Administrative Department of the President of the Russian Federation under Yeltsin, and immediately after that, Putin allegedly refused to disclose compromising information on him. Then, when working under the late Yevgeny Primakov, Head of the FSB Vladimir Putin refused to set up informal surveillance over Igor Malashenko, then Head of NTV, as was requested by the Prime Minister, having not found sufficient justification, and then advised the influential Primakov to hire a private security company.

We can conclude that Putin had long been **"a loyal man of his boss"**, a *"samurai"* in some sense, who truly preserved principles of subordination and devotion to duty. For instance, in his youth, Vladimir Putin resisted the pressure of his university coaches and remained faithful to his old sports trainer and club. This is explained by judo principles cultivated since his childhood.

The behavior etiquette on a tatami is subject to strict observance of the "senior-minor" hierarchy. It appears that **Putin has internalized this system, having made it a principle of life**, which is very common among those practicing oriental martial arts.

In public service, Putin felt quite comfortable on the sidelines, deliberately depriving himself of the external attributes of power. For example, as Director of the Federal Security Service (FSB), that is, occupying the position of General of the Army, Putin did not initiate the process to bring his military rank (lieutenant colonel) in accordance with his position.

At the same time, Putin proved his ability to act "outside the team". Thus, he once stood up for Lev Savenkov, the Deputy Mayor of St. Petersburg, who was accused of smuggling precious metals, and even wrote an article in his defense, which at that time was a significant manifestation of political courage.

Putin's reaction to the case of Yury Skuratov was rather typical: Skuratov, then Prosecutor General, found himself at the center of a scandal, in which a "man resembling the Prosecutor General" appeared on tape engaging in sexual activity with two ladies of "easy virtue". In spite of his personal friendship with Skuratov, Putin's reaction was unambiguous: in the light of what happened, the Prosecutor General was to resign. Putin thus **demonstrated the strict appreciation and observance of the officer's honor**.

It is also revealing that in the early days of his political career, responding to an attempt to blackmail him with his KGB past, Putin gave an extensive interview to then Leningrad TV, openly discussing his career as a KGB officer, eradicating **any possibility of blackmail in the future**.

Unlike the majority of high-ranking officials, Vladimir Putin is said to be **patient and unpretentious**. This trait is well illustrated by an episode, which happened to him in the autumn of 1999, during a visit to Primorye. Putin spent a night on the missile cruiser Varyag; someone failed to switch off the speaker in his cabin and then Prime Minister Putin was consigned to listen to the team's banter, including rather scabrous content, through the entire night. The mishap was discovered only in the morning, but Putin made no complaints to the captain.

Putin's unpretentiousness in life is offset by a specialized routine of serving food and drinks. Putin usually uses Japanese warmed-up towels before he starts eating, even if European cuisine is served. He prefers green tea and still water. These observations give away the fact that the President is **highly careful of his health**, aiming to keep the functionality of the body for as long as possible.

It should be noted that Putin **has an outstanding, albeit somewhat flat, sense of humor**. For example, after the above-described case, at the conclusion of the subsequent heartfelt speech of then Governor of Primorye Yevgeny Nazdratenko, Putin said, "*Yevgeny, you praised me so much that I* *thought I was dead*". At that, it was completely impossible to understand by Putin's face whether he was joking or not. Incidentally, there was a time when Putin liked telling jokes, which unfortunately were sometimes stale. Since 2015-2016, he has almost ceased doing this.

Putin often cites examples from the private life, highlighting his appreciation for non-standard situations, and further uses them in conversation as life examples (with characteristics of his acquaintances and friends).

A special feature of Vladimir Putin's personality is his **high emotional sensitivity in any given situation**. According to accounts, he keenly feels certain events. Public appearances, despite long-standing practice, had cost him a great nervous tension in the early days of his public activity. Back in the "St. Petersburg period", Sobchak remarked, *"Putin came from a meeting - I had never seen him in such a state: for some reason, he was all blue and seemed to have lost a few kilos"*[40].

This predicament has a reverse, positive side: thanks to his susceptibility, Putin easily enters any kind of conversation, even in conditions absolutely new to him. He **has great powers of intuition**, which he uses in *behind-the-scenes games* on both the domestic and foreign policy tracks.

In serious crisis situations, Putin displays enormous self-control. Thus, before the appointment as Acting Prime Minister, Vladimir Putin lost his father, but never showed his feelings.

In practice, very few factors can destabilize Putin's nerves. Among these are threats to the President's family and the direct betrayal by his associates. It seems that his negative attitude towards Mikhail Khodorkovsky and Leonid Nevzlin are of just such nature[41].

Some of Vladimir Putin's friends noted that after he rescued his daughters from a burning dacha in the suburbs of St. Petersburg, **his religious feelings started to amplify**. He is said to wear a next-to-skin cross, which allegedly did not melt in the fire at the dacha; the cross was

---

[40] Kommersant, 14.09.1999.

[41] According to sources, for a long time during each visit to Israel, Putin used to raise the issue of extradition of Nevzlin, who was sentenced in Russia to a long term of imprisonment for organizing a murder and is hiding in Tel Aviv.

presented to Putin by his mother and consequently consecrated during his visit to Jerusalem.

When performing public duties, Putin is said to **prefer acting in a calm atmosphere, when all the participants of a situation have already showed their worth and abilities**.

In extreme situations, Putin demonstrates a genuinely "demonic" calmness, bordering on complete apathy. **He prefers to postpone a decision** in the short or even the long term, guided by the following purpose: if the need for the decision remains, it will be taken based on the analysis of the situation; if the need to decide disappears – the issue will be closed.

Another interesting trait of Putin's character lies in the fact that he has never changed his opinion about people based on a change of their status (up or down the career ladder).

Putin apparently likes to create a *semblance*, a false view of himself, among people who communicate with him. Then, he starts to deal with the consequences of this false opinion. He is said to enjoy this process (of changing public opinion and exploding myths).

Some sources also note the fact that Putin sometimes suffers from bouts of laziness. Detractors pointed out that his reluctance to work, to engage in current affairs, had led to the fact that he delegated many of his powers to certain trustees. The latter included Alexei Kudrin, before his dismissal from the post of Finance Minister, and Igor Sechin, whose exceptional work ethic is legendary. Furthermore, Putin often and willingly gave (temporarily) broad authority to Elvira Nabiullina, the current Chairwoman of the Bank of Russia, German Gref, the current Chairman and CEO of Sberbank, and other ministers.

Regardless, when it comes to subjects of personal interest – specifically energy and security, Putin prefers to engage in them personally. For example, he has repeatedly struck well-known experts in gas and oil business with the depth of his knowledge on the subject. It was alleged that Putin could personally calculate the number of energy carriers to provide, appoint persons to monitor the supply processes, etc.

It is indicative that Putin is still **actively involved in sports; among many reasons, in order to maintain his "virile" status**. He is said to be interested in the practice of extending life activity in general.

According to Head of the Medical Center under the Administrative Department of the President of the Russian Federation Sergei Mironov, Vladimir Putin sometimes performs a series of gymnastic exercises, works out with weights, swims in the pool and takes a lot of walks. All this helps to maintain his vigor at the proper level and to de-stress after heavy work loads[42].

Putin's passion for sports, of course, has had a great influence on the formation of his personality and his political career.

Putin started practicing martial arts at the age of 13, due to the fact that he fell ill often and for long periods of time, but in process of training, he recovered and strengthened his health, which is typical of martial arts practice. (In the Soviet times, his practice was limited to sambo[43], because Japanese martial arts were banned from widespread practice in the USSR.) Putin practiced sambo at the Turbostroitel Club, coached by **Anatoly Rakhlin**[44].

At a professional level, Putin began practicing judo, as well as swimming, at the university. At that time, in the Soviet Union, the Japanese martial arts were the prerogative of the KGB employees - only they could officially practice them. Putin's success in martial arts is impressive: in 1973 he became a master of sports in sambo, in 1975 – in judo.

Currently, Vladimir Putin's sporting interests include **mountain skiing and ice hockey**. He has recently started training with a team of veterans as a member of the so-called *Night Hockey League.*

Putin also regularly swims in the pool. He considers it is a good way to do effective cardio training. He also visits a gym to practice **judo**, where Olympic champions often act as his sparring partners.

In our opinion, it was judo in particular which helped incline Putin toward the **shaping of Russian power verticals** (and partially forming of

---

[42] Incidentally, the Medical Center is engaged in physical and psychological rehabilitation of Putin. Viktor Rovnov is said to lead the group of his doctors.

[43] SAMBO is an alliteration that means "self-defense without weapons". This is a combined martial art, invented at the dawn of the formation of internal affairs and intelligence agencies of Soviet Russia.

[44] Anatoly Rakhlin died in July 2013, and Putin attended the funeral of his mentor. The ceremony was arranged in a special way (the President walked all alone in the street, he had gone by for practice routines).

his world-view, as previously mentioned) **into a strict hierarchical structure**.

Ever since his first presidential term, vacations are extremely important events for Putin. This is a special psychological feature of his personality. There have been known several conflicts in his narrow circles, in particular with Alexei Kudrin, who received additional powers as Minister of Finance just so as not to disturb Putin on vacation.

The favorite vacation spots of Vladimir Putin and his family are, first Finland, and then – Sochi. In the later period, his trips to Sochi have become so regular that the Kremlin began to speak of a "third capital" in the south of Russia.

There was a period, when Putin actively skied in Krasnaya Polyana, Sochi. In his inner circle, it was considered obligatory to ski with the President, if you regarded yourself a "confidant". In Yeltsin's time, there was a similar tennis "club".

The list of Vladimir Putin's hobbies also includes:

Music (classical, as well as Russian pop music, mostly of the Soviet period; Putin is currently learning to play the piano);

Books (he quotes by heart the early Vladimir Mayakovsky; has read Heinrich Böll in the original; in his youth he liked to visit bookstores; from among the Russian classical writers, Putin likes Lev Tolstoy and Vladimir Nabokov; reads foreign detective stories – by Agatha Christie and James Chase; recently has focused on philosophical works);

Chess and backgammon (sources claim that he has played these games since the childhood);

Russian-sauna house (banya) (only with close friends, including Gennady Timchenko and Yury Kovalchuk);

Fishing (not hunting, as is widely believed);

Soccer (sometimes he watches soccer broadcastings - there is always a sports channel with soccer switched on in the residence; he also visits stadiums);

Car racing and horseback riding (in his youth, he drove a Zaporozhets and, by his own admission, was a reckless driver, once running down a man, who luckily did survive; today he prefers horse riding in the Altai region)[45];

Jokes on friends and acquaintances (as a method of combatting his self-consciousness).

Mysticism (in the middle of the 2000's, he visited the Arkaim, an esoteric center-city in the Altai).

Curiously, according to sources, **children used to be afraid of him**. However, after certain work on self-improvement, Vladimir Putin repeatedly demonstrated to the public that this was no longer true. The public was particularly strongly impressed when he *kissed a boy in the stomach*, which happened spontaneously, judging by the reaction of protection officers and press service, at a meeting with citizens.

It is important to note that Putin's personal characteristics as a KGB officer were seriously influenced by the fact that he was fluent in German. Later, already in the presidential post, Putin also learned English, though for a long time he preferred not to speak it, unless absolutely necessary.

All the distinguished traits emphasize the obviousness of the main goal of Vladimir Putin – **the aspiration to gain power and apply it to change the world in accordance with his own perception of right.**

---

[45] Putin's first car was a Zaporozhets model, which he won in a lottery in 1974, according to his classmate Sergey Kudrov. According to another classmate, Alexander Nikolayev, Putin's father won the car and gave it to the son, as he could not drive it. The latter version was confirmed by Vladimir Putin himself. Later, Putin brought a second-hand Volga from Germany, and was said to be very proud of it. Soon, to replace the Volga, he bought a dark blue VAZ of the sixth model, very fashionable in its time. His friends remembered that Putin was much impressed by a special car vacuum cleaner, an accessory in short supply, presented him by one of them.

Personality cult: basic features and myth debunking

Putin's detractors often spread the rumor that he loves being idolized. They have even discussed the establishment of a **cult of personality** (by analogy with the cult of Stalin), specifically formulated as condoning the creation of the cult. Putin commented on the matter as follows: "*Everything must be in moderation; but in Russia, unfortunately, this depends on the level of general culture. Nothing can be done about it. I view it as a negative.*"[46]

Among the most striking phenomena of "presidentophilia" we distinguish the following interesting or just curious ones.

Phenomenon: Judo-mania
Forms: A book "Learning Judo with Vladimir Putin"
Remarks: Putin willingly patronizes not only judo, but also other sports activities. There is a joke: *an ad in a newspaper: "A state official will immediately exchange two tennis rackets for a kimono."*

Phenomenon: Monument to Putin
Forms: An equestrian statue
Remarks: According to some data, a wood equestrian statue of Vladimir Putin is located in the Novgorod high security colony № OYa 22\07.

Phenomenon: Portraits of Putin
Forms: Traditionally, very common in the offices of state officials
Remarks: The most famous include portraits by Nikas Safronov and others.

Phenomenon: Badges with the image of Putin
Forms: Gold and silver images
Remarks: The badges are produced by a jeweler Viktor Furman in the Chelyabinsk region.

---

[46] Profile, 7.10.2002.

Phenomenon: The image of Putin on carpets and cakes, as well as on suits and tee shirts

Forms: Putting the image of Putin on household items and confectionery products is one of the more extreme forms of the people's love

Remarks: The practice of putting Putin's image onto carpets exists, for example, in Turkmenistan and Tajikistan. Such carpets also appeared in the Perm region. Suits depicting Putin were seen in Izhevsk (Udmurtia). After returning Crimea to Russia, prints on t-shirts in the style like "The politest of the people", etc.) gained particular popularity

Phenomenon: Songs about Putin

Forms: Songs performed by a band "Poyushchiye vmeste" [Singing Together] and other enthusiasts, for example, the band "Beliy Oryol" [White Eagle]

Remarks: It is another form of "stepping into eternity"

Phenomenon: Books

Forms: Printed goods about Putin – one of the most common forms

Remarks: Books about Putin are divided into propaganda and analytics. The former are published with the aim of attracting the attention of the President or his entourage; the latter attempt to sum up the current events

Phenomenon: Textbooks

Forms: A textbook for primary school pupils

Remarks: The textbook was published in September 2000 in St. Petersburg at the initiative of the local branch of Unity. Some pages are devoted to the description of the childhood of Vladimir Putin, who "feared no one" and "never let anyone down", "helped good people and disliked bad people very much"

Ten "weaknesses"

1. Putin's love for his children resulted in the **"sealed" regime of his private life**. Attempts to break the regime and endanger his family have ended very badly for their initiators.

2. The **divorce** of Vladimir and Lyudmila Putina became a serious political hindrance for his potential voters.

3. Putin made mistakes[47] at the early stages of his presidential tenure. At the beginning of his first term, for example, following **the tragedy of the nuclear submarine Kursk** in August 12, 2000, Putin did not interrupt his vacation for the entire period of rescue operations and commented on the tragedy in a rather cynical way. In reply to the question "What happened to the submarine?", he stated: "It sank". He has never repeated such mistakes.

4. The **"Chechen problem"** had long served as a psychological trigger, bringing the President out of balance (from 1999 to 2008). The reason was Shamil Basayev, who undertook a raid into Dagestan. Since then, Putin had considered the "Chechen problem" his personal mission, which he completed. According to operational information, Basayev had "put Putin on a hit list"; in particular, there was a message put up in the Internet promising an award of 2,500,000 U.S. dollars for murdering Vladimir Putin.

5. **Complicated personal relations with Boris Berezovsky** (until the latter's death). Berezovsky publicly declared that it was he who "made" Putin the President. According to the press, journalists comprise many of

---

[47] According to some reports, a Decree on the security safeguards for Boris Yeltsin and his family was Vladimir Putin's first decree. Incidentally, in June 2000, Putin signed a law passed by the State Duma regarding amnesty for all criminals and those under investigation (including on cases not yet disclosed) awarded with any Soviet or Russian Orders - for all crimes, including corruption ones. The "Putin's amnesty" deprived virtually all cases against officials of the Yeltsin era of any perspective, since almost all of them had either Soviet or Russian Orders. This decree, according to numerous testimonies, played a very negative role in the voters' attitudes.

Putin's personal enemies: Yevgeniya Albats (The New Times), Roman Anin (Novaya Gazeta), Roman Shleinov (Vedomosti), as well as a number of journalists who wrote about his daughters at different times.

6. Vladimir Putin regarded **the actions of George W. Bush in 2003-2005 as a betrayal**. During the period of development of their personal relations, the U.S. president presumed to neglect various agreements that had been reached tête-à-tête. Putin's disappointment culminated in his famous "Munich speech" in February 2007 at the Russia + NATO Summit, when the Russian president clearly pronounced his staunch opposition towards Anglo-Saxon policies.

7. It is known that Putin's relations with **Ramzan Kadyrov**, the Head of Chechnya, are quite warm. Detractors often use the defiant behavior of Kadyrov's son Akhmad against the Russian president.

8. Putin reacts emotionally to **accusations of authoritarianism**. In fact, the President often exploits authoritarian notions, combining them with very liberal statements to mislead interlocutors. As a result, authoritarians often believe that he is deeply authoritarian, whereas liberals regard him as their own. (Incidentally, the Medvedev Cabinet of 2012 was full of liberals.)

9. Putin's passion for **extreme activities** draws the public attention and is a cause for concern on the part of the FSO and the presidential press service (examples include the flight on a military fighter, descent on a bathyscaphe to the bottom of Lake Baikal, etc.).

10. Putin eschews references to his master's thesis due to the fact that it was found to contain **plagiarism**[48].

---

[48] Putin is a Candidate of Economic Sciences. The subject of the thesis presented at the St. Petersburg Mining University in June 27, 1997 was "Strategic planning of reproduction of the mineral resource base of a region in the conditions of formation of market relations. St. Petersburg and the Leningrad region". According to some data, Valery Serdyukov and Sergei Glazyev were among the reviewers. Two scientists, one of whom – of Russian origin, the other - an American, discovered large plagiarized abstracts from a monograph published in the 1970s. To date, the scandal has not spread widely.

Ten "displays of force"

1. Vladimir Putin is stubborn, prone to analytical conclusions and is fiercely competitive in argument. At the same time, he relies on intuition even in simple conversation. Today, he is **rather self-confident**, but still capable of changing his position after hearing and agreeing with opponents' arguments.

2. He is **unceremonious with interlocutors** whom considers not particularly competent, rarely misses an opportunity to reveal a weakness in his opponent's position and to point to it in public.

3. He prefers a **collective process of making difficult decisions**, and, despite accusations of authoritarianism, rarely takes full responsibility for such decisions, but **has a sense of duty**, even rather exaggerated.

4. Putin is **a good psychologist**, who hates being mistaken about people; at the same time, he can skillfully hide his disappointment. The list of people with whom Putin was disappointed at different times includes Viktor Cherkesov, the former Head of the Federal Service for Control of Illegal Trafficking of Drugs; Viktor Ivanov, the former Deputy Head of the Presidential Executive Office for Human Resources; Nikolai Patrushev, the former Director of the Federal Security Service, and others[49].

5. **He is sardonic towards opponents**, using irony as a weapon, and merciless towards those who criticize him unreasonably. He treats the so-called "snakes in the grass" (who do not show their dislike of him outwardly, but, according to his information, are nevertheless hostile) with

---

[49] The three mentioned persons participated in the so-called "war of special services" in 2007. It was a public ideological confrontation between the Federal Drug Control Service and the FSB, which ended in staff movements for all participants in the conflict, and even in withdrawal of some of them out from the political field.

the greatest hostility – **it is preferable to be an open enemy of Putin than his latent opponent**.

6. Putin is inclined to **public speaking**. Prior to 2003, he had shown no such inclination, and in fact avoided public appearances, but **had since overcome himself**. Since the mid 2000's, he holds the so-called "Direct lines with the President" (during the period of Putin's premiership in 2008-2012 the program was called "Discussion with Vladimir Putin"), whereby he performs an informational marathon of 4-5 hours without a break, talking to the public on a variety of topics. Apparently, he considers it useful practice and his political achievement.

7. Putin **uses figurative language**, metaphors and literary images (Rudyard Kipling and others), quotes from poets (Omar Khayyam). In our view, he generally likes Sufism, the religious-philosophical branch of Islam. He is **artistic**.

8. He **professes Russian nationalism**. Putin has claimed in private to be a "Russian nationalist", much more so than some open nationalists.

9. He **treats with respect his own and others' authority figures**: Yury Andropov, Anatoly Sobchak, Yevgeny Primakov. Among historical leaders, he gives prominence to Peter I and Stalin. Putin has thoroughly studied the role and activity of Ivan the Terrible, though he had not publicly acknowledged this until 2017.

10. He has traditionally revered the **German political style** and had developed a system relying on Germany as Russia's agent country in the European Union. (This was a success and led to the fact that Italy, and to some extent France, became interested in a similar system of relations with Russia). Today, the "German style" is merged with the **"Asian style"**, which develops through building close relations with the Chinese, Japanese and other authoritative leaders in Asia.

Ten "features of style"

1. Vladimir Putin **feels a constant need to prove his masculinity** and to conceal any internal agitation. His inclination towards risk plays a catalytic role in building his image as a popular politician and promotes the growth of his influence in society.

2. He **professes adherence to principles and fidelity to given promises**, even to the detriment of political ratings. He operates within moral and ethical categories with absolute seriousness. In 2013, observers concluded with certainty that **Putin has learned to forgive his enemies**. Signs of this psychological characteristic appeared as early as 2011–2012, but became fully apparent only in 2013, when the President pardoned and released Mikhail Khodorkovsky to the latter's dying mother.

3. Putin **takes care of loyal associates, friends and even acquaintances, who have rendered him services.** He does not leave them in trouble and distress.

4. He considers **informal communications a priority** to address formal matters: Putin has maintained his friendship with the former Stasi official Matthias Warnig, Italian Prime-Minister Silvio Berlusconi, despite the vicissitudes of his career, Romano Prodi, and others.

5. Putin is proud of the fact that in the early 2000's he helped **to prevent a real threat of disintegration of the Russian Federation**. He considers himself a true guardian of the freedom of speech in Russia and seems to become offended when the West accuses him of "suffocation" of this freedom.

6. **Putin takes the credit for the victory over the "color revolution" by pro-Western NGOs in Russia.** Since 2006, the Kremlin worked on the systematic neutralization of the efforts of foreign agent NGOs. By 2012 these efforts resulted in the practically unconditional victory for the Kremlin. Even the financing of human rights activities had been recaptured

by the President through a system of special funds – grantors supported by the Kremlin.

7. Putin **considers himself young**. There are many boyish expressions in his lexicon – "we should not meddle there"; "more trouble than it's worth to offend us"; "get out while the getting is good"; "pasted them seriously"; "the horse that draws best is most whipped"; "worked like a galley slave". He often displays **machismo**, as well: the notorious "rub them out in the outhouse".

8. On the one hand, Putin is prone to categorical thinking, underscored by high emotionality; on the other hand, he is persistent and reserved. The combination of these qualities **can give the impression of stiffness, which in fact bears no relation to reality**.

9. **Putin is inclined to ritual actions**, but also prefers to break the ritual himself. For example, he is well known for his late comings, even to the most important official meetings. This is explained in different ways, but today is used as a strong trait – anticipation forces the other party to concentrate on the main theme of the meeting, everything secondary is swept aside.

10. Putin **appreciates a hierarchical view of life and integrity in people** and disdains contraventions of settled plans. In this context, he tends to **sacralize his own power**, highlighting its attributes: complete public support, attention to rituals emphasizing the absolute nature of the power and so on[50].

Resume. *Vladimir Putin changed dramatically over his first presidential term. During his second term as president and during the premiership, the process of change of his personality almost stopped. By the third presidential term, his*

---

[50] This approach was required to remedy the situation that arose during the presidency of Dmitry Medvedev, who greatly lowered the status of the President because of his peculiar behavior, having allowed his entourage to become overly familiar with him.

personality traits began to change again. That is why, in our opinion, he won the presidential election, having won almost 64% votes without much difficulty.

The credit of trust, which he received from the population of Russia, in spite of the powerful demotivating and discrediting campaign waged by liberal groups, the United States and the European Union, left a great impression on him. ***Putin's tears*** after the announcement of his victory on the Manezh Square in 2012, in our opinion, were a sincere expression of feelings.

His gait no longer sways like that of a fighter. He has gained a little weight. ***His face became more compelling and more weary.*** Putin began to ***look in the eyes of an interlocutor for a long time***, a practice, which he reported avoided in the past. He is also said to have ceased consuming hard alcoholic drinks and to dislike public feasts, ***preferring solitude and peace.***

The president has retained ***the habit of working a lot and resting a lot.*** His custom of being catastrophically late for a meeting has remained untouched (in extreme cases - 2-2.5 hours in Russia). The same happens abroad. In 2002, he was late for 12 minutes for an audience with the Queen, 8 minutes – with the King of Malaysia, and for 45 minutes – with the Pope in 2015.

The psychological and emotional state of president Putin can be called solidly stable. There are very few people who cause him severe emotional stress today. In the past the subject of confrontation with the United States, the "Chechen issue", the "Yukos case", or the "creative class" with their requirement for Putin to step down in 2011-2012, would provoke sharp antagonism. Of all these themes, only the relations with the United States remain a genuinely sensitive issue.

CHAPTER 3.
PUTIN'S ASSOCIATIONS AND INTERACTIONS

Putin's associations and interactions with those who surround him fall into certain conditional **segments**. It is commonly accepted that there exist the "inner circle", the "external circle" and the "persons of interest". This division is rather arbitrary, since Putin periodically brings some individuals closer into his circle, keeping representatives of his entourage on the edge.

The "inner circle" segment includes **people bonded with Putin by a common past – those who enjoy his unconditional trust.**

The "external circle" segment includes people, with whom **Putin is obliged to communicate in his professional capacity.**

The "persons of interest" includes not only those who sympathize with Putin and draw his attention due to their particular characteristics, but also his **competitors and even overt adversaries.** Putin observes these intently, even when personal communications are kept to a minimum.

The institution of Putin's "trusted confidants", which appeared in the not too distant past, refers to the **artificial creation of a circle of people from different social strata and creative groups**, who were called upon to "represent the interests" of presidential candidate Putin during his election campaigns.

In between his election campaigns, the president pays scant attention to his opponents, focusing instead on interacting with the members of the so-called "All-Russian People's Front" (ARPF), an association considered to be Putin's main foundation for cultivation of bureaucrats and the so-called **"nationalization of elites"** on both the federal and regional levels.

The ARPF is a special institution - with no registered membership - that helps the Russian Presidential Administration to resolve ongoing problems of governance and to settle crisis situations in the regions.

Another format clearly favored by the president is the *Direct Line with Vladimir Putin* – a special politico-technological instrument that allows him to plainly and visually demonstrate his connection with the society and its people. This tool is continually perfected by technology. The particulars of topic selection and the contingent involved in these events underscore the extent, to which **simple voters welcome the principle of "manual governance" of the country**.

Who makes decisions in Putin's team?

"Who makes the decisions in Putin's team?" is a most pertinent question for those interested in Russia's modern history. The situation is simple and simultaneously complex.

Current and operational policy **decisions are made collectively by the permanent members of the Russian Security Council**, which is held on a weekly basis every Friday. Recent history has seen an increase of extraordinary meetings, thanks to the vigorous activity of Russia's "Western partners" aiming to achieve its political destabilization and the destruction of its economy through the so-called "sectoral" sanctions.

In addition to the President, the Prime Minister, and the Speakers of both houses of the Russian parliament (the State Duma and the Federation Council), permanent members of the Russian Security Council include the "siloviki" – heads of the agencies responsible for the country's security (the Ministry of Defense, the Ministry of Internal Affairs, the Federal Security Service, the Foreign Intelligence Service). The Council also includes the Minister of Foreign Affairs, the Chief of Staff of the Presidential Administration of the Russian Federation, as well as the Special Presidential Representative for Environmental Protection, Ecology and Transport. This post was taken up by Sergei Ivanov, the former Chief of Staff of the Presidential Administration. This, in actuality, completes the circle of people who make the key decisions on state governance.

Fundamental political decisions that influence the country's future at the geopolitical level are also made by the Security Council, but these are resolved with greater depth, using the help of experts recruited through the Presidential Administration or other agencies, depending on the relevant sphere of competence for each particular issue.

On the one hand, **the decision-making is certainly collegial**; on the other hand, **Putin often takes personal political responsibility for the result**, as happened with Crimea and Syria.

There have been known cases of Vladimir Putin's utter disappointment with his close associates: examples include the former Deputy Chief of Staff of the Presidential Administration Viktor Ivanov, the former Head of the Federal Service for Combating Illicit Trafficking in Narcotic Drugs Viktor Cherkesov, the former Head of Russian Railways Vladimir Yakunin. These persons never managed to win back Putin's confidence and regard and were forced to leave the Russian "*power Olympus*".

There are people, whom Putin trusts unconditionally and whom he treasures: Foreign Minister Sergei Lavrov, Defense Minister Sergei Shoigu, Director of the Foreign Intelligence Service Sergei Naryshkin, Special Presidential Representative for Environmental Protection Sergei Ivanov. Vladimir Putin is said to have repeatedly discouraged these persons from resigning and transferred them to those areas of governance that he considers most difficult and challenging.

In this regard, there is reason to believe that those who consider Putin an authoritarian leader inclined to make decisions on his own are mistaken, to put it mildly. Most likely, they confuse the concept of "authority" with that of "authoritarianism".

Yes, Putin is popular: his appearance in public is always a sensation, he is a superstar in the Western sense of that term. This is his strength and, in a way, a curse, since he has obviously had no personal life for the longest time. In essence, it seems, *the modern world is built on the envy of beautiful women and the hatred of strong men...*

Of course, the President has a circle of advisers. This circle is changed regularly, from one presidential term to another.

In practice, the very process of making policy decisions in Putin's administration always implies the involvement of concrete executors who, collectively or one-on-one with the President, develop the conceptual measures in any given direction. The initiator of a policy quite often acts as its executor, while the President exercises control, helps with administrative and political resources, and shares responsibility.

Vladimir Putin's team is divided into spheres of activity, organized by "projects" and resembling the system of "Olympic gods", where the president acts as *Zeus the Thunderer*, while the other participants in the process play the role of *sectoral gods* responsible for specific projects and directions.

In Russia, this system is called the *"manual governance of the country"*. Whether one endorses this concept or not, it was exactly this system, created under Stalin, that led to the rise of the USSR, despite extremely difficult conditions and innumerable losses.

At the current stage, Putin's team has its own *"immortal / immutable gods"* and even *"demigods"* – those new members of the team who are on a "probation period", though obviously enjoying the favor of the Russian president. They have prospects within the framework of the 2018-2024 project, as nobody can abolish the natural aging of the current "golden team" of Kremlin figures.

The "presidential talent pool" of the Russian president is a novel concept that has emerged only recently. This is a rather official list of people, compiled, extended and shortened by a special department in the Presidential Administration, which contains the main reservoir for officials appointed by the head of state. In 2017, for example, this list consisted of 135 people who met special requirements and possessed a considerably high professional level.

It is obvious that **Vladimir Putin is in search of a worthy successor**. He has recently confessed this in a conversation with the children from the Sirius Educational Center. This brings extreme indignation to the Russian liberal public, who advocate an unconditional and regular alternation of power, as well as to Russia's foreign partners, who find the current President, to put it mildly, a difficult interlocutor because of his intransigence. (It seems that Mikhail Gorbachyov and Boris Yeltsin had established a certain model concept that a Russian president must necessarily give way to his "Western partners".)

Incidentally, it was thanks to Putin that the expert and political community began to call Russia's foreign partners in the West as "*our Western partners*" (with a known touch of irony, implying that realistically they are not our partners at all...).

A rumor has been generated somewhere from the entrails of Russia's liberal community that Putin's entourage has long considered him a "tsar". Rumors about the return to the institution of a monarchy in the country, albeit a constitutional monarchy, abound as well. Such rumors, eagerly picked up by the liberals' foreign colleagues, are regarded by the Russian president with irony, drawing his ridicule over those who spread them.

In 2013-2014, the Kremlin effectively resisted the attempt to create a "personality cult" of Putin by analogy with Stalin. Curiously, his opponents were the most avid supporters of this cult creation. It is likely that they hoped that the "cult" would hasten the disappointment with the national leader among the majority of Russians. However, the opposite effect was observed in the end: the image of Joseph Stalin with his so-called "personality cult" seemed to have layered onto the image of the incumbent Russian president and strengthened him in the perception of Russians. Eventually, the images of Stalin and Putin practically merged in the citizens' eyes, and they began to expect that the head of state should act as Joseph Stalin would act at the present stage. This translated into a popular expression "Stalin would have dealt with you properly!" and the unequivocal expectation of reprisals against those representatives of the Russian establishment who did not meet the Russians' longing for justice.

Surprisingly, these trends became clearly visible as early as 2013, whereas the external informational pressure on Putin mobilized not only his supporters, but also those social groups that had previously showed no interest in him. As a result, Putin regularly receives the overwhelming support from the Russian population, which is registered through opinion polls. Results of these polls are undisputed by most of Putin's political opponents.

The so-called "inner circle" of the Russian president has changed little over the past 10-15 years. Thus, Head of Rosneft (the country's largest taxpayer) **Igor Sechin** is still one of Putin's closest associates, despite the application of the sanctions regime against him by the United States.

Having said that, we should note that the imposition of sanctions on members of Putin's team only resulted in this "inconvenience" being generously set off by the top leadership – by admission of those affected to large-scale projects inside the country, which made them considerably more wealthy. For instance, preferences were given to Gennady Timchenko, the Rotenberg brothers and the Kovalchuk brothers – all representatives of the president's "business circle" from among his acquaintances long before 2000, when Putin became the head of state for the first time.

Perhaps, it was Sechin's activity that has been the subject of the closest scrutiny by experts and detractors in recent times. Sechin has been working to compose a strategy for the development of Russia for both its near and distant future – according to his own understanding, of course. His partners, Glenn Waller from ExxonMobil (Russia) and Robert Dudley from BP, are trying to help him in this undertaking, while, naturally, pursuing the interests of their own companies.

Not long ago Sechin managed to get a toehold in the West, where he had a highly ambiguous reputation after the so-called "Yukos affair" that destroyed the business empire of Mikhail Khodorkovsky. However, the introduction of the "anti-Russian sanctions" has completely changed the situation. From the moment the sanctions were applied against Sechin personally, communication with him has become very risky and some of his foreign partners, except the closest ones, simply gave up on him.

Sechin's weak point is considered his susceptibility to Putin's harsh remarks about the former's excessive enthusiasm for PR projects, which make the President suspect Sechin of an aspiration for greater independence in making key decisions. Nevertheless, it is obvious that the CEO of Rosneft enjoys the confidence of the Russian president and is a member of the "inner circle".

Clearly, Rosneft itself is Putin's favorite "Teddy Bear". One of the tasks, assigned to and capably fulfilled by Sechin, was **making the company the main source of the state budget reinforcement.**

Personal friends of Vladimir Putin play a big role in the "inner circle" of the president. These include the above-mentioned **Yuri Kovalchuk** (banking, insurance, Gazprom, media) and **Gennady Timchenko** (an oil and gas trader, NOVATEK, investments). They are the president's confidants on economic issues and their political weight is only expected to increase. The Rotenberg brothers (construction, banking) are also especially close to Putin.

Valery Golubev (Gazprom, investments), **Alexei Kudrin** (financial and audit expert – in May 2018, appointed Chairman of the Accounting Chamber of the Federal Assembly of the Russian Federation, a body that monitors the due expenditure of state funds), **Sergei Naryshkin** (the Director of the Foreign Intelligence Service), **Vyacheslav Volodin** (the Speaker of the State Duma), **Sergei Shoigu** (the Defense Minister) and **Sergei Sobyanin** (the Mayor of Moscow) have likewise recently strengthened their positions.

Sergei Ivanov (former chief of staff of the presidential administration, who became the Special Presidential Representative for Environmental Protection, Ecology and Transport, but retained his seat as the permanent member of the Russian Security Council) and **Valentina Matvienko** (the Speaker of the Federation Council) have recently receded into the background, though without any considerable loss of political weight.

Russian Foreign Minister **Sergei Lavrov** enjoys the role of a popular media persona close to the president. Lavrov regularly ranks at the top of various popularity ratings and number of references. His political prospects were narrowed, however, due to his professional specialization.

A special place near Putin is occupied by his partner in the so-called "ruling tandem" (2008-2012), the "eternal" Prime Minister **Dmitry Medvedev**. Since 2012, from time to time Putin demonstratively spends his free time with Medvedev, drinking tea, riding bicycles, walking together. This is done in order to alleviate the bureaucratic tension that periodically arises in the Russian establishment because of persistent rumors about Medvedev's impending dismissal. Putin has gone out of his way to establish that Medvedev enjoys his unconditional confidence and support.

The Putin opposition movement (Putin being its "main target") in Russian society, which garners so much time and attention from the

American, British and European diplomats, has experienced regular periods of reformatting since 2012. Representatives of the "non-systemic opposition" have been incapable of "exploding" (in a positive sense) their election campaigns. Of course, they place the entire blame for their political failures on "Kremlin intrigues". At the same time, they pointedly neglect the fact that the protesters oppose a leader who is the hyper-popular among the ordinary Russian population, which, of course, brings to naught their efforts to more or less convincingly win at least one election.

The protest groups regularly try to engage external factors to support their efforts – the U.S. and the EU, which are likewise extremely interested in discovering the "weaknesses" of the Russian president, who in recent years has demonstrated an extreme degree of intransigence in all areas, political and economic.

However, it is apparent that the intelligence and law enforcement agencies are thwarting – and will continue to thwart – any attempts to create such an "alliance". On the other hand, it should not be expected that there will be total suppression of the opposition: their potential is too valuable for Putin for keeping the power verticals on their toes (in anticipation of a possible replacement of certain structural elements that fail to stand the moral pressure of the "protest groups").

Despite the efforts of the president and his administration, the situation in the Russian social strata makes it obvious that **in the future, "political fatigue" with the Russian leadership can serve as a serious stimulus to the downgrading of Putin's personal rating**.

As a result, **the so-called potential "successors" of Putin may well come to the fore in the information field** to create *"the impression of a consistently stable future"* among the population and major elite groups.

In addition, Putin and his political strategists have big plans for the protest groups. Generally controlling the process, they plan to mobilize more and more new loyal groups of the population around the presidential team, thus increasing Putin's personal popularity.

In order to balance his influence in the society, Putin has also **started to distance himself from his business environment**, although it is quite clear that he does not plan to completely break off relations with his "support groups": not only the Kovalchuks, but also the Rotenbergs are now starting to form powerful media pools (with the aim of influencing the public opinion).

There is a high probability that Putin will eventually "purge" his political environment; all the prerequisites are already in place, and, in fact, this process is under way.

Putin's team is mainly replenished through the recruitment of provincial elites and the involvement of young people.

Russian society today is entering an active phase; this is especially felt against the backdrop of the symptoms of the global financial and economic crisis that has lasted since 2008.

Any mistake committed by the authorities today can lead to serious economic losses and, as a result, to political damages. In this regard, members of Putin's entourage strongly feel the strain and anxiety over their future. The president uses (and encourages) these emotions to emphasize **the importance of his figure as a stabilizer of relations within the power group.**

It is obvious that Prime Minister Medvedev took a step back in his own political development in order not to interfere with Putin's political development and dominance over the other participants in the processes. Then again, Dmitry Medvedev generally stood no chance in 2012–2017, because his team actively supported the so-called "liberal political wing", which includes the former Head of the Yeltsin administration Alexander Voloshin and other iconic figures from the Yeltsin past.

Moreover, **Vladimir Putin continues to fashion a system of strategic management of the country's politics and economy,** parallel to that led by Medvedev, but **of a dominant nature**.

In fact, a whole network of agencies has been created in the Kremlin for the ideological support of the President, which suggests that the "new Putin" of the third term has developed an **ideology of state governance** that is altogether different from that of Medvedev.

Putin has also intensified the development of personnel at the Presidential Executive Office, which many call the "Administration of the president" by analogy with the American White House. For a long time, sources have considered **Yevgeny Shkolov** the chief "Kremlin personnel officer". The ex-Deputy Minister of Internal Affairs and ex-Head of the

Economic Security Department of the Ministry of Internal Affairs, Shkolov was appointed Aide to the President. (We would note that he had been dismissed from the Ministry of Internal Affairs at the initiative of then President Medvedev and appears to have a score to settle.) However, in 2018, Shkolov left this post in favor of **Anatoly Seryshev**, a former FSB officer.

As a result, **along with the build-up of Putin's administrative power, a process of withdrawal of Medvedev's associates from the decision-making system in the Kremlin and other government bodies is evident.**

It is believed that for some time Medvedev seriously took his role as a modernizer of the administrative system in general and the United Russia party in particular. The rating of the "ruling party" started to increase for the first time after the shuffle on September 24, 2011. The prime minister's entourage immediately associated this fact with Medvedev's leadership in the party, which he has chaired from May 2012.

Eventually, there emerged the concept of the **"Medvedev clan"**, consisting of those officials who are dissatisfied or weary of the rules and notions established by Putin. There are persistent rumors that all of them have certain agreements with Medvedev. A massive group of "oligarchs" and other businessmen, who categorically disagree with the rules of distribution of the financial and resource flows set by Putin, have formed around these officials.

It is also reported that the first to join the "Medvedev clan" were the "oligarchs" who originated from the Caucasus and Central Asia. Having unlimited financial resources, the latter dole out money to all the officials who have joined the clan, including Medvedev himself. Sources also argue that "old-style oligarchs", such as Pyotr Aven, Mikhail Fridman, Roman Abramovich, Viktor Vekselberg, and others, allegedly sympathize with these principles: arguably, they are also dissatisfied with the distribution of financial and resource flows.

In any case, **Dmitry Medvedev has not yet emerged from the "political shadow" of Vladimir Putin and focuses mostly on non-committal routine activities.** Being in this "shadow", the prime minister allowed sources to profess very warm relations between him and the President. However, despite concessions on the economic branch of the Russian Government

(Putin made concessions almost everywhere), Arkady Dvorkovich (Deputy Prime Minister until May 2018) and Igor Shuvalov (First Deputy Prime Minister until 2018), both close to Medvedev, were separated from the "real" economy supported by state-owned holdings, and were relegated to mostly organizational processes and general issues.

Besides, Medvedev has to establish a new system of relations with each of the new ministers (all of whom are relatively young professionals). If the prime minister plans to use his standard approach of administrative pressure, then, in the end, the work of these departments may be hindered or even paralyzed, which will certainly affect the socio-economic performance of the new cabinet.

It must be noted that **Medvedev had secured for himself certain levers in the real economy** – when heading the Russian Government, he replaced Putin as Chairman of the Supervisory Board of VneshEconomBank (VEB).

In Putin's circles, they note that the pressure exerted to subordinate him to the interests of different players – the U.S., the U.K., Germany and China – will only mount. Perhaps, that is why Putin has actively "disconnected" those Medvedev associates who had a pro-American reputation and has surrounded himself with varied kinds of government and civil institutions, securing thus the needed substantial support from those loyal to him. Clearly, **Putin tried to debug and fine-tune the system for implementation of the projects of his third presidential term.**

The search for a successor and/or the nomination of Vladimir Putin himself resembles the situation of 2006/2007 yet characterized by a kind of the *discourse with masochistic dimension* imposed from the outside. It appears that the opponents of the incumbent President in advance sought a pretext *not* to be nominated. A similar phenomenon took place in 2004, when instead of the traditional participants (Vladimir Zhirinovsky, Gennady Zyuganov), the campaigns were waged by their "backups".

In this regard, Putin has demonstrated an interesting quality: he expressed a most sound idea about the ratings ("*the key is not to be their hostage*"), reasoning that as soon as a politician falls into dependence on the ratings, his actions become inadequate and weakly correlated with practical goals. Such a politician does not take well-considered and sober decisions, but proceeds from the current state of affairs. The fact that Putin understands this is a very valuable quality for the organization of work within his team. Meanwhile, the main idea of the interview was as follows: *keep calm, don't worry, Russia is ready for an information – and even a hot – war, but does not want it.*

Putin's associations inside the country

Having published their "sanctions list" in 2014, the U.S. authorities themselves assigned Vladimir Putin his inner circle, figuratively speaking.

It is noteworthy that **the President of the Russian Federation is not on this list – he was "given a pass" to emerge from the difficult situation.** However, **so far, the personal sanctions only helped to consolidate Putin's team,** since the degree of dependence on him by these associates personally increases.

Currently, the circle of people who take part in the formation of the economic agenda jointly with the President, includes the following officials:

- Prime Minister Dmitry Medvedev,
- Special Presidential Representative for Environmental Protection, Ecology and Transport Sergei Ivanov,
- Aide to the President (for macroeconomics) Andrei Belousov,
- Chairman of VneshEconomBank Igor Shuvalov (First Deputy Prime Minister until 2018),
- First Deputy Prime Minister and Minister of Finance Anton Siluanov,
- Chairman of the Central Bank Elvira Nabiullina.

If special closeness to Putin is evaluated from the point of view of **emotional ties,** the criterion being the degree of emotional involvement and attention paid by the president to certain persons, an analysis of his communications shows that the circle of those really close to Putin includes the following persons:

- Director of the Foreign Intelligence Service Sergei Naryshkin,

-Special Presidential Representative Sergei Ivanov,

-First Deputy Chief of Staff of the Presidential Administration Alexei Gromov,

-Press Secretary Dmitry Peskov,

-Minister of Defense Sergei Shoigu,

-Head of Rostec Holding Sergei Chemezov,

-Minister of Foreign Affairs Sergei Lavrov,

-Chairman of the Accounting Chamber of the Federal Assembly Alexei Kudrin (the economic reform ideologist).

The circle of businessmen-confidants, with whom Putin makes decisions on the social and economic development of Russia, includes the following persons:

- Yuri Kovalchuk (joint-stock bank Rossiya),
- Gennady Timchenko (NOVATEK),
- Valery Golubev (Gazprom),
- Arkady Rotenberg (SPM-Bank),
- Igor Sechin (Rosneft).

The circle of politicians-confidants includes the following persons:

-Prime Minister Dmitry Medvedev,

-Deputy Prime Minister Dmitry Kozak,

-Chairman of VneshEconomBank Igor Shuvalov,

-Speaker of the Federation Council Valentina Matvienko,

-Speaker of the State Duma Vyacheslav Volodin.

The circle of the "siloviki"-confidants includes the following persons:

-Minister of Defense Sergei Shoigu,

-Director of the Federal Security Service Alexander Bortnikov,

-Director of the Foreign Intelligence Service Sergei Naryshkin,

-Director of the Federal National Guard Troops Service (Rosgvardia) Viktor Zolotov,

-Minister of Internal Affairs Vladimir Kolokoltsev,
-Secretary of the Security Council Nikolai Patrushev.

Familial relations again began to play a big role in the current political landscape. The fact is that the stability of elite groups gradually led to the situation whereby the children of top Russian officials and businessmen began to marry each other, thus forming real *dynasties*. This will make it extremely difficult in the future to organize any anti-corruption struggle.

Rumors of this nature were spread after the divorce of Vladimir and Lyudmila Putin. It seems that this direction was chosen by the detractors of the incumbent president of Russia as the most demotivating for his support groups.

Strangely enough (for the U.S. and the EU), **it was the information attack from outside that consolidated the Russian society and strengthened Putin's personal position.** Without the "sanction war", it would be difficult to rationalize the obvious mistakes and the ineffectiveness of Medvedev's Cabinet of Ministers. Instead, the aggressive rhetoric of Barack Obama and Angela Merkel had extended the *expiration date* of Putin's personal power indefinitely.

We would like to recall that a similar situation, though in a milder form, took place when Obama decided to "aid" Medvedev to reach a decision on the possible nomination for a second presidential term in 2012 and announced Washington's full support of him. After such an "aid", the Russian political circles simply refused to even consider this option.

Actions of various NGOs, intrigues in the course of the "sanctions war", "world marches", and the dubious circumstances surrounding Mikhail Khodorkovsky, produced an expected announcement: the latter announced his readiness to become President of Russia.

The statement was hardly politically responsible, as Khodorkovsky's nomination is technically impossible under the Russian law, given his previous criminal convictions. Therefore, it would be logical to assume that the announcement was made under the influence (or pressure) of certain circumstances. Similar circumstances apparently faced Mikhail Kasyanov in 2003, when the latter resigned as prime minister and suddenly, unexpectedly for his associates, picked up the opposition banner, though he had previously claimed to start up a consulting business and even registered a business firm for this purpose – MK-Analytics.

Khodorkovsky has lost all political independence. Most likely, he seeks to uphold **a reputation of the "fighter against the regime" in the West, of which he became a hostage.** As a result, he was forced to revive the Open Russia Foundation (OR)[51] and to conduct basically anti-Russian activities during the so-called "Ukrainian crisis". **Khodorkovsky formulates the ultimate goal very simply: change of the regime.**

The hyperactivity in the ranks of Khodorkovsky's supporters is explained by the need to attract new funds to organize a full-scale information attack against Putin personally.

Khodorkovsky no longer hides the fact that his task lies in the gradual destabilization of the situation in Russia with the aim of seizing political power. On the other hand, his associates say that Khodorkovsky has no presidential aspirations. Allegedly, he is guided by a mere desire to attract additional funds from the outside for his team.

Khodorkovsky's business partners have swindled him and are now working to tap Russia for money without his involvement. According to the same sources, **he lives on a tight budget,** and therefore intends **to deploy the "revolutionary propaganda" at the expense of outside investors** interested in the process, following the example of the late Boris Berezovsky[52].

Khodorkovsky and Putin may eventually become political sparring partners. But today, Putin is generally skeptical of the representatives of the opposition, the so-called "protest movement": he doubts its probity.

---

[51] From the organizational point of view, the new Open Russia will resemble the Committee of Civil Initiatives of ex-Finance Minister Alexei Kudrin. That means that the organization will not receive funding and register with the Ministry of Justice. Khodorkovsky announced creation of a network organization on the basis of Open Russia; in his understanding, it should replace the parties of today. A similar idea was already sounded by Mikhail Prokhorov (a Masonic type party of 500 lawyers, etc.). Nothing good came from this: he had to abandon the idea.

[52] Mikhail Khodorkovsky's visit to the U.S. was quite revealing in terms of his prioritization. The official goal was to get acquainted with the nature and society of this country. In deed, if not in name, he aimed to establish relations with a part of the American establishment on a personal basis. In this regard, there is reason to argue that the voyage is very much resembles a traditional roadshow to attract financing for current political projects.

This view of the Russian leader is fully justified: since 2011, the "creative class" has failed to formulate a positive agenda (their requirements to the authorities) and has continued to play on the citizens' negative emotions.

Putin's associations outside the country

On the foreign policy track, Vladimir Putin appreciates when his partners and associates have a clear position, consider national interests (integrity is particularly appreciated in this sense), and can formulate a mutual benefit from cooperation.

For instance, the situation with the nearest neighbor, Poland, was rather tense at the time when the Kaczynski brothers (President and Prime Minister) were under the US protectorate. Once Donald Tusk came to power, Putin's attitude towards Warsaw turned highly sympathetic, despite the fact that Tusk came to power under pro-European slogans.

As we have already noted, many foreign diplomats point out **the transparency of the foreign policy** based on Russia's real capabilities.

If Boris Yeltsin conducted his foreign policy looking up towards the U.S. and "friend Bill", Putin turned to closer neighbors, "friends" Jacques Chirac, Gerhard Schröder and Silvio Berlusconi. At the same time, Putin never failed to keep the Middle and Far East out of his radar[53].

The gradual and considered manner of acting when resolving subtle political or economic issues is a hallmark of Putin, who acts quite decisively in other cases. For example, a visa regime for the citizens of Georgia was introduced immediately in response to that country's anti-Russian policies.

---

[53] Back in September 2000, Russia formally fully recognized the provisions of the Soviet-Japanese Joint Declaration of 1956, in which Moscow expressed its willingness to transfer two of the four South Kuril Islands (more precisely, the uninhabited Habomai ridge and Shikotan Island) to Japan after the signing of the peace treaty. Japan, claiming all four islands, met this step with restraint. On March 25, 2001, Putin signed the so-called joint Russian-Japanese "Irkutsk Statement", in which the two sides declared their intention to "speed up further negotiations" to "address the issue of the nationality of the islands of Iturup, Kunashir, Shikotan and Habomai" with the mention of the 1956 Declaration. Since then, there have been no developments.

Rather complex relations have developed between Putin and **Alexander Lukashenko,** because for a long while the president of Belarus did not perceive his Russian counterpart as an equal partner and tried to impose on him certain agreements that he allegedly had reached with Boris Yeltsin. It came to the crunch when Putin reportedly slammed the telephone on Lukashenko, "freezing" Russian-Belarusian relations for some time.

Eventually, Putin and Lukashenko managed to reach an understanding, largely thanks to the fact that Russian pressure groups began to position their stakes on other Belarusian authoritative leaders (Viktor Sheiman, Viktor Lukashenko, the son of the president of Belarus) and Lukashenko Sr. had to stop playing with the European Union for a while.

There are several emotional complications in Putin's relations with **Nursultan Nazarbayev.** The most significant of these is Putin's active use of the "Eurasian project", the authorship of which is claimed by Nazarbayev. In this context, the latter has expressed rather strong criticism for his Russian counterpart, albeit privately.

The fact that Putin tries to establish primarily an emotional connection with leaders of other countries has worked often (Gerhard Schröder, Silvio Berlusconi, Jacques Chirac), and the Russian president succeeded. There were flat failures, too: Angela Merkel, Nicolas Sarkozy, Francois Hollande, with whom he did not manage to establish relations. Relations with the new French President Emmanuel Macron are just taking shape, but some sources in the Kremlin believe that the French President has yet to show off his treachery.

Barack Obama was the most difficult partner for the emotional Putin. Although it fell to Dmitry Medvedev, while he was president of Russia, to build the initial dialogue with the U.S. President, relations between Putin and Obama went sour right away. Both were very wary of each other and clearly experienced a personal animus. In the Kremlin corridors, they mentioned that Obama could not forgive Putin his constant tardiness for meetings.

It is likely that **Donald Trump** will be unable to establish his own special relations with Putin, because he is too crotchety, to the point of eccentricity. Unwillingness to compromise is a trait that Putin does not recognize in his partners at all.

Putin's relations with **Silvio Berlusconi,** nicknamed "Cavalier", the former Prime Minister of Italy, are perhaps the most researched and high-profile. It is known that the Russian president is extremely kind to his Italian friend and that the feeling is mutual. Berlusconi almost always spoke about Putin in a complimentary way. In difficult times, when Berlusconi was threatened with lengthy imprisonment, it was Putin who stood up for him publicly, without denying that he was doing it out of friendship.

It is clear that this friendship had caused much grievance in the Western world and may serve as the reason for the misfortunes of both "dear friends". The relations between Putin and Berlusconi became especially close after the latter's attempt to establish a friendly relationship between the Russian President and **George W. Bush.**

Relations with Bush were quite complicated. At first, they showed all possible rapprochement. Putin was one of the first leaders who expressed condolences to his American counterpart about the tragic events in New York on September 11, 2001 and strongly supported the U.S. in its attempts to exact revenge on terrorists. However, after the attack against Iraq under the pretext of responding to the terrorist attack, as well as the de facto liquidation trial of Saddam Hussein, Putin's relations with Bush Jr. came to naught and became confrontational. The Russian president considered himself deceived, as he admitted in private.

Much later, after then President Medvedev, under the American spell of Barack Obama, approved of the UN Security Council resolution against Libya, which resulted in air strikes on Muammar Gaddafi and his extrajudicial liquidation, Putin again admitted to his associates that he had warned Medvedev that the Americans would first use him in their own interests and then deceive him.

Putin early on developed warm relations with German Chancellor **Gerhard Schröder,** who had a positive attitude towards Russia and believed that Germany should embrace Russia despite the obstacles put up by the United States.

Schröder apparently tried to exploit this friendship, and Putin was not always comfortable with this. Once, during a public meeting with Putin, Schröder tried to force the discussion of the allocation of significant funds for environmental needs. It was quite obvious that Putin did not wish to make any obligations in public, but Schröder insisted... Nevertheless, Gerhard Schröder continues to be a welcomed guest in Russia and a member of numerous joint projects (Nord Stream, etc.). After the relations between Germany and Russia deteriorated, Schröder was often criticized in his homeland for his closeness to Putin.

Perhaps Putin's relations with **Angela Merkel,** the current German Chancellor, who replaced the pro-Russian Schröder, are the most controversial and tragic ones.

Experts in Russia believe that the underlying reason for Merkel's negative attitude towards Russia as a whole, and Putin in particular, is that the chancellor comes from the eastern part of Germany, the GDR, and holds prejudicial views against successors to the USSR. In addition, there is suspicion that Merkel's prejudice towards Russia is strongly influenced by the U.S. intelligence agencies – the wiretapping of the German Chancellor caused a massive public scandal, which was promptly "extinguished" by the German intelligence agencies.

However, it should not be discounted that Merkel expresses her chilly attitude towards her eastern neighbor with such extreme emotion because of a number of personal circumstances. One of them was a joke that Putin is said to have played with his German counterpart: being aware of Angela Merkel's panic fear of dogs, he did not prevent his home Labrador Kony from approaching the chancellor during one of the official visits to his residence.

There exists other anecdotal evidence. According to one story, during Merkel's first official visit to Russia, at a reception in the Kremlin, she criticized the policies of Putin and his team with such severity that, for some time, those present in the audience joked: "*It seemed it was not Merkel speaking, but Condoleezza Rice*" (the well-known critic of Putin, the then U.S. Secretary of State). In other words, the relations had a rough start.

Putin has recently established particularly warm relations with Shinzo Abe, the long-time Japanese Prime Minister, and Xi Jinping, the Chairman of the People's Republic of China, who has recently extended his powers for another term.

The Russian President's relations with Shinzo Abe are quite peculiar, as the Russian side is well aware of their underlying reason – "the island issue", or the problem of the return of the "northern territories", as the Japanese put it. Nevertheless, the heads of the two states have worked intensively to established personal ties. The Japanese Prime Minister even invited Putin to his native city, a sign of a great goodwill.

President Putin is on favorable terms with Xi Jinping; they call each other friends. Theirs is a highly strategic alliance, albeit with very serious reservations. In fact, China uses Russia in its geopolitical games, and Russia uses the PRC. That being said, the sincerity of the leaders' good relations is not doubted by observers.

Resume. *It is obvious that **Putin is accustomed to developing relationships for the long term. He is ready to forgive his partners' mistakes, but he will never forget their breach of agreements, reached with him personally** (basically, this is the "Japanese style" of communication).*

*On the foreign policy track, Putin **appreciates the personality factor, soulful relations,** and personal bonds.*

*On the internal political track, Putin **has long been above the fray** of various pressure groups in the country and, recently, has **partly distanced himself from his following.***

Today, he faces serious challenges on the internal track. For instance, after his win in the March 2012 election, the implementation of Putin's election platform encountered certain difficulties. The first reason was the position of the Russian government led by Dmitry Medvedev, which favored spending on innovation and the modernization of economy over social programs. The second reason was the position of the regional authorities, which failed to cope with the increased functions transferred from the federal level.

The fulfillment of the social obligations assumed by presidential candidate Putin in 2012 was also hampered by the active anti-corruption struggle. Another obstacle lay in the aggravating economic situation: the fall in energy prices and the difficulties experienced by the systemically important Russian companies – Gazprom, Rosneft and others.

*The fact that **Putin continues to insist on the social orientation of his policy** is regularly confirmed during meetings and various direct lines.*

Nevertheless, there is a certain (specific) **"fatigue" of the Russian population with Putin the politician.** *From the political psychology point of view, this midset derives from natural causes: the country's population personifies the supreme power to a great degree, completely shifting on it the responsibility for its own problems, including household ones.*

Several analysts considered the appointment of Dmitry Medvedev as prime minister a failure that has resulted in a seriously negative attitude among the public. However, the President has not only defended "his" prime minister, but also gave his team a chance to realize their potential. In part, that helped to "remove the problem" by 2015. Nevertheless, his failure to implement the President's "May Decrees" may well radically change the situation for the worse, for both Medvedev and Putin.

The President's distancing himself from the executive vertical is less noticeable, but still tangible: it is obvious that the current cabinet of ministers, concerned with their own business problems and projects, do not particularly care about the fulfillment of the tasks assigned to them by the President.

The anti-corruption campaign actively stimulated by the supreme power is a source of pride for Putin today. *According to the Kremlin, it is conducted in a consistent manner, which fuels the expectation of positive results. Putin believes that the anti-corruption struggle should become not just a campaign but a permanent component of public policy, forcing the government bodies to rotate.*

Putin's decision to tighten the rules of the game for government officials (e.g., a ban on the ownership of foreign accounts and assets) should "squeeze" out those civil servants who are oriented toward personal enrichment from the officialdom.

This initiative, which was called the **"nationalization of the elites",** *was positively received by the population, but it requires serious improvement and constant monitoring by the supreme authority. Loss of control can lead to negative consequences: the disappointment of the population closely watching the behavior of corrupt officials will adversely affect the popularity of the President and weaken his political position.*

This policy inevitably encounters **bureaucratic resistance,** *which will contribute to the de- popularization of the president's activity (civil servants and their family members make up about 25-30% of the population in Russia).*

Evidently, Putin will not seriously rely on the support of the parliamentary parties, which are clearly unable today to launch the mechanisms of social regulation. That requires elements of "manual governance", which can only be generated by the supreme power. At the same time, **the power verticals will continue to be renewed,** which is to boost social processes as strongly as possible. The President will need new support groups, which he apparently intends to transform into a system of civil institutions, which in turn help the authorities to debug the social sphere through a gradual reduction of the state participation in this process. At the same time, the state is not disconnected from the process at all, as it happened in the 1990's, resulting in a serious social catastrophe.

The social demand for the development of the social state has long existed in the Russian society and neglecting this demand will inevitably result in the authorities' loss of legitimacy in the eyes of Russian citizens.

CHAPTER 4.
PUTIN IS FROM THE 1990'S: THE SECRET OF POPULARITY

The obsession of Moscow citizens with the *romance of protest* in 2011-2012 has deep roots, well beyond the youth culture.

The collapse of the political and economic system of the USSR in the late Soviet and post-Soviet periods of 1983-1993 (prior to the adoption of the Russian Constitution in December 1993) was a time when **the official influence of authorities and public institutions on both the youth and the older generations was extremely limited.** During this period, when the state completely repudiated its social and political obligations, Russia's population fell mainly under the impact of *the free market ideas and the consumer culture of the Soviet Union's opponents.*

Against this background, various new socially and politically active groups were actively forming, including the so-called new bureaucracy, the new "political class" (represented by the newborn business community), and organized crime (criminalization of culture, business spheres and even government authorities was palpable).

The lack of ability to adapt to social changes due to the forced de-idealization of political processes and the abandonment of social obligations by the state during the 1990's led to partial (and in some cases complete) **destruction of traditional value systems,** in particular those that still remained from the Soviet times.

This became possible because of **the waning social immunity under the powerful information technologies of the consumer society.** By and large, the post-Soviet (Russian) society divided into two parts:

– the socially, creatively and business active part that was well-adapted to the new life conditions, and

– the socially passive, gradually marginalized part that was poorly adapted to these conditions.

The socially active part became the environment, which generated new *opinion leaders* and became the source for recruitment to business and government bodies. Among other things, this fostered the notorious *"means of social mobility"* (the existence of which most in Russia refuse to believe, obeying their political orientation). The renewal of a significant part of various social groups, overturning sharply in the 1990's and then gradually through the 2010's, testifies to the availability of such means: the State Duma (not just deputies, but also their numerous assistants), business, sports and even intelligence agencies provided a very diverse contingent the opportunity to penetrate to the top levels of power.

In the 1990's, transfers from one social group to another were relatively easy: initially due to the collapse of the Soviet system of social mobility, and later due to the permeability of the boundaries of these social groups.

The division of the population into the wealthy and the poor in the early 1990's (and the ensuing social trauma), intensifying as time passed, has become a salutary medium for the development of various *socio-political diseases* and the spread of *an altered state of mind* within Russia's civil society as a whole.

In summary, **the fundamental deformation of public consciousness** occurred in the 1980's (and earlier), worsened in the 1990's, and finally took shape, so to speak, as a complex of "political inferiority" in the 2000's. As a result, the country clearly split into those who believe that the Russian society is *guilty* of inaccurate adherence to the "Western patterns" of market development, and those who insist that the country ought to proceed along its own, special path.

As a side effect, there emerged a **social creed of chasing "easy money"**, with little respect for labor and the law. In the 1990's those who succeeded were examples emulated by the youth. This once again led to a conditionally ideological (and completely false) division of the Russian society. As a result, **the public's resentments began to accumulate rapidly** in both the professional and marginal social strata, which emerged in the following forms:

- hatred of the substantial property owners (primarily the *"oligarchs"* and then the *civil servants who do not hide their luxurious lifestyle*);
- hatred of the representatives of the authorities in general and at all levels;
- hatred / envy of successful people in general.

It only remained to wait for the formation of those influence groups, which would be able to take advantage of this social tension by turning it into political potential. If we sought to model this situation, it could be vividly demonstrated with the behavior of motorists on the roads:

*If everybody complies with the traffic rules, **an advantage is obtained by those who violate them.** Looking at the latter, others also begin to violate the rules, on the basis of on their own vision of justice.*

The traffic police (the authorities), which cannot or do not want to force everyone without exception to observe the traffic rules (and even violate them themselves), become the object of ridicule, hatred and contempt. At the same time, representatives of the traffic police enjoy a priority on the road, so these feelings are blended with a burning desire to enter into the category of those having immunity over other road users.

As a consequence, spontaneous actions to express their attitude towards the situation on the roadway may well turn into mass actions of public disobedience.

Such grievances and resentments resulted in changes to everyday language and appearance of special sardonic terms, which became prevalent in the political environment. Examples include "prikhvatizatsiya" (grabby privatization), "dermokraty" (shitocrats), "demshiza" (democratic schizophrenia), etc., underscoring the emotional component of contemporary political discourse.

Concurrently with the authorities' attempts to recruit people from the regions to gradually improve the quality of elites at the federal level (such attempts have become systemic since 2004), a formation process of the *"counter-elite"* began taking shape. The latter rejected the very possibility of creating a social state on the basis of the political system established by President Vladimir Putin in early 2000's.

Some variances of this politically and socially active group, of course, existed earlier. In the 1980's, in certain circles it was known as "demshiza", in the 1990's – a contingent of various exotic parties and movements, in the 2000's – a disappointed and, in part, marginalized intelligentsia.

In 2011, the latter actively manifested themselves during the protests, organized by the self-pronounced **new leaders of public opinion.** These new leaders had to engage in a hidden but very tough competition with the previous opposition leaders, proving their right to become not only the *"face of protest"* but also *"the genuine counter-elite"* (in essence, its latest edition).

The main obstacle to the recruitment of regional elites and the formation of civil institutions was defined as **"social infantilism"** caused the overly rapid destruction of the Soviet social security system, in which the state assumed practically all the functions of supporting the life of each member of the Soviet society. In a way, the effects of this phenomenon are still visible today. Low levels of education and family values, as well as insufficient pedagogical work in general and special educational institutions, provoke various social cataclysms: "financial pyramids", civil unconsciousness in elections and others.

Nevertheless, one cannot deny the very existence and stability of civil society in Russia. Indirectly this was confirmed by a high level of social mobilization at the beginning of 2000's, when disintegration of the country was actually halted, as well as in 2014, when the "sanctions war" was levied upon Russia.

The main cause of the tense political situation in 2011 was **the global financial and economic crisis** resonating since 2008, whose serious consequences subjected the political, economic, and financial institutions to the test in Russia and across the globe. Against the background of aggravating economic conditions and under the influence of the growing social tensions there emerged various **political pressure groups.**

These groups are still today divided into "**systemic**" (parliamentary parties, civil society organizations, including the All-Russia People's Front, and various expert groups, such as the so-called "Kremlin pool"), and "**non-systemic**" (unregistered parties, social groups participating in protest actions, the party Yabloko, the "network" organization Open Russia, etc.). **This division exacerbated in the period from 2011 to 2016,** specifically in light of the "*Crimean consensus*", the so-called "*anti-Russia sanctions*", and the aggressive behavior of NATO countries.

The "systemic" groups gradually consolidated around the supreme power in the person of Vladimir Putin, while the "non-systemic" groups commenced attacking the same, directing their attacks personally against the president of Russia and representatives of his team. Notable consolidation took place despite the expectations of external pressure groups, which initiated the "sanctions" pressure on Russia, and the attacks of the internal "non-systemic" opposition, which emerged as **caricature "agents of Western influence"**, a status that will be extremely difficult for them to alter under current political conditions.

The "non-systemic" groups actively used foreign ideological and financial support in their activities, despite the fact that **the authorities provided all the basic conditions for the opposition to conduct legal political activity.** Regardless, it was external support that drove the formation of stable "protest groups"[54]. The groups had the appearance of either political parties, or public associations, or were represented by specific individuals.

In the period from 2011 to 2016, the so-called "protest potential" had finally matured, as it seemed to the organizers, and even managed to evolve, ready to use the post-crisis situation and social tension to their advantage.

Various protest figures' circle and degree of participation in political events was determined by recruitment activities carried out by Western

---

[54] The West's money in Russian politics is more terrible than the Islamic state. Vedomosti, 11.10.2017. https://www.vedomosti.ru/politics/articles/2017/10/11/737341-dengi-zapada; Evidence of the work of the non-systemic opposition for Western countries. Ruxpert. http://ruxpert.ru//Доказательства_работы_несистемной_оппозиции_на_стра ны_Запада

NGOs, the U.S. State Department and other organizations. Ukrainian and Georgian experts, who had experience in organizing "color revolutions" in their own regions, also began to work with them.

Following a "crackdown" period during **"sovereignization" of the Russian democracy and the so-called "era of special projects"** of Vladislav Surkov from 2004 to 2011, political liberalization led to the multiplication of political parties and civil society organizations[55].

These organizations received an opportunity for broad financing in the form of *"presidential grants"*. Organizations, which had traditionally opposed the federal and regional authorities, also gained access to the financial resources allocated by the Russian leadership.

The potential emergence of a new constructive opposition through the declared liberalization of the party and political space was met with a neutral-hostile attitude by the established "systemic" parties, which had passed into the State Duma and felt a serious competitive threat represented by *young party members.*

The Communist Party and the Liberal Democratic Party of Russia (LDPR) were particularly anxious; their leaders expressed their concerns directly[56]. Infant party projects faced serious resistance from "senior party comrades", especially at the regional level. As a result, in spite of party diversity and a significant number of new projects, none of them could become competitive against the parliamentary parties.

Under these conditions, understanding that the parliamentary parties will in every possible way hamper the political development of their young competitors in the regions, the Presidential Administration of the Russian Federation reached a principled decision to secretly support the "youth". This included such unconventional methods as the transfer of votes

---

[55] For the first time, the concept of "sovereign democracy" was disclosed by Vladislav Surkov in 2006: "Our, Russian model of democracy is called "sovereign democracy". We are building an open society, not forgetting that we are free... We want to be an open nation among other open nations and to cooperate with them by fair rules, and not be controlled from outside. Sovereign Philology. Lenta.ru, 13.09.2006. https://lenta.ru/articles/2006/09/13/surkov/

[56] Single-mandate deputies return to the State Duma: a test and a hidden threat. RIA Novosti, 1.03.2013. https://ria.ru/politics/20130301/925372038.html; United Russia and the Communist Party are asked to move over. Kommersant, 21.01.2014. https://www.kommersant.ru/doc/2388514

necessary for registration in regional elections from United Russia to their political opponents. For example, such assistance was provided to Alexei Navalny in the mayoral election in Moscow in 2013, when his headquarters could not collect the necessary number of votes to clear the so-called "*municipal filter*".

Of course, this policy was perceived quite ambiguously by the members of the "ruling party" both in Moscow and in the regions. However, from the standpoint of political strategy, the move turned out justified: opponents were forced to recognize the priority of the "ruling party" unafraid of its rivals to such an extent as to even provide them with political support.

Later this approach was applied at the elections of 2016, when United Russia, having won the election, shared the posts of chairmen and their deputies in the Duma Committees with other parties that passed into the State Duma. Such parliamentary party tactics proved highly effective: the 2016 State Duma remained split between only four parties, which was interpreted by a number of experts as a sign of political stability.

From 2011 to 2016, mainly as a result of preventive actions by the federal authorities, protests that were dubbed "Bolotny"[57] or "white-ribbon" began to take on various new forms, such as the Russian Opposition Coordination Council, short-term party alliances (for example, the Democratic Coalition), etc. Nevertheless, their attempts to unite and mobilize in the form of the so-called "*Marches of Millions*" proved unsuccessful: the marches gradually degenerated into "protest walks", then came to naught.

Thus, by 2017, in search of social reasons to make people take to the streets, the protest groups began to engage in open provocations, trying to mislead minors, attracting them to agitation, which is directly prohibited by law[58].

The "non-systemic" opposition has acquired the following characteristics:

---

[57] During this period, a white ribbon on the lapel was the symbol of the protest - in commemoration of the first mass protest on the Bolotnaya Square in Moscow, the success of which, incidentally, has yet not been repeated.

[58] By this time, the "non-systemic opposition" was finally marginalized, having occupied a very specific and small section of the political field.

1) they do not accept any form of cooperation with the authorities (that make them similar to professional criminal organizations, which also under no pretext cooperate with representatives of the law);

2) they focus exclusively on the federal agenda and are unable to form an agenda understandable in the regions, which is the reason for their continued failure in regional elections;

3) they focus exclusively on criticism of the government and the negative picture, thus earning an unofficial name "haters";

4) they are unable to offer more or less intelligible programs for the country's development alternative to official ones.

It should be noted that throughout this period the federal authorities represented by the Presidential Administration of the Russian Federation actively seized the anti-corruption initiative from the opposition, having launched a systemic fight against corruption in 2012 and a project of "nationalization of elites".

In the end, the protest environment generated **professional revolutionaries,** not very numerous, inclined to unconditionally overthrow the existing authorities acting beyond the framework of legal political processes. The remaining significant part of the representatives of the protest groups either emigrated (under the guise of the so-called "*political emigration*", though it was obvious that they openly used their opposition status and hypertrophied the alleged persecution by the authorities to receive "political asylum" in the countries with more comfortable living conditions), or withdrew from the protest activity, or chose the path of legalization at the municipal level in representative authorities.

Against the background of aggravating crisis conditions in the world, the following **new political pressure groups** began to form in Russia under the influence of the emerging social tension:

1) groups influencing the authorities (including the protest groups, the self-proclaimed "*creative class*", "*angry citizens*", etc.) and

2) groups protecting the government ("*protectors*"), scattered around many party-political projects, regardless of the right-left bias.

The relative stability of the current political system can be seen in the fact that the authorities do not enter the zone of direct conflict with the protesters, but offer their basic principles for *changing the social order* and even a new system for *recruiting the elites*[59]: the liberalization of the party and political field, the systemic struggle against corruption on a new level, the toughening of control over civil servants in the form of the "nationalization of elites", etc.

By this time, the Russian regions have gone through several waves of "rejuvenation" of top executives, one of which was organized by President Dmitry Medvedev, and another already completed during Vladimir Putin's current term. Personnel rotation in the regions in 2016-2017 was accompanied by a massive arrival of "young technocrats", the youngest of whom was the 31-year-old Anton Alikhanov, interim Governor of Kaliningrad, and the oldest – the 45-year-old Alexei Dumin, interim Governor of the Tula Region.

The stability of the current Russian political system is not the result of its stagnation, but, on the contrary, the result of a "*social backlash*" in this unequivocally rigid construction, which allows *simulating "dismantling of the regime"*, but not allowing its destruction. Moreover, the presence of the "means of social mobility" (for example, when a large part of the deputy corps changed after the State Duma elections in 2016) **allowed this political system to develop actively** in this period.

In the meantime, Vladimir Putin's team remains quite monolithic and includes primarily experienced politicians, "heavyweights". All external attempts to destabilize the situation have been unsuccessful: **the mobilization potential of the country's population turned out to be big**

---

[59] From the monograph "Personnel Reserves of Russia. Members and features of formation of elites." // Authored and compiled by A.B.Shatilov, A.V.Yudelson, S.V.Doichenko; edited by A.A.Mukhin - Moscow, the Center for Political Information, 2006.- 199 p.

enough to prevent the development of events by analogy with other countries – Georgia, Ukraine, Moldova, Syria etc.

Putin and the opposition: uneven relations

In the period from 2011 to 2016, the "non-parliamentary" field had gone through its own evolution, dynamic in relation to its electorate, similarly to the experience of the parliamentary parties. The main factors that influenced the "non-parliamentary" forces were as follows: the liberalization of the political space, the so-called "*Crimean spring*", and the sharp deterioration in the relations with the United States and the European Union.

During this period, the "non-systemic" part either degenerated, or switched to a fundamentally different state – immigrated or fell into political oblivion.

The first indicator, which determined this division of the political field, was the attitude of a party or an association to Vladimir Putin personally, as well as to the foreign and domestic policies that he pursued. **Shifting of the responsibility for all the negative events taking place in Russia on to Putin personally and to his closest associates became the main political credo of the "non-systemic" opposition.**

The "systemic" part of the political field generally stood in solidarity with the course pursued by the head of state, though some of them did not support the activity of the RF Government and the Prime Minister, as well as held different attitudes towards the "ruling party". At the same time, the "systemic" opposition was ready to conduct a dialogue with the authorities at various levels. Against this background, **the "non-systemic" opposition stood in stark contrast, wishing to obtain powers by any means, including unconstitutional ones.** Representatives of the "non-systemic" opposition expressed and still express their opinion through holding rallies, public appeals to sabotage the decisions or the operation of the government bodies, and sometimes appeals to overthrow them.

As a rule, instead of an open dialogue, the "non-systemic" forces use a well-established scheme of provocative influence, which consists of the following typical steps:

1. A newsworthy event (as a rule, focused on a humanitarian problem, understandable to an ordinary Western individual) is addressed to a person in power in the judicial or law enforcement bodies or in the political environment.

2. A campaign is launched to blatantly defame the object, who may, in case of a lucky coincidence, respond to the attacks (for example, the Head of the Russian Investigative Committee Alexander Bastrykin used to respond emotionally to the information attacks by the oppositionists).

3. As a result, step by step, the public influence of this person is devalued and the atmosphere of psychological discomfort around him/her is created. In the future, any actions of the authorities aimed at protecting this person turn the "public opinion" (or rather, the opinion of a specially selected audience) against the representatives of the authorities themselves.

Speakers of the protest groups often and willingly use a widespread and, at first glance, harmless method – the *substitution of notions*. This involves the making of a certain statement, which rapidly gains "comments", then passing it off as a fact that is allegedly "already recognized by everybody". Gradually such substitution of notions became the main tool of the protest movement. Those detained for participating in the riots on May 6, 2012 within the "Bolotnaya case" were dubbed "political prisoners" by the protest environment. In fact, they were accused of specific criminal acts – aggressive behavior towards law enforcement officers, and not of the ideological struggle with the regime.

Concluding the description of this scheme, we note its key goal: **the protest participants aim to obtain the so-called "public immunity"**, whereby any actions of law enforcement and investigative bodies against them, even quite legitimate, are presented as "politically motivated".

The next distinguishing feature of the non-parliamentary political field of Russia is its permeable **ideological self-identification, when a public or**

political association occupies a certain niche in the political system according to the lobbied set of values. With all the diversity of ideologies in Russia, sometimes it turns out that a party or a movement cannot, does not want, or does not know which ideological niche to join. Sometimes there is an informal change of values or a combination of several, even mutually exclusive, political attitudes, which is more characteristic of the parliamentary field.

This happens, as a rule, to expand the electoral potential or to change the "exhausted" landmarks that do not follow the trends in the society. The "non-parliamentary" field, unlike the "parliamentary" field, does not widely use methods of combination or transition to different ideological levels. At the same time, some protest groups have displayed a tendency to not occupy any ideological niche, being neutrally "civil", and their leaders position themselves simply as "civil activists".

The "non-systemic" opposition is characterized by a kind of division of labor, since each of the opposition elements is mainly seeking to take the most radical position possible to contrast against the background of other political forces. Since the lobbied values are so "radical", it is impossible for any of them to be combined. For example, nationalists by definition would not be able to uphold the rights of the LGBT community, and generally "look askance" at the entire liberal "get-together".

In the mid-2000's, the bulk of the Russian "non-systemic" opposition was represented by Mikhail Kasyanov, Boris Nemtsov, Vladimir Ryzhkov, Garry Kasparov, Eduard Limonov, among others. By the electoral cycle of 2011-2012, these "old school" oppositionists became exhausted and lost their former popularity even among their own supporters. Nevertheless, most of them actively participated in a series of protests.

The development of internet technologies has made it possible to bring young opposition leaders to the forefront. They contrasted with the old ones in that they formulated more acute and urgent issues, organized "creative" actions, actively used social networks, etc. They represented the whole ideological spectrum, from nature protection activists to nationalists, having become recognizable in a short time by the urban intellectual and so-called "creative" milieu (in contrast, their recognition in the regions was traditionally low)[60].

The names most often mentioned in the media included Aleksxei Navalny, Ilya Yashin, Dmitry Gudkov, Yevgenia Chirikova, Sergei Udaltsov, Dmitry Dyomushkin, and others. The majority of figures in this category stuck to the formula *"a problem required a protest; protest means work; the more protests – the more jobs."*

In other words, certain protest leaders' lack of the necessary level of education, as well as political and administrative experience, **provided natural conditions for such leaders to migrate into the social group of "professional revolutionaries"**. The ultimate stage of the evolution of the new protest groups could be defined as *"protest for the sake of protest"*.

Former politicians, who had been in the position of power in the past, represented a separate category of protest leaders or speakers. These included Boris Nemtsov, Mikhail Kasyanov, Vladimir Milov, and others. The representatives of this group had a certain political baggage, which was often used against them, making it difficult for them to become leaders in the new youth protest environment. Apart from this group stood Mikhail Khodorkovsky, who actively joined the political process after his release from prison thanks to that pardon granted by the Russian president.

Although everyone has their own motivation for participating in the protest movement, the movement is united by the common desire to take **political revenge**. Many of these people are well known in the West, as they regularly attend various meetings and conferences and speak out there with criticism of Putin and his team.

The "old guard" in the protest movement is also represented by Russian human rights defenders, renowned since the 1990's and even earlier: Lev Ponomaryov, Lyudmila Alexeyeva, and others. Nevertheless, the latter played virtually no part in the 2011-2012 protest, being busy with their professional activities.

The new leaders of the opposition, unburdened with heavy political karma, receiving grants or simply financial aid, were mostly young, universal and mobile. As was previously noted, **opposition-minded people often use a conflict situation around them as a "horizontal lift" to a**

---

[60] "Creative class" is the self-styled name of protest figures in 2011-2012, when these groups felt the need for self-identification. Subsequently, the term did not take root.

purportedly better life in Europe. At the slightest signs of impending, often imaginary, threat, they apply for political asylum, since this status brings a substantial permanent income and allows them to continue carrying out opposition activities while living in comfortable European conditions.

Wealthy Russian oppositionists with funds in the Western banks, and with "closet skeletons" in the form of their unsuccessful political past, are less odious but more predictable, since **the Western intelligence agencies likely control their finances.** This would explain the strange behavior of, for example, former Prime Minister Mikhail Kasyanov, who abruptly changed his plans to engage in lobbying through his registered company MK-Analytics, dismantled a well-organized office with employees and became an oppositionist. Similar oddities could be observed in the behavior of Mikhail Khodorkovsky, who has started to gain momentum in the opposition movement[61], despite the initially declared non-participation in politics after his pardon.

The next mainstream trend in the evolution of the 2011-2016 protest movement was **the process of self-expression ("performance") of individuals or groups through defaming the acting authorities.**

As a rule, members of the group *"protest as self-expression"* belong to the creative intelligentsia and the elite youth. Likely, the reasons for such unusual self-expression lie not in a real desire to receive certain political dividends or financial support, but in the field of psychology, determined by an internal creative crisis. Ideologically, such persons belong to nihilistic groups.

In the period from 2011 to 2013, it became *trendy* in the urban environment among different groups of intellectuals to oppose the authorities. A category of "celebrity" children emerged immediately: Ksenia Sobchak, Maria Gaidar, Dmitry Gudkov, Maxim Vitorgan, Vladimir Kara-Murza Jr., etc.

Groups of creative intellectuals, who showed interest in the protest, included representatives of the cinema and music industry, writers, journalists and media hosts. Most of them took an active part in protest

---

[61] Khodorkovsky and the opposition discussed the "fate of Russia" in London. Izvestia, 11.11.2015. http://iz.ru/news/595515

actions: Boris Akunin, Olga Romanova, Yury Shevchuk, Oleg Basilashvili, Leonid Parfyonov, Viktor Shenderovich, and others.

It is worth noting, however, that many representatives of creative professions, though not sharing the policy of the authorities, were ready for a normal dialogue and behaved constructively.

Some representatives of the intelligentsia decided to reinvest the "profit" received in the form of media promotion on the wave of protests in 2011-2012 during the *"Crimean spring"*[62], but badly miscalculated the vector of the trend. To their regret, they lost the support of the most part of their adherents and actually became personas non grata at political and cultural events held in Russia.

The development of the Internet space created another form of self-expression, based on a simple formula *"the more disgusting, the more sensational"*. This form of self-expression tried to institutionalize as presentations of "modern art".

For example, creativity of a group Pussy Riot, known for its scandalous "performances", was not appreciated in Russia: it was unpopular, caused misunderstanding and rejection among the vast majority of its citizens. By contrast, the West recognized Pussy Riot as "prisoners of conscience" and generally gave them a special place in the world of the modern art, placing them on a par with outstanding thinkers[63].

Piotr Pavlensky competed for "oppositionist" status with the young ladies from Pussy Riot during this period. His "creative" actions were likewise noted by both the opposition and foreign observers, who later granted him a "horizontal lift" to France, on the ground of alleged political persecution in Russia[64]. The symbolism of his creations may be little understood by an ordinary art connoisseur, but some prominent protest leaders hailed it as the highest form of the contemporary Russian art[65]. Still, even within the opposition environment, there are those who disfavor Pavlensky and believe that his performances serve to discredit the

---

[62] "Crimean spring" refers to the process of returning the Crimea to Russia.

[63] The FP Top 100 Global Thinkers. Foreign Policy. 26.11. 2012. http://foreignpolicy.com/2012/11/26/the-fp-top-100-global-thinkers/

[64] Pavlensky was granted political refugee status in France. RIA Novosti, 04.05.2017. https://ria.ru/world/20170504/1493684654.html

[65] The victory of Russian modern art. Alexei Navalny's official website, 08.06.2016. https://navalny.com/p/4903/

opposition[66]. The content of Pavlensky's works, their coverage in the media, as well as the expressions of support by many creative and "artistic" oppositionists, appeared to bring to light the worst of the essence and methods of political protest.

In the eyes of an inexperienced citizen, the works of Pavlensky, associated with the opposition forces, could be represented by his action "Fixation", in which not only the "quasi-artist" himself, but **the opposition in general had its genitals nailed to the Kremlin pavement**, as if to underscore their lack of prospects for reproduction and the future[67].

It is worth noting that the development of the new "insane" protest trend created a "window of opportunity" for gay activists and LGBT community defenders who either participated in the protests of 2011-2013 or held their own single-person protests. This activity intensified in 2017, when the waves of mass protests had long receded, and only algae and foam remained on the obscure political shore.

The "change of generations" in the opposition was accompanied by an obvious degradation; most of the modern protest leaders, despite the best prospects at the start, are doomed to a short political life. The "old guard" went through the hard school of life in the 1990's, earning their political and financial capital in harsh conditions of the political reality, and therefore have a strong personality backbone. However, referring to the biographies of the young protest leaders, one finds that, as a rule, none are distressed in their environment. They are mainly "*angry citizens*", primarily from the capital of Russia, less often from other large cities, the "elite youth" or representatives of the intelligentsia[68]. At a certain stage, it even turned out that the protest actions involve *Moscow rentiers*, people who do not work anywhere on a permanent basis, rent out their "extra" apartments and, accordingly, have a lot of free time to implement political projects. Maria Gaidar was the brightest representative of this group; she

---

[66] The collision of Pavlensky or the conversation in different languages. Garry Kasparov's Facebook account. https://www.facebook.com/KasparovHome/posts/1136959649659988

[67] Nailing the opposition with genitals. Dni.RU, 11.11.2013. https://www.dni.ru/polit/2013/11/11/263774.html

[68] "Angry Citizens" is an attempt at self-identification of the protesting groups in 2011-2012. "Elite youth" are children of fulfilled, wealthy parents, not burdened with the need to earn a living, who are active participants in various political events.

openly admitted that the main source of her income is the rental of her Moscow real estate[69].

In the midst of the "non-systemic" opposition, it was widely believed that the clean-up of the political party field in the 2000's **led to the emergence of a vacuum** that needed to be filled. They counted on the emergence of a free protest electorate in the country, as well as on foreign financial assistance for organizing the public activity.

Financing of political parties from abroad was forbidden, of course, but NGO's could receive foreign funding in that period, albeit in a limited format. That is why the measures taken by the government in this direction – further restricting financing from abroad – were so painfully perceived in the protest and human rights environment.

On the eve of the electoral cycle of 2011-2012, attempts to create specific party associations for the purpose of nominal participation in the political process were resumed by the "non-systemic" opposition. The opposition really intensified their efforts to institutionalize after the procedures for registering parties were simplified and they found a simple solution for the difficult situation with raising money for organization of protest activity – **crowd funding**[70].

Relying on the compilation method of financing, **the protest gradually passed under the control of professional groups.** The demonstrative and mostly irrational hatred for the State Duma and for the elected president of the Russian Federation became the main drivers for the protest.

During this period, key centers of power began to emerge in the protest environment. There were four main protest groups: Alexei Navalny's group (general civil position), Yevgenia Chirikova's group (the "greens"), Eduard Limonov's group (the nationalists), and Sergei Udaltsov's group (the

---

[69] Where will Maria Gaidar go after her resignation? Komsomolskaya Pravda, 11.05.2016. https://www.kp.ru/daily/26527/3544488/ Maria Gaidar is the daughter of Yegor Gaidar, a prominent economist who had a strong influence on the process of reforming the post-Soviet economy of Russia. He is extremely unpopular in today's Russia because he was the ideologist behind the so-called "price liberalization" in the early 1990's, which led to a massive impoverishment of the country's population.

[70] Crowd funding is the collective cooperation of people (donors) who voluntarily pool their money or other resources together, usually via the Internet, to support the efforts of other people or organizations (recipients). This form of concentration of funds "to battle the regime" boomed in 2016-2017.

leftists)[71]. The other active persons from the protest movement were mainly represented individually: Boris Nemtsov, Ilya Yashin, Oleg Kashin, Ksenia Sobchak, etc., – without "political coloration".

After a series of popular protests in mid-2012, the opposition leaders decided to unite and legitimize themselves in the form of the **Russian Opposition Coordination Council (ROCC).** The virtually exhausted protest agenda served as a catalyst for its establishment. It became clear that the State Duma would not be dissolved and the slogan "Against Putin!" failed to garner the expected response from the public, gradually turning into a "boring mantra" unsubstantiated by any weighty arguments.

Perhaps the main reason for this consolidation attempt was the fact that in 2012 **the "parliamentary" opposition had by this point fully separated from the "non-systemic" part,** and the latter was clearly made to understand that their place was alongside political marginals, unburdened by legitimacy.

In turn, the protest contingent nurtured plans for creating parallel power bodies (a proto-parliament, a constituent assembly, etc.), imitating governmental activity in every possible way. In return for their rejection of street struggle the parliamentary parties had also been subjected to defamation by the oppositionists; this was "targeted" defamation, addressed to the entire Lower House of the Parliament. It was the State Duma in general, not only United Russia, which gradually became the main object of hatred in the opposition environment. They even came up with a mocking equivalent of its name "*Gos.Dura*" (literarily means "a state silly woman") and called it the "*delirious printer*".

Even before the idea of the "proto-parliament", **the ROCC tried to adopt a form of quasi-government.** At the meetings, they discussed creating a central executive office of the ROCC, as well as sectoral committees, following the example of sectoral ministries in the executive branch of the government. In this regard, the Council members made some typical statements that the ROCC was planning to engage in the development of specific positive action platforms (for example, the program to transform

---

[71] The ideological classification was carried out in accordance with the "ideological curiae", the same principle was used when the ROCC members were elected.

from a resource-based economy or a transition program assuming the dismissal of Putin and the re-election of the State Duma). In public rhetoric and in informal conversations, the representatives of the ROCC increasingly compared the Council with the *"interim government"*[72]. Later on, nothing was heard regarding these projects.

Opinions with respect to anti-Putin slogans quickly diverged in the ROCC: the so-called "civil activists" (Ksenia Sobchak, Dmitry Bykov, and others) were more moderate and advocated taking into account the public interest and refraining from using unpopular slogans. The more radical group (Boris Nemtsov, Andrei Piontkovsky, and others) did not want to reduce the degree of emotion and continued to call for waging the "anti-Putin" campaign. It is noteworthy that Mikhail Khodorkovsky, who was still in prison then, but was influential in the opposition circles (and was expected to become the main sponsor of the protest), took the position of the moderate part of the ROCC, having noted that the opposition should focus on *"realistic, implementable slogans."*[73]

The ideological differences among the participants of these processes became immediately apparent in the open election to the ROCC. The election itself was held in accordance with ideological quotas, which included the general civil list, the "left forces", the "liberal" and "nationalist" forces. The general civil list included all the remaining ideological diversity.

However, it was not so much the ideological diversity, but **the hypertrophied ego of every opposition representative in this body that became the main problem for the work of the ROCC.** Their competition with each other was so intense that the protest leaders could not work effectively within the framework of the joint project. Later on, the so-called **Opposition Expert Council** (OEC) appeared next to the ROCC. It was formed by ambitious activists, who failed to get in the ROCC[74]. Even these attempts to duplicate the government functions proved to be a failure, and

---

[72] The Russian Opposition Coordination Council forms an interim government. Izvestia, 12.11.2012. http://iz.ru/news/539377

[73] Mikhail Khodorkovsky: to the attention of the Russian Opposition Coordination Council. Echo of Moscow,, 29.11.2012. http://echo.msk.ru/blog/echomsk/958318-echo/

[74] Statement by a group of former candidates on the situation in the ROCC. Official site of the Opposition Expert Council. http://esovet.org/organisation/.

as a result, neither the ROCC nor the OEC were able to exist for more than one year. They reached no practical decisions and remained somewhere in the imaginary world.

In parallel with the work of the ROCC, the "non-systemic" opposition used the liberalization of the party and political space to **institutionalize in the form of party projects.**

Generally, these projects can be divided along ideological lines. The liberal parties of the non-systemic opposition began to "awake" by the end of December 2012. The Congress of the People's Alliance (later – the Party of Progress) was held in mid-December 2012; they represented themselves as a centrist party for the middle class and supporters of the European development path of the country[75]. Vladimir Ashurkov was one of the leaders of the party; later it was headed by the group's real leader, Alexei Navalny (the group concealed his leadership from the Ministry of Justice before registration, believing that his official role may impede registration).

Another organization that was not registered, the Party of 5th December (Roman Dobrokhotov and others) was a direct competitor to the Party of Progress. The first congress was held on December 8, 2012. The backbone of the Party of 5th December was formed by some members of the Solidarity movement, who entered the new party under the pretext of a response to the entry of the movement leaders, Boris Nemtsov and Ilya Yashin, into the leadership of RPR-PARNAS[76].

These two young parties were formed and led by neophyte oppositionists. Basically, they consisted of people who were far from professional politics, which in general affected the content of their platforms and the recognition of the parties. Both parties were not registered as party formations because of various violations or shortcomings in their platforms.

---

[75] Party of Alexei Navalny's associates "People's Alliance" presented a draft platform. Vedomosti, 29.11.2012. https://www.vedomosti.ru/politics/articles/2012/11/29/novye_centristy

[76] The founding congress of the Party of 5th December held in Moscow. Vedomosti, 10.12.2012. https://www.vedomosti.ru/politics/articles/2012/12/10/bolotnye_dekabristy?

Another party, Democratic Choice, first led by Vladimir Milov, managed to obtain the official registration in September 2012. The leader of Yabloko Grigory Yavlinsky, who considered Democratic Choice a suitable ally or a candidate for a joint political bloc, regarded the new party with favor[77]. However, the party did not exist long under Milov, who was removed from the leadership in 2015 because of internal disagreements with the party activists.

Far more serious forces of the so-called liberal wing of the "non-systemic" opposition gathered around the newly formed RPR-PARNAS party. It would be more accurate to say that one of the oldest, by Russian standards, Republican Party of Russia (RPR) teamed up with a young coalition of Russian "non-systemic" political organizations that adhered to liberal ideology (PARNAS)[78]. The new alliance united three leaders of the liberal wing of the opposition – Mikhail Kasyanov, Vladimir Ryzhkov, and Boris Nemtsov; but they did not manage to stay in a single party "team" for a long time[79].

In general, **RPR-PARNAS tried to become the flagship in issues of unification** among the newly formed parties of the "non-systemic opposition".

It must be noted that **the "non-systemic" oppositionists constantly attempted to unite before the elections at various levels**; they tried to unite not only among themselves, but also with "old" players, for example, with the Yabloko party. It was a sort of ritual, but all the attempts were unsuccessful.

Most of the representatives of the "non-systemic" parties of the liberal wing supported the so-called "Euromaidan" in Ukraine; in one form or another, they opposed Russia's support of the People's Republics of

---

[77] Yavlinsky announced his cooperation with the Democratic Choice association. Interfax, 22.01.2012. http://www.interfax.ru/russia/227075

[78] It is worth mentioning that before the association with PARNAS, the RPR challenged the decision of a Russian court in the ECHR, which rendered dissolution of the party unlawful.

[79] Ryzhkov was the first who withdrew from RPR-PARNAS. After the murder of Nemtsov, Kasyanov became the sole chairman of the party. According to mass media, the withdrawal of Ryzhkov was associated with his disagreement on the nomination of Alexei Navalny as the RPR-PARNAS candidate for mayor of Moscow. Despite this disagreement, Navalny was nominated.

Donetsk and Lugansk, as well as the accession of the Crimea to Russia. Later, however, Alexei Navalny recognized the Crimea a part of Russia[80].

In addition to Navalny, Sergei Udaltsov spoke in favor of the recognition of the Crimea return, appealing to the will of the people[81]. This division on the basis of the principle *"Crimea is ours!"* became very typical for all groups of the "non-systemic" opposition, including even the nationalist forces[82]. The largest number of opponents to accession of Crimea clustered in its liberal wing.

The relative majority of the "non-system" opposition representatives expressed a more carefully-worded opinion on the *"Crimean issue"*. Mikhail Kasyanov stood in stark difference to them; he spoke not just for the unconditional transfer of the Crimea to Ukraine, but also for the supply of lethal weapons and the introduction of the UN mission to the Donbass[83]. Thereby, the former prime minister, a very experienced politician with the understanding of political risk, shut the door on his political future. On the other hand, this is consistent with the assumption that Kasyanov joined opposition ranks not of his free volition.

In the end, the only party from the "non-systemic" opposition, RPR–PARNAS, won only 0.7% in the 2016 elections to the State Duma.

The so-called "systemic" non-parliamentary parties have undergone multiple internal changes. They included parties that exited the Just Russia (the Russian Party of Pensioners, the Russian Environmental Party "Greens", Rodina), spoiler parties (the Communist Party of the Soviet Union, etc.), patriotic parties (Great Fatherland Party), liberal projects (Yabloko, Right Cause (since 2016 - the Party of Growth), Civic Platform, etc.)

---

[80] Navalny recognized the Crimea as a part of Russia. Lenta.ru, 15.10.2014. https://lenta.ru/news/2014/10/15/crimea/

[81] Udaltsov supports the decision of the Crimeans to make the peninsula a part of Russia. TASS, 10.08.2017. http://tass.ru/obschestvo/4474082

[82] Why Russian nationalists fight each other in Ukraine. Moskovsky Komsomolets, 23.06.2015.
http://www.mk.ru/politics/2015/07/23/dva-lica-russkogo-nacionalizma-oba-s-travmoy.html

[83] Kasyanov said he would return the Crimea to Ukraine without a doubt. RIA Novosti, 21.05.2015. https://ria.ru/politics/20150521/1065843615.html

Some parties, for example Yabloko, actually came to a state of decline, without practically any means to maintain their existence. Incidentally, Yabloko is actually the only party from the systemic field that did not support the accession of the Crimea and even included the issue on its return back to Ukraine in its election platform, which was practically *political suicide*[84] and affected the party's result in the federal campaign of 2016 – 1.9% plus the deprivation of state funding.

Resume. *On the eve of the electoral cycle of 2011-2012, attempts to establish party associations for the purpose of nominal participation in the political processes were resumed by the "non-systemic" opposition. However, **the intensification of party building stimulated splits and disagreements between former comrades.** As a result, the leaders of the "non-systemic" opposition tried to create new or revive old formats of interaction with potential electoral groups. The protest groups, using the fruits of liberalization, even attempted **to institutionalize in the form of new party projects:** People's Alliance, Party of 5th December[85]. However, the specificity of their generally destructive position did not allow them to establish themselves in the legal sense and they stayed in a narrow section of the political field, in its marginal part.*

*As a result of the development of the protest movement in 2011-2012, the so-called "systemic" opposition finally distanced itself from the "non-systemic" part. The leaders of the "non-systemic" groups, using increased informatization and media mobility of the society, became recognizable in the urban intellectual and "creative" environment in a short time. However, this formed quite **narrow borders for the expansion of their political influence** - the protest did not expand to the regions, despite their obvious compulsion for criticism towards the authorities. The reason was the low quality of the protest leaders (and speakers) and their inability to entice potential supporters. The high standing of the supreme power also prevented them from entering the new electoral niches.*

---

[84] Yabloko included the item on the referendum in the Crimea in its draft electoral program. TASS, 01.07.2016. http://tass.ru/elections2016/article/3421997/

[85] In the same period, representatives of several dozen protest groups held negotiations in the Moscow region to create an organization that would ensure the interregional coordination of the opposition campaigns. The initiators called themselves the "Civil Federation". The "systemic" liberals also intensified their activity; having failed at the federal level (the failure of the Right Cause project), they tried to take revenge in the regions.

In 2012-2014, **the protest gradually passed under the control of professional groups;** and the demonstrative and mostly irrational hatred for the State Duma and for President Putin became their main driver. The political peculiarity of these groups was manifested in a **steady reluctance to formulate a constructive or at least positive agenda.** The narrow field was an obstacle for the development of protest moods: the competition with each other was so intense that the protest leaders could not work effectively even within the body they elected – **the Russian Coordination Opposition Council.** This led to the emergence of another competing body – **the Opposition Expert Council,** formed by ambitious activists, who failed to get into the main body. This "generating plurality" was supplemented by a persistent inability to agree with each other, which ultimately led to a serious demoralization of their supporters.

Vladimir Putin's secret is simple. **For a large part of the population of the country that supports him, he has saved Russia from collapse,** which threatened the country as a result of the reforms initiated by Russian liberals in the 1990's. Since then, the liberal ideas and their proponents are not just unpopular, but frankly scorned by almost all social groups.

Putin was the first speaker from the "high tribune" who pondered the perniciousness of the collapse of the USSR and once again increased his popularity, especially in the regions of the country.

The "Crimean Consensus" finished off the opponents of the Russian president, in the image sense, and **turned Putin into a legend.**

CHAPTER 5.
THE INFORMATION WAR AGAINST PUTIN

The Munich speech of Vladimir Putin, delivered at the summit on security policy in Munich, Germany, on February 10, 2007, was shrewd and seamless. In it the Russian president articulated his attitude to the so-called "double standards" policy, which, in his opinion, the G7 countries professed (then still the "Group of Eight", as Russia was part of the G8 at that time).

Russian observers of Putin's speech particularly enjoyed the faces of the so-called "Western partners" of Russia during this speech: they clearly expressed discomfort and moral suffering[86]. Inside the country, Putin's speech sharply increased his political capital.

The success of the speech was strengthened by the Russian president on October 24, 2014 with the so-called **"Valdai speech"**, as well as by **the speech of Vladimir Putin at the UN General Assembly** on September 28, 2015, when he posed his accusatory question, "*Do you understand now what you have done?*"[87]. In sum, Putin has regularly used public speeches to formulate his claims to his "Western partners", alternating between the straightforward and the cautious manner.

---

[86] The Munich speech of Vladimir Putin. Wikipedia. https://ru.wikipedia.org/wiki/Мюнхенская_речь_Владимира_Путина

[87] Vladimir Putin at the UN General Assembly: "Do you understand now what you have done?". BUSINESS Online, 29.09.2015. https://www.business-gazeta.ru/article/142022

Assange and Snowden as unwitting helpers of Putin

Later on, Putin acquired unwitting helpers: **Julian Assange and Edward Snowden** – the "nightmare" of the US intelligence agencies and the U.S. State Department. Idealists, who have come to believe in justice in this world and in the idea that they can restore this justice, are **a perfect weapon against intelligence agencies,** because it is impossible to detect in advance such unreliable elements in the ranks.

Former hacker Julian Assange was forced to shelter in the embassy of Ecuador from direct threats to his freedom and life in response to exposing the corrupt and criminal activities of the leadership of different countries and, in particular, the U.S. State Department, on his WikiLeaks portal. Part of the information that he published pertained to Russia and the State Department activities in that state. WikiLeaks had also mentioned the author of this book, Alexei Mukhin, who regularly met for discussion with the staff of the U.S. Embassy in Moscow. The day before the publication of the State Department's reports on the website, the U.S. Embassy in Moscow actually apologized to him for the State Department being unable to stop this publication.

It is interesting that later, some foreign media used the image of Putin that Mukhin created during an interview with the embassy staff. Answering the question of a State Department official, regarding the relations between Putin and his entourage, Mukhin mentioned the term alfa-dog[88], implying the dominant role of the Russian president in his team: other team members clearly model themselves upon his example, using even his facial expressions and gestures.

Created in 2006, the resource WikiLeaks proclaimed its goal of exposing undemocratic governments, and even published a number of materials against the Russian authorities, as well. However, the resource sprung into

---

[88] "The picture of Russia's "alpha-dog" ruler eyeing another Kremlin term corresponds to the assessment of U.S. Ambassador to Russia John Beyrle who cast Medvedev as playing "Robin to Putin's Batman," according to leaked U.S. diplomatic cables". Russia's Putin considering Kremlin return: sources. Wikileaks. https://wikileaks.org/gifiles/docs/17/1786580_-os-retag-russia-more-russia-s-putin-considering-kremlin.html

popularity after the materials compromising the actions of the U.S. government in the Middle East were published in 2010. The publication was unprecedented, both in terms of volume and content. In fact, it had exposed the policy of "double standards" pursued by the U.S. authorities, which Putin proclaimed in February 2007 in Munich.

Until 2010, the Western media had always vigorously, pointedly and in an accusatory vein discussed problems in "non–Western" democracies. Although the world community surmised the existence of problems in the "strongholds of democracy", the governments of these countries were not subjected to any criticism.

The activity of WikiLeaks fell upon a fertile ground – the exposure of U.S. government actions inevitably became sensational. And when, shortly after the publication of the U.S. documents, an international warrant was issued for Assange's arrest in connection with allegations of sexual assault in Sweden, Putin overtly called the charges politically motivated. Thus, at a press conference after the talks with French Prime Minister Francois Fillon, then Chairman of the Russian government said: *"As far as democracy goes, it should be a complete democracy. Why then did they put Mr. Assange behind bars? Is this democracy? There's an American saying: He who lives in a glass house shouldn't throw stones. So, I want to shoot back the puck to our American partners."*[89]

The administration of Barack Obama never reconciled with the unmasking activities by WikiLeaks and, subsequently, within the political rhetoric of U.S. authorities (primarily Democrats), WikiLeaks was intrusively linked to Russian intelligence agencies, on which they hung the responsibility for the information leakage from the U.S. authorities.

The active phase of the information war against the Russian authorities occurred in 2016, the year signified with the election for the presidency of the United States. Then, in the midst of the election campaign, **WikiLeaks published tens of thousands of emails from John Podesta, campaign chairman for the Democratic Party candidate Hillary Clinton**[90]. First

---

[89] Putin about the persecutors of Wikileaks: He who lives in a glass house shouldn't throw stones. Vedomosti, 09.12.2010. https://www.vedomosti.ru/politics/news/2010/12/09/putin_o_presledovatelyah_wikileaks_chya_by_korova_mychala

[90] Spirit Cooking dinner and hot dogs: the strange world of Hillary Clinton's

portion of the emails was published by WikiLeaks on October 7, just one month before the Election Day. As a result, predictably enough, the Russian authorities were accused of the attempt to influence the outcome of the election campaign in the United States through "Russian hackers", who allegedly hacked Podesta's mail box. On October 11, Barack Obama's Administration openly announced its intention to produce a *tit-for-tat response* to Russia's cyberattacks[91].

Russian authorities have repeatedly pointed to the undeniable absence of any evidentiary basis for these accusations by the U.S. authorities. The Russian president has also drawn attention to the fact that the hysteria around the new publications of WikiLeaks was aimed at "***diverting the attention of the American people from the essence of what was exposed by the hackers***", which was in essence itself a "***manipulation of public opinion.***"[92]

The attacks by the representatives of the Democratic Party on Putin appeared to have become the key in their strategy to regain their political positions after the explosion of compromising materials from the Podesta e-mails. In fact, the Democrats resorted to the most popular way of mobilizing the supporters – **formation of the image of an external enemy: Russia in general and Putin in particular.** But the situation turned out to be extremely ambiguous for the Democrats. Earlier, in July 2016, the U.S. Democratic Party National Committee announced the hacking of its computers and warned about the upcoming leaks. The same month, **a programmer Seth Rich, the employee of the DNC,** was killed under strange circumstances. According to the official police report, Rich was killed during a robbery, but this version was called to question, since cash and all documents were left untouched with the victim[93]. At the same time, the media drew attention to how the death of Rich fit within a series of tragic

campaign chairman. Russia Today, 04.11.2016. https://russian.rt.com/world/article/330382–podesta-pisma-wikileaks

[91] Media: The CIA is preparing cyberattacks against Russian institutions. Rossiyskaya Gazeta, 15.10.2016. https://rg.ru/2016/10/15/smi-cru-gotovit-kiberataki-na-rossijskie-uchrezhdeniia.html

[92] Putin: the hysteria around the hacker attack is pumped out to divert attention. RIA Novosti, 12.10.2016. https://ria.ru/world/20161012/1479053638.html

[93] Killed under mysterious circumstances: another WikiLeaks informant was named. Vesti.RU, 17.05.2017. https://www.vesti.ru/doc.html?id=2888765

events surrounding Clinton opponents[94]. Soon after Rich's murder, Assange, without any exhaustive explanation, announced a reward of $20,000 for any information regarding the circumstances of his death.

WikiLeaks is recognized for hiding the identity of its informants for the sake of their safety and the safety of their loved ones. Therefore, Julian Assange's refusal to comment provides another argument to support the version that the DNC data leak was carried out by Seth Rich. In any case, the FBI still has not published any convincing evidence to support the version that there was a hacker attack.

Assange's statements made on various media platforms (including his official Twitter account), in which he criticized the actions of Western authorities, were cited as evidence of WikiLeaks' ties with Russia. In addition, the Western media like to recall that Julian Assange was the author of a **project called "The World Tomorrow"** – a series of television programs in four languages, English, Spanish, Arabic, and Russian, which were aired on the RT channel for several months in 2012[95]. In his defense, Assange noted that the choice of RT resulted from the fact that other channels refused to cooperate with him, whereas RT agreed to publish his material on his terms without any censure "from upstairs"[96].

The fact that WikiLeaks did not expose the actions of the Russian government was also said to supply evidence of its ties with Russia. Assange has explained in his interviews that Russia had its own organizations, a form of *competitors to WikiLeaks*, which were engaged in exposing cases of human rights violations, corruption schemes, etc. (Assange named the politician Alexei Navalny and the famous Russian opposition newspaper Novaya Gazeta among the critics of the Russian authorities.) Furthermore, Assange has stressed that WikiLeaks had no

---

[94] Five mysterious deaths of Hillary Clinton's opponents. Komsomolskaya Pravda, 15.08.2016. https://www.kp.ru/daily/26568.5/3584396/

[95] Assange TV, Presented by the Kremlin. The New York Times, 13.04.2012. https://thelede.blogs.nytimes.com/2012/04/13/assange-tv-presented-by-the-kremlin/

The World Tomorrow: Julian Assange proves a useful idiot. The Guardian, 17.04.2012. https://www.theguardian.com/media/2012/apr/17/world-tomorrow-julian-assange-wikileaks

[96] The Prisoner as Talk Show Host. The New York Times, 17.04.2012. http://www.nytimes.com/2012/04/18/arts/television/julian-assange-starts-talk-show-on-russian-tv.html

Russian-speaking employees, and that the organization was mainly focused on the English-speaking audience.[97]

In any event, none of this prevented WikiLeaks from passing compromising materials about certain representatives of the Russian elite to its official partner Novaya Gazeta in the end of 2010. In September 2017, WikiLeaks published a series of documents called **"Spy Files Russia"**[98], which reported on a company that provided the FSB and the Russian Ministry of Internal Affairs with access to the data of Russian subscribers of mobile operators. Therefore, until proven otherwise, the accusations of Assange's biased attitude towards Russia should be considered baseless.

Not everyone has fallen into the mass hysteria about the "Russian hackers". For example, after the Catalan referendum on independence from Spain, for which Russia was also blamed, Yana Toom, an Estonian member of the European Parliament, stressed that the accusations against Russia were **an attempt by the European authorities to shift the blame for their own mistakes on someone else**[99].

In contrast to Julian Assange, Edward Snowden became rather a victim of circumstances.

Snowden was actually stuck in the transit zone of Sheremetyevo Airport in Moscow when the U.S. authorities annulled his passport, notified the authorities of Hong Kong and Russia, and demanded that Russia deport their citizen. Originally, Snowden planned to go from Moscow to Latin America (different sources also reported it was Ecuador, which had sheltered Julian Assange in its embassy in London, Venezuela, or Cuba), but because of the canceled passport he had to place his fate in the hands of Russian authorities.

Temporary asylum and, soon after, a residence permit granted to Snowden allowed the Russian leadership to earn many political "points" among those who did not sympathize with the USA. For example, China, contending with the U.S. for world leadership, assumed their traditional

---

[97] Julian Assange: "Donald? It's a change anyway". L'Repubblica, 23.12.2016. http://www.repubblica.it/esteri/2016/12/23/news/assange_wikileaks-154754000/

[98] The official website of WikiLeaks. 19.09.2017. https://wikileaks.org/spyfiles/russia/

[99] Yana Toom: Putin and Assange have nothing to do with the Catalan referendum. Postimees. 18.10.2017. http://rus.postimees.ee/4262809/yana-toom-putin-i-assanzh-k-katalonskomu-referendumu-otnosheniya-ne-imeyut

extremely moderate stand: on the one hand, the Chinese authorities did not provide Snowden with refuge; on the other hand, they allowed him to stay in Hong Kong just as long as he needed to pass on the remaining secret documents and urgently leave the country.

Subsequently, Beijing officially confirmed that the Hong Kong authorities acted in accordance with their protocols[100], and they had no way to prevent Snowden from flying away. China did not shelter Snowden in light of the U.S. indictment against him, but the fact that they allowed Snowden to avoid deportation caused deep dissatisfaction of the Americans. Then again, technically the American authorities had no cause to blame the Chinese. At the time, the media speculated on the possible collusion between the Russian and Chinese intelligence agencies (this was implied in the threats by Secretary of State John Kerry regarding "consequences" for China and Russia in case it was revealed that the authorities of these countries had deliberately let Snowden aboard the plane)[101]. Yet having allowed Snowden to leave Hong Kong, China avoided an open confrontation with the United States. Nevertheless, the only thing that is clear is that Snowden could hardly manage to get to Russia if he had not cooperated somehow with the Chinese authorities.

In 2017, in an interview with the American film director Oliver Stone, Vladimir Putin admitted that Russia initially did not intend to support Snowden[102]. Snowden's arrival in Moscow forced the Russian authorities to contemplate further actions. Dmitry Peskov officially announced on June 11 that if Snowden's application for asylum were received, it would be *considered* by the Russian authorities[103]. This, of course, in no way

---

[100] "The United States, without reasonable justification, questions the legitimacy of the actions of the Hong Kong administration. The accusations against the central government of China are also groundless. The authorities of Hong Kong once again confirmed that Snowden had left the country legally as an ordinary tourist. Hong Kong had no legal grounds to detain him, since the immigration department of the Hong Kong Special Administrative Region has not yet received a notice from the U.S. government about the cancellation of the passport of the ex-employee of the U.S. Central Intelligence Agency Edward Snowden." Statement of Foreign Ministry spokeswoman Hua Chuning. China and the US quarreled over Snowden. Interfax, 25.06.2013. http://www.interfax.ru/world/314686

[101] From Moscow by plane. The fugitive CIA informer disappeared after arriving at Sheremetyevo. Lenta.ru, 24.06.2013. https://lenta.ru/articles/2013/06/24/snowden/

[102] Putin said that Russia initially was not ready to support Snowden. RIA Novosti, 14.06.2017. https://ria.ru/politics/20170614/1496438349.html

guaranteed a positive response to such an application. At the same time, it was obvious Snowden's extradition to the United States would carry practically no benefit for the Russian authorities.

Snowden, in turn, despite the claim that he had handed over all physical information-carrying media with relevant materials before heading to Russia, later nevertheless became a valuable resource for Russia.

First, Snowden could share technology with Russian intelligence agencies and advise them on issues of interaction with American counterparts. Second, the granting of asylum to Snowden was a successful bet against the ongoing campaign for a real demonization of Putin in the Western press.

Both the American and the world community as a whole split into two camps: on the one hand, Snowden was guilty of divulging state secrets; on the other hand, the ex-employee of the American intelligence agencies stirred up sympathy for having acted in accordance with the higher principles of morality, in the interests of mankind, when exposing U.S. espionage practices. Ultimately, the second camp was much more numerous, though its political weight was extremely low.

Putin's Administration had well played the sympathy card. As early as 2013, Putin justified the refusal to extradite Snowden with the lack of an agreement with the U.S. regarding the mutual extradition of criminals, which, according to the President, the Russian side had repeatedly offered to conclude. At the same time, Putin sympathized with the fate of Snowden, calling him "a strange guy" and his actions - "noble"[104]. At the St.-Petersburg Economic Forum in May 2014, the President declared from the official rostrum: *"Russia is not the country that hands over fighters for human rights"*[105]. Thereby, **Russia in the person of Putin had seized the U.S. initiative to attract political dissidents.**

In the interview with Oliver Stone mentioned earlier, Putin noted that he did not consider Snowden's act a betrayal of his country's interests,

---

[103] Russia is likely to shelter the CIA betrayer and truth-teller Snowden. NTV, 11.06.2013. http://www.ntv.ru/novosti/621237/

[104] Putin: I thought about Snowden, he is a strange guy. Vedomosti, 04.09.2013. https://www.vedomosti.ru/politics/articles/2013/09/04/putin-ya-dumal-o-snoudene-on-strannyj-paren

[105] Putin about Snowden: Russia is not the country that extradites fighters for human rights. Vesti.ru, 23.05.2014. https://www.vesti.ru/doc.html?id=1611339

since he "*did not pass any information, the leakage of which would be disastrous for his own country or for his own people*". However, when asked whether the President agreed with what Snowden did, Putin answered in the negative.[106]

Despite his utter dependence on the Russian authorities (it is obvious that the door outside of Russia, where there is a real threat to his life, is closed for Snowden; the US authorities still do not consider the possibility of granting the ex-employee of the U.S. intelligence services a pardon, despite appeals from the American public), who hold power over his residence status in Russia[107], Snowden openly criticizes not only the actions of the Government of the Russian Federation, but also Putin personally. In particular, accusations of human rights violations in Russia were repeatedly posted on his Twitter account; in 2016, he openly criticized the so-called "Yarovaya Law" (a package of anti-terrorist amendments introducing greater control by law enforcement agencies over the telecommunications industry), calling it "The Big Brother Law"[108].

The interest of the Russian authorities and the public in the fate of Snowden and Assange was dictated by long-term strategic goals.

First, both persons are in open confrontation with the authorities of Western states. Thereby, they serve as a kind of *litmus paper* for revealing the shortcomings of these political systems, which previously claimed to be exemplary democracies. In fact, **Snowden and Assange struck one of the cornerstones of Western democracies – transparency,** having exposed the populism of Western leaders in this regard.

Second, the support for Snowden and Assange is one of the manifestations of the "soft power" of the Russian diplomacy and Putin personally. By granting the political asylum to Snowden, Putin attracted a

---

[106] Putin refused to call Snowden a traitor. Lenta.ru, 02.06.2017. https://lenta.ru/news/2017/06/02/snowden/

[107] The last time the residence permit was extended in January 2017 for another two years, according to the representative of the Russian Foreign Ministry Maria Zakharova. Zakharova reported on the extension of Snowden's residence permit in Russia. Lenta.ru, 18.01.2017. https://lenta.ru/news/2017/01/18/snowden/

[108] The official account of Edward Snowden on Twitter. https://twitter.com/Snowden/status/751019610258964480?ref_src=twsrc%5Etfw &ref_url=https%3A%2F%2Fru.insider.pro%2Fopinion%2F2016-09-12%2Fkak-edvard-snouden-stanovitsya-obuzoj-dlya-putina%2F

huge interest towards Russia, forcing many to take a fresh look at the country.

It is not surprising that calls to stop demonizing Russia and to establish a constructive dialogue with the state have been heard more and more often from the "left" and "alternative" forces in the political spectrum of Europe and the United States in recent years. Providing Snowden and Assange with the opportunity to self-express also worked for the benefit of the Kremlin's "mouthpieces" – **Russian news agencies Russia Today and Sputnik.**

By and large, the accusations of WikiLeaks in relations with Russia and personal sympathies for Putin were originally aimed at discrediting the resource. Subsequently, the Western media began to regard WikiLeaks as an information war tool. The same fate befell Edward Snowden, who, after receiving the residence permit in Russia, was called a Russian spy in certain circles, which, to put it mildly, has no relation with reality.

In any event, it is necessary to recognize one indisputable fact: no matter how intensely WikiLeaks and Snowden were flagellated in American political discourse, in fact, the exposures did not lead to any fundamental changes in either world politics or the domestic politics of certain countries. The same Hillary Clinton was initially accused of the events of 2009-2013 during her term in office of the U.S. Secretary of State, when her competence was compromised by leaks carried out solely by U.S. citizens.[109]

---

[109] How Clinton's email scandal took root. The Washington Post, 27.05.2016. https://www.washingtonpost.com/investigations/how-clintons-email-scandal-took-root/2016/03/27/ee301168-e162-11e5-846c-10191d1fc4ec_story.html?utm_term=.83b19f4553b5

Tragedy of MH-17

On July 17, 2014, **Boeing 777 flight MN-17 flying from the Netherlands to Malaysia was shot down** over the territory of Donbass. All the passengers died.

Literally within hours of the tragedy, Ukrainian authorities officially laid the blame for shooting down the Boeing on the Donbass militia that were beyond Kiev's control, and, peculiarly, on Russia itself. The sheer striking awareness of Kiev on this issue raised unsettling questions at the time.

According to the data of objective control presented later by the Russian military, the Boeing changed the trajectory of its normal flight path under pressure of Ukrainian air-traffic controllers and was directed by them into the combat zone. Moreover, by the order of the Ukrainian controllers, the aircraft had lowered its altitude prior to the attack. Earlier, the reconnaissance unit of the militiamen received purported intelligence information that a Ukrainian military transport aircraft AN-26 would follow along that very course.

The Russian side, represented by the Almaz-Antey Concern, which produces the Buk systems, carried out a full-scale simulation of the circumstances and, with the help of advanced technology, proved that the MN-17 jet could not have been shot down from the territory controlled by the militia, but was rather shot down from the territory controlled by the Armed Forces of Ukraine (AFU).

Regardless, an information campaign against Russia was launched immediately after the incident and long before the findings of the official commission convened with no hurry under the auspices of the Netherlands (Russia and Malaysia were de facto excluded from participation in the investigation). The campaign has been the most large-scale in recent years and served as an information background for the introduction of the so-called "sanctions" against Russia, bypassing the UN Security Council. Subsequently, the United States literally forced the European Union to join these "sanctions" and to extend them every six months.

Many oddities were revealed as the investigation progressed.

First, the investigation itself proceeded extremely slowly (members of the commission could not get to the territory where the parts of the Boeing and the victims' bodies were located – this territory was under active fire by the AFU for half a year, despite the readiness of the militia to provide all the data for the investigators) and inaccurately – some of the remains and the ruins of the jet were just left in the place of the crash.

Second, despite the fact that formally the crash had no relation to Russia (having occurred over the territory of Ukraine, and suspects in crime being citizens of Ukraine, etc.) and the fact that Russia had a significant amount of objective data about what happened, the information provided by Russia to the commission was entirely neglected.[110]

Third, in contrast, the information provided by Ukraine was taken into consideration, but the key persons – the Ukrainian air-traffic controllers – were never interrogated (their location is unknown since then), and radar data and other technical data were seized by the Security Service of Ukraine and never released to the investigators. Moreover, evidence indicating concerted attempts to destroy physical evidence from the scene of the tragedy was exposed.[111]

Fourth, Ukraine could not explain the recorded deployment of its Buk systems in the immediate vicinity of the area of the incident (the militiamen do not have aviation), as well as the loitering of military aircraft of the AFU in the air near the Boeing – a fact, which Kiev tried to hide.

As a result, the Netherlands, which were tasked with conducting the investigation, delayed it in every possible way in order to postpone the announcement of the final verdict of the commission for as long as possible.

---

[110] The findings of the expert examination by the Almaz-Antey Concern (presented to the public on June 2, 2015) have never been taken into account. They suggested that the missile that shot down the Boeing was not the one indicated in the conclusion of the international commission, which cast doubt on the competence of that commission. The crash of the Malaysian Boeing near Donetsk. Ruxpert
http://ruxpert.ru/Гибель_малайзийского_Боинга_под_Донецком

[111] "Destroy the facts of conducting a special operation". Published: 22.05.2017 http://www.sovsekretno.ru/articles/id/5703/. Four "top secret" documents of the Ukrainian Security Service: "Conduct special measures to destroy the facts of conducting a special operation"; "Carry out effective preventive measures among witnesses to the special operation on July 17, 2014"; "Establish and detain witnesses of the civil aircraft explosion"; "Regroup soldiers who served in the territory of the village of Grabovo, the Donetsk region"; "Within the framework of a special operation, destroy all materials that indicate the presence of a combat aircraft performing combat missions in the specified area on July 17, 2014".

Since 2015, there have been attempts to create a special tribunal on the air crash. Russia has vetoed these attempts, justly believing that, absent the public exposure of the evidence regarding the incident, such a tribunal would likely resemble a *political kangaroo court*. This sense is informed, among other things, by the case of Slobodan Milosevic, who died in confinement, having never learned of his posthumous acquittal by the Hague tribunal.

As previously mentioned, the MN-17 air disaster was exploited by the U.S. in order to impose the inaugural so-called "sanctions" on Russia (bypassing the UN Security Council). In essence, these sanctions have become a tool for one WTO member country (the USA) to exert the pressure on other member of the WTO (Russia).

American experts have openly admitted that the purpose of the "sanctions" was an attempt to split the ranks of the Russian establishment and to direct the discontent with these "sanctions regime" against Vladimir Putin personally.[112]

The "Sports War" against Putin

Sport is not only one of Vladimir Putin's favorite hobbies, but also an integral part of the social policy, conducted at the initiative of the Russian president. In this regard, in recent years, Russia has repeatedly hosted international sports events: the 2013 Summer Universiade in Kazan, the 2014 Olympic Games in Sochi, and the 2018 FIFA World Cup. Thus, **Russian sports have long passed into the political field.**

---

[112] Thus, the former coordinator of the sanctions policy of the U.S. State Department, an expert of the Washington Atlantic Council, Daniel Fried reported that the process of selecting individuals against whom the sanctions were imposed "consisted in that we went to experts and found out from them, who are those the closest financially to Putin, who helped him to become rich. The names of these people are well-known, they were disclosed in open sources long time ago. All the departments of the U.S. government participated in the preparation of the sanctions lists". Daniel Fried: we could impose sanctions against Vladimir Putin. Voice of America, 27.07.2017. https://www.golos-ameriki.ru/a/russia-sanctions-putin-state-department-/3960464.html

Leaders of sports organizations,
representing the Russian authorities or big business[113]

Russian Boxing Federation

Yevgeny Murov (Head of the Federal Security Service of the Russian Federation)
2007 – 2009 *President*

All-Russia Swimming Federation

Sergei Naryshkin (Head of the Central Office of the Government of the Russian Federation, Head of the Administration of the President of the Russian Federation, Chairman of the State Duma, Director of the Foreign Intelligence Service)
2006 - 2009 *President*
2010 – 2016 *Chairman of the Supreme Supervisory Council*

Russian Rowing Slalom Federation

Sergei Lavrov (Minister of Foreign Affairs of the Russian Federation)
2007 – 2009 *President*

Russian Taekwondo Union

Vladimir Shamanov (Commander-in-Chief of the Airborne Forces of the Russian Fedeartion)
2008 – 2009 *President*

St.-Petersburg Tennis Federation

Valentina Matvienko (Governor of St.-Petersburg)
2004 – 2009 *President*

---

[113] The posts and positions of these persons are relevant as of the period of their leadership in a sports federation.

Winter Olympic Sports Association

Vladimir Kozhin (Head of the Department of Presidential Affairs of the Russian Federation)
2004 – present time *Chairman of the Council of Presidents*

All-Russian Sailing Federation

Dmitry Zelenin (Governor of the Tver Region)
2008 – 2009 *President*

National Badminton Federation of Russia

Sergei Shakhrai (Head of the Central Office of the Accounting Chamber of the Russian Federation)
2005 – 2009 *President*

Russian Table Tennis Federation

Igor Levitin (Minister of Transport of the Russian Federation)
2006 – 2009 *President*

Russian Chess Federation

Alexander Zhukov (Deputy of the State Duma, Deputy Prime Minister of the Russian Federation)
1999–2003 *Vice- President*
2003 – 2009 *President*

Judo Federation of Russia

Alexei Gordeev (Minister of Agriculture of the Russian Federation)
2004 – 2009 *President*

Arkady Rotenberg (a Russian entrepreneur; assets: Stroygazmontazh, Minudobreniya, TPS Avia, SMP Bank)

2003 – present time *Chairman of the Supreme Council of the National Judo Union*

2017 – present time *Development Manager of the International Judo Federation (IJF)*

National Karate Federation of Russia

Sergei Shoigu (Minister for Civil Defense, Emergencies and Elimination of Consequences of Natural Disasters)

2000 – 2004 *President*

Aikido Federation "Aikikai of Russia", Russian Union of Martial Arts

Sergei Kiriyenko[114] (Head of Rosatom, First Deputy Chief of Staff of the Presidential
Administration)

2001 – present time *President of the Aikido Federation "Aikikai of Russia"*

2005 – present time *Co-Chairman of the Russian Union of Martial Arts*

All-Russian Volleyball Federation

Nikolai Patrushev (Director of the Federal Security Service, Secretary of the Security Council of the Russian Federation)

2004 – 2009 *President*

All-Russian Sailing Federation

Alexander Kotenkov (Presidential Plenipotentiary Envoy to the Federation Council of the Federal Assembly of the Russian Federation)

2000 – 2008 *President*

---

[114] Sergei Kirienko is the co-Chairman of the Russian Union of Martial Arts jointly with Yuri Trutnev (Minister of Natural Resources of the Russian Federation, Plenipotentiary Envoy of the President of the Russian Federation to the Far Eastern Federal District).

VTB United League

Sergei Ivanov (Chief of Staff of the Presidential Administration of the Russian Federation)
2011 – 2014 *President*

International Fencing Federation

Alisher Usmanov (Russian entrepreneur, the founder and principal shareholder of USM Holdings)
2008 – present time *President of the International Fencing Federation*
2001 – 2009 *President of the Russian Fencing Federation*
2005 – 2009 *President of the European Fencing Confederation*

Artistic Gymnastics Federation of Russia

Andrei Kostin (Russian banker and financier, President-Chairman of the Management Board of the Foreign Trade Bank (VTB))
2006 – 2014 *President*

Continental Hockey League

Gennady Timchenko (Russian businessman, a member of the Board of Directors of Novatek and Sibur)
2012 – present time *Chairman of the Board of Directors*
2011 – present time *Chairman of the Board of Directors, President of the SKA Hockey Club*

Ice Hockey Federation of Russia

Arkady Rotenberg (Russian entrepreneur; assets: Stroygazmontazh, Minudobreniya, TPS Avia, SMP Bank)
2015 – present time *Chairman of the Management Board*

Eventually, step by step, Western politicians, media and institutions began using elite sports as an instrument of pressure on Russia to compromise the reputation of the country and its political leadership.

First attempts to discredit the Russian sports on the global level took place in 2013, on the eve of the Olympics in Sochi. It is indicative that many Western media linked the Olympics in Russia to the personality of Vladimir Putin. Thus, at the threshold of the Olympics Putin appeared in the headlines of Western magazines in the following light: *"Putin' Dirty Games"* (Internazione, Italy), *"Putin is a Super-Tsar. The Task of the Olympic Games"* (L'Express, France), *"Sochi is Putin's Ice House"* (Vrij Nederland, Netherlands).[115]

In Russia, the negative accents of Western media found support among the Russian opposition circles. Their criticism was often reduced to the desire to condemn Putin and the upcoming Olympic Games. For instance, in December 2012, Olga Romanova, an opponent of the authorities posted on Twitter: *"There was an earthquake in Sochi. I hope everything collapsed"*[116]. It must be said that the official authorities were relatively calm about this activity of the opposition, preferring not to react to such statements.

As for the accusations by the West, they touched upon many aspects of the Russian internal and foreign policy. The Western politicians and media even called for boycotting the sporting event, rationalized by Russia's actions in Syria, oppression of the opposition, and even the relations of the Russian authorities with Edward Snowden. In general, all such arguments were often rather removed from the world of sports.

The main themes, sounded by the Western politicians and media most often, boiled down to the following:

"Russia will not have time to prepare for the Olympics." The fact that Russia will run out of time to prepare for the main sporting event of the planet was one of the main topics of the foreign media.

---

[115] Campaign against the Olympics in Sochi. Ruxpert. http://ruxpert.ru/Kampaniya_protiv_Olimpiady_v_Sochi

[116] There was an earthquake in Sochi. I hope everything collapsed. Olga Romanova, Twitter, 23.21.2012. https://twitter.com/oooromanova/status/282844298859384832

For instance, just before the start of the Olympics, one of the main critics of Sochi-2014, The Washington Post, published an article "15 Signs that Russia is not Ready for the Olympics"[117], relying on "unconfirmed" facts about the situation in Sochi.

In reality, it became clear that the Olympic facilities would be ready on time as early as the second half of 2013; their construction was under the personal control of Vladimir Putin. At that time, the Western media and bloggers decided to stoop so low as to discuss minor household defects that could have been committed during the finishing works at certain facilities: this inevitably reached a point when fake evidence of plumbing faults in the infrastructure facilities began to appear on the Internet.[118]

Despite the fact that many understood that the Western media were trying to squeeze the most out of the topic from the materials that were at their disposal, the negative publicity still managed to serve a particular role: the atmosphere created around the Olympics forced many Western guests of Sochi-2014 to arrive with a clearly prejudiced attitude. Nonetheless, after the Olympics Opening Day (after the foreigners have had enough time to evaluate the offered services and appreciate the scope of the event), it became obvious that Russia had exceeded the expectations of the observers, and even major U.S. and European media outlets had to recognize the success of the organizers and to report either positively, or in a restrained manner, without negative comments.

Thus, a Canadian television channel CBC called the opening ceremony "*a wonderful and mysterious show*"; the New York Times noted that the ceremony "*embodied all the hopes of Russia related to the Winter Olympics*"[119]; USA Today noted: "*Who would have thought of it, but the only problem was the unrevealed ring.*"[120]

---

[117] The Washington Post: 15 signs that Russia is not ready for the Olympics. Postimees, 2.11.2017. https://rus.postimees.ee/2688336/the-washington-post-15-priznakov-togo-chto-rossiya-ne-gotova-k-olimpiade

[118] 8 Viral Sochi Olympics Photos That Are Total Lies. Paleofuture, 2.06.2014. https://paleofuture.gizmodo.com/8-viral-sochi-olympics-photos-that-are-total-lies-1517429839

[119] The most terrible review about the Olympics was written by The Washington Post. Delovoy Kvartal, 9.02.2014. http://ekb.dk.ru/news/samyj-zhutkij-otzyv-ob-olimpiade-napisali-v-the-washington-post-236829930

[120] During the opening ceremony of Sochi-2014, one Olympic ring failed to opened with a delay, which became the subject of multiple jokes during the Olympics

American athletes, who arrived in Sochi, also defended Russia. They wrote in their accounts in social networks: *"The Russians do everything very well"*. They also noted that the Olympics were criticized by those who could not give an objective assessment of the situation: *"It amazes me that 98% of people criticizing the Olympics are not even here."*[121]

"The Olympics in Sochi are the most expensive Olympics ever." According to certain estimates, the Olympic Games in Sochi cost Russia 51 billion U.S. dollars[122].

The general accent of claims regarding this issue can be expressed by the following quotation from USA Today: *"Such grandiose shows can only be afforded by such countries as Russia and China, because no democracy will allow to spend so much money."*[123]

The Russian opposition, as well as Western politicians and media, quite quickly tied this amount to a high level of corruption in Russia, having missed two important facts.

First, as representatives of the Russian establishment, including Putin himself, repeatedly noted, such a large amount is justified by the fact that the winter Sochi was built "practically from scratch," and a significant part of the funds was spent on **the development of the city's infrastructure**. In this context, it should be noted that Sochi has traditionally been considered a summer resort in Russia, whereas the implementation of the Winter Olympics project transformed it into a vibrant year-round tourist destination.

Second, it is important to pay attention to the future effect of the Olympics project implementation. Unlike many countries, where the Olympic facilities fall into disrepair within a few years, the opposite happened to Russia. Interest in the city as a winter resort among the Russian population increased so greatly that hotels were barely able to cope

(the humor was appreciated by Western journalists), and Audi even used it in its advertising slogan – "When four rings is all you need".

[121] Sochi a year later: the Winter Olympics, which debunked the myths. Russia Today, 6.01.2015. https://russian.rt.com/article/72247

[122] Is it true that Sochi cost $50 billion? Let us take a closer look at the figures. InoPressa, 2.11.2017. https://www.inopressa.ru/article/11feb2014/wp/sochi_1

[123] Foreign media about the Olympic Games opening ceremony in Sochi (review). RBC, 8.02.2014. http://www.rbc.ru/rbcfreenews/20140208083222.shtml

with the flow of tourists in the region in subsequent years, despite the "above average" price segment. To appraise the situation in bigger-picture terms, the city of Sochi also brought the idea of vacationing in Russia back into fashion for the Russian population, which had a positive impact on domestic tourism as a whole.

According to Deputy Prime Minister Dmitry Kozak, a close friend of Putin, as a result of the Olympics, the proceeds exceeded costs by 800 million rubles (taking into account the Russian government's net investment in the Olympic project).[124]

"Abuse of the LGBT rights." Another critical issue discussed in the run-up to the Olympics was the condemnation of Russia for discrimination of the LGBT community (which, according to Western media, was expressed in the 2013 law implementing fines for promoting homosexuality among minors).

Questions on this issue were repeatedly raised at press conferences with Putin; he always responded in a rather restrained manner.

As expected, during the sports event there was not a single case of harassment of the LGBT community. The sole exception was the owner of a gay club in Sochi who complained that the Western journalists hammered him for over 200 interviews, interfering with the regular work of his club.[125]

"The threat from the Caucasus." The campaign launched by Western journalists, who warned of terror in the North Caucasus that could spread to Sochi in 2014, also struck the reputation of the upcoming Olympic Games on the eve of the event. Thus, in 2011 Bloomberg published a material titled *"Terror in the North Caucasus threatens the Olympics in Sochi"*[126]; in 2014, Time recalled the incident at the 1972 Olympics in Munich when

---

[124] Proceeds from the Olympics in Sochi exceeded costs by 800 million rubles. Russkiy Dozor, 16.04.2014. http://rusdozor.ru/2014/04/16/doxody-ot-olimpiady-v-sochi-prevysili-rasxody-na-800-mln-rublej/

[125] The owner of the Sochi gay club complains about the influx of foreign journalists. Newsru.com, 10.02.2014. http://www.newsru.com/russia/10feb2014/geysochi.html

[126] Terror in the North Caucasus threatens the Olympics in Sochi. Inosmi.ru. http://inosmi.ru/social/20110225/166848325.html

Israeli athletes were killed in an article titled *"The Ghost of Munich hanging over the Sochi Olympics"*.[127]

For obvious reasons, Vladimir Putin could not allow even a hint of a terrorist threat against residents of Russia and foreign guests of the Olympics in Sochi in 2014. In this regard, a great part of his "security branch", that is, intelligence, security, defense, and law enforcement agencies, worked to ensure security for the guests of the Olympics – more than 100,000 employees overall. As a result of their seamless efforts, no incidents occurred, and none of the participants and guests of the Olympics noted a sense of tense security.

There were many reports that the Russian Olympics was highly appreciated by observers in both the media and social networks (mainly from foreign athletes who could objectively assess the situation in Sochi). The Head of the Olympic Committee Thomas Bach noted during the sports event: *"I enjoy it, because there are first-class conditions for athletes here. So far, I have not heard a single complaint from the participants of the Olympics."*[128]

As for the boycott of the Olympics, none of the national teams refused to visit Russia to take part in the Games, unlike 1980. The only boycott, if it can be called as such, manifested itself in the refusal of a number of national leaders to visit Sochi.[129]

It is also noteworthy that despite the massive information war, actual attempts to initiate a boycott of the Russian Olympiad were not perceived positively. For example, even Senator John McCain, who often takes a tough anti-Russian stance, publicly stated: *"Our past experience of refusal to participate in the Olympic Games had not brought us anything good."* [130]

Having encountered the skillful organization of the Olympics in Sochi in 2014, Putin's opponents preferred to drop this card. But just a year later,

---

[127] Time: the ghost of Munich looms large over the Sochi Olympics. Postimees, 1.01.2014, https://rus.postimees.ee/2647672/time-prizrak-myunhena-navis-nad-sochinskoy-olimpiadoy

[128] Sochi a year later: the Winter Olympics, which debunked the myths. Russia Today, 6.01.2015. https://russian.rt.com/article/72247

[129] Boycott or not: who and why did not go to Sochi. Forbes, 01/02/2014. http://www.forbes.ru/sobytiya-photogallery/vlast/249961-boikot-ili-net-kto-i-pochemu-ne-poedet-v-sochi?photo=1, 1.02.2014.

[130] Six reasons for boycotting the Olympics in Sochi. Inosmi.ru, 22.07.2013. http://inosmi.ru/world/20130722/211160247.html

another international scandal involving Russian sports and the representatives of the Russian political leadership, including Vladimir Putin, came to fore. We refer to the conflict unleashed by the World Anti-Doping Agency (WADA), which accused Russian athletes of using doping at international sports competitions. As of the date of writing, the conflict has not been resolved yet.

In autumn 2015, WADA simultaneously initiated two processes against the Russian athletes. In November 2015, the agency published the report of its investigation, which accused the whole body of Russian athletes of using doping in the course of a number of international competitions.

After the publication of the report, the Russian anti-doping agency RUSADA lost its WADA accreditation. This was followed by allegations of corruption against both the International Association of Athletic Federations (IAAF) and the Russian Athletics Federation (RusAF). Sanctions were applied to the Russian athletes; in November 2015, they were denied the opportunity to take part in international tournaments.

In January 2016, WADA published the second part of the report, which had political implications, as the focus was made on the corruption in the IAAF, with the Russian government's involvement. The report dropped hints of Putin's personal involvement in the scandal.

The second process was initiated by the international agency in September 2015. WADA decided to ban the use of the drug "Meldonium" (effective as of January 1, 2016), and in 2016, a number of Russian athletes were accused of using this drug.

At first glance, this situation would seem quite fair: the athletes violated the rules of the international federation and were disciplined accordingly. However, if a number of factors and various nuances are taken into account, the situation appears in an absolutely different light.

Although the swift reaction of WADA in applying the sanctions to the Russian athletes in November 2015 could surprise observers, it was difficult to judge at that time whether the investigation was objective. The accuracy of the data on doping usage in RusAF was also questioned. But the objectivity of the decision on the "meldonium" case even then caused a lot of questions in the international community, and the very situation with the ban on the drug had many signs of political overtones and double standards applied to Russia by the West.

Contrary to popular belief, stoked by the scale of the scandal, "meldonium" is not a drug. It is aimed at maintaining the work of the cardiovascular system of an athlete when peak loads are achieved. In addition to being freely available in many countries, in Russia it is also included in the register of "Essential Medicines"[131]. In the West, "meldonium" did not achieve popularity: in the U.S. and Western Europe they preferred to use alternative drugs, albeit with the absolutely similar effect.

It was this disparity that caused the Russian society to formulate the opinion on this issue assuming that the ban on "meldonium" was a consequence of the U.S. lobbying aimed at discrediting Russian athletes, and later – the Russian authorities. Moreover, the scheme used by WADA and the people interested in this scandal is quite simple: search and ban a drug that is actively used predominantly in Eastern Europe and Russia, then fuel a scandal to trigger pressure on Russia at the sports track. It should be noted that the fact that the new rules regarding "meldonium" were introduced unexpectedly played into the hands of Putin's opponents. Many athletes did not stop taking the medicine in 2015 because they were not aware of the impending ban, and the excretion period of "meldonium" is so long that it was easy enough to catch the athletes "using" it.

The theory that the actions of WADA were dictated by the desire to create an artificial conflict to discredit both the Russian athletes and the Russian leadership was also supported by the fact that the scandal began at the end of 2015, that is, less than a year before the Summer Olympics in Rio de Janeiro in 2016: it became an important instrument of pressure on Russia and the **ban of its Olympic team from participation in the Olympics.**

Having received a chance to further unwind the situation around the use of doping by the Russian athletes, Russia's opponents in international sports organizations, as expected, quickly initiated a discussion of admission of the Russian athletes to the Olympics in Rio.

---

[131] The Order of the Government of the Russian Federation N2199 of December 7, 2011. Rossiyskaya Gazeta, 16.12.2011. https://rg.ru/2011/12/14/lekarstva-site-dok.html

The Russian track and field athletes were hit first, though there were rumors that the entire Russian national team could be excluded from participation in the Games. For example, the German Der Spiegel released an article in June, which predicted: *"Russia is threatened with complete exclusion from the Olympics in Rio"*[132].

In the second half of July, less than a month before the Summer Olympics, a report by **Richard McLaren** on the use of doping by the Russian athletes was published; it was also expected to influence the final decision of the International Olympic Committee (IOC) on the admission of the Russian Olympians to Rio-2016. As a result, the IOC decided in late July not to exclude the entire Russian national team from the Olympic Games, but instead left the final decision regarding the Russian athletes to the relevant international federations. The IOC decision did not concern the Russian track and field athletes, who were still under the sanctions due to the events of November 2015. As a result, 281 Russian athletes out of 387 who planned to attend the Olympics were eventually admitted to the Games, and Russia took the 4th place in the overall medal standings.

On the other hand, Russian Paralympic athletes, who often show high results in international competitions, were entirely excluded from the Paralympics. The full International Paralympic Committee (IPC) decided to exclude the whole national Paralympic team from sport competitions based on the McLaren report.

Two parts of the McLaren report, published in July and December 2016, aroused a strong response. In them, the author accused the Russian athletes of using doping at numerous international competitions (including Sochi-2014). Representatives of the Russian establishment, a number of Russian state institutions (such as the Ministry of Sports and the Russian Olympic Committee), as well as Russian intelligence agencies were also accused by the author of active participation in the falsification of the athletes' doping tests and assistance in the athletes' use of banned drugs.

It is noteworthy that the former head of RUSADA, **Grigory Rodchenkov**, took an active part in the preparation of the report. He became one of the

---

[132] Der Spiegel: Russia is threatened with complete exclusion from the Olympics in Rio. Russia Today, 19.06.2016. https://russian.rt.com/inotv/2016-06-19/Der-Spiegel-Rossii-grozit-polnoe

most controversial figures in this conflict. Thus, according to the WADA investigation published in November 2015, Rodchenkov was accused of deliberately destroying athletes' doping test samples, extorting money from the athletes, thereby strengthening corruption in the Russian anti-doping agency, and allegedly acting under the full control of the Ministry of Sports and the Russian law enforcement agencies.

It would be expected that, given the range of the charges raised by WADA against Rodchenkov, he would be enemy number one for the Western authorities. However, in 2016 Rodchenkov migrated to the USA and became an informant to WADA and McLaren, who was then working on his first report.

It is not surprising that Rodchenkov cleverly changed his status from a major corrupt official in the world of sports to *"the Russian version of Snowden,"*[133] according to film director Bryan Vogel. Vogel, seeking fame on Rodchenkov's coattails, authored the "Icarus" documentary, released worldwide on Netflix in August 2017. The film, allegedly based on real facts, is dedicated to the Russia's state-sponsored Olympic doping program.

In December 2016, after the publication of the second part of McLaren's report, Vladimir Putin spoke out quite strongly against Rodchenkov at one of his press conferences, calling him a "scoundrel". Noting that the world of sports should be extremely open, Putin compared WADA and its policies to the "defense industry"[134]. The Russian president was accurately referring to the October 2016 hack of WADA's servers that resulted in leakage of information.

The hacker attack revealed that a number of well-known western athletes, including tennis players the Williams sisters, who legally took illegal drugs with the permission from WADA. Putin bluntly noted: *"We do not approve of what the hackers do, but what they did cannot but be of interest to the international community."*[135] But, as expected, there was no due interest

---

[133] Is the doping whistleblower Grigory Rodchenkov a Russian Edward Snowden? Inosmi.ru, 20.07.2016. http://inosmi.ru/social/20160720/237255933.html

[134] "He carried all sorts of nasty things from USA to Russia." Putin commented on the doping "leaks" by the "informer" Rodchenkov. Znak, 23.12.2016. https://www.znak.com/2016-12-23/putin_prokommentiroval_dopingovye_slivy_informatora_rodchenkova

[135] Putin commented on the doping scandal and cyberattacks on WADA. RIA

from the sports associations, while at the same time, one of the most famous Russian tennis players – **Maria Sharapova** – had already been disqualified for 15 months for the above-mentioned meldonium.

At that stage, for many observers in Russia, the doping scandal already began to transform from the "dubious actions of the West" into "an aggressive policy of double standards towards Russia." In December 2016, the second part of McLaren's report amplified this effect, and here the situation began to take a completely different turn.

In February 2017, an open letter by the IOC (which, as shown above, had already made objective decisions towards the Russian athletes) reported: *"WADA has acknowledged that in many cases there is not enough evidence to investigate the use of prohibited drugs to the end."*[136] In response to this statement, Vladimir Putin, as if exchanging compliments, acknowledged: *"The system of control over the non-use of doping, the Russian one, did not work, and this is our fault, we need to say this straight and recognize this."*[137] It is noteworthy that later the head of WADA called the open publication of the IOC letter "counterproductive" and a "sucker punch".[138]

In early September 2017, more unexpected things happened. First, the Head of the Independent Public Anti-Doping Commission **Vitaly Smirnov**, after a meeting with McLaren, said that the latter *"withdrew his accusations of state interference."*[139] Nine days later, WADA dismissed 95 out of 96 cases against the Russians mentioned in McLaren's report.

Prior to this, investigations against some Russian athletes mentioned in the report had also been halted.[140] After these news, Rodchenkov's lawyer said in an interview with the New York Times that the main reason for

---

Novosti, 16.09.2016. https://ria.ru/sport/20160916/1477149465.html

[136] WADA called evidence in the McLaren report insufficient. RBC, 25.02.2017. http://www.rbc.ru/society/25/02/2017/58b159b19a79478198ba2f96

[137] Putin acknowledged the state's fault in the failure of Russia's anti-doping system. RBC, 1.03.2017. http://www.rbc.ru/politics/01/03/2017/58b674989a7947cb9c6d314b

[138] Head of WADA called the IOC's letter on the McClaren report a "sucker punch". RBC, 3.03.2017. http://www.rbc.ru/rbcfreenews/58b919d59a7947e6136a4a9a

[139] The Kremlin responded to the reports on the changed position of McLaren on doping. RBC, 4.09.2017. http://www.rbc.ru/politics/04/09/2017/59ad72a49a794701e35f68a8

[140] Without proof: WADA dismissed the investigations against 95 Russians from the McLaren report. RIA Novosti, 14.09.2017. https://rsport.ria.ru/blog_rian/20170913/1125669704.html

dismissing these cases was "Rodchenkov's inaccessibility". In other words, WADA could not get in touch with its informant.[141]

As for the WADA decision, the Russian side naturally accepted the dismissals of investigations against practically all the Russian athletes as a positive step. However, beside the fact that the RusAF, the Paralympic Committee of Russia and the RUSADA have not yet been restored in their rights, and Russia has missed the chance to host of a number of international sports competitions,[142] there remains the moral side of this issue.

The Olympics are the most prestigious event in the world of sports. For many athletes, participation in it can be one of the most important events in their lives. Having accused the Russian athletes of doping, WADA deprived them of the opportunity to participate in the Olympics, and then admitted that they could not prove their guilt. At the same time, WADA entrusted one single person, working on the basis of data provided by a sole Russian fugitive, with the responsibility of accusing almost all athletes. The limited portions of Rodchenkov's proof, which have been released to the public, suggest that McLaren wrote his report almost verbatim from the words of Rodchenkov.

As a result, WADA, as expected, forsook the responsibility for further actions against the Russian athletes, which the integrity and professionalism of the agency remains under a big cloud.

It is clear that WADA expects the Russian authorities to assume responsibility for the creation of the doping system described in the McLaren report. The ultimate goal of such demands is obvious: **for the Russian authorities, including Putin personally, to self-discredit.** It is also evident that the whole conflict was completely politically motivated, which, incidentally, was eventually revealed after Rodchenkov's withdrawal of his testimony.

---

[141] Rodchenkov's refusal to cooperate was confirmed by representatives of WADA in late September 2017.

[142] Due to the doping scandal, Russia was banned from hosting some international competitions on its territory, including the world championships in bobsleigh, skeleton and biathlon.

Resume. On the one hand, the USA managed to show that its political influence on the world arena and lobbying potential can reach even international sports institutions, which can be used to initiate conflicts in the political sphere.

On the other hand, many are rather impressed by the restrained style of Russia, which has been tolerating the West's attacks with respect to international sporting events for several years, acting in this case as the party interested in distancing sports from politics.

Information attacks against Russia in the sphere of sports continued in 2017: countries under pressure from the United States collected "votes" to prevent Russia from participation in the 2018 Olympics in South Korea.

"Chinese Project" of Vladimir Putin: love at first sight or marriage of propriety?

Despite the attempts to present Russia as a predominantly Asian country, the European community nevertheless recognizes it as its main partner and, in general, adequately perceives its European identity. However, the expansion of cooperation first with the countries of Europe, and then with the countries of Asia is a consequence of not only the intensive cultural exchange between the countries, but also objective trends in the world economy.

The main trade and economic partner of Russia, the European Union, demonstrates the desire to diversify energy suppliers, actively invests in energy conservation and the search for alternative energy sources.

On the other hand, China is already the world's largest consumer of energy resources; its energy demand will most likely increase in the near future, in particular, within the framework of the unique project "*The New Silk Road*".

In addition, Russia, at the initiative of Vladimir Putin among others, has serious views on India as a vast future market.

It should be noted that under peacetime conditions **the nature of the trade and economic reorientation of Russia to the east would be much slower and more cautious.** Today, expanding the cooperation with the countries of Asia, the Russian leadership is solving several strategic tasks.

First, Russia's economic security is being strengthened through the diversification of economic ties.

Second, the expansion will propel the development of the Russian Far East, whose natural resources, according to strategic documents, should form the basis for implementing highly profitable projects and creating vast new production facilities to produce and process high-tech products.

Third, by virtue of their relatively close geographic position, Russia and China share similar geopolitical challenges. For example, China is interested in providing security in the relatively troubled Xinjiang Uygur Autonomous Region, while one of the security priorities for Russia is to ensure stability in the countries of the Central Asian region, whose destabilization can negatively impact the security of its own borders.

Fourth, cooperation with Asian countries in high-tech industries is mitigating the consequences of the U.S. attempts to isolate Russia technologically. After Western countries imposed restrictions on the sale of high-tech products to Russia some Russian companies that previously actively purchased these products found themselves on the brink of collapse. Expanding cooperation with Asian countries, primarily with China, which has achieved serious success in technological development, provided an immediate solution prior to the import substitution policy. Drawing further on these successes will allow Russia to avert the threat of deepening technological inferiority.

Fifth, the alliance of the actively developing BRICS countries (Brazil, Russia, India, China and South Africa) serves as a special factor and at the same time a mechanism for expanding the Russian-Chinese cooperation.

Nevertheless, in order to meaningfully cooperate with China, **Russia needs to boost its own industrial and trade potential.** Efforts in this direction are already being made. Thus, after initiating the procedures for establishing economic cooperation and creating free trade zones (the EurAsEC and the Customs Union), Russia, Kazakhstan and Belarus turned towards gradual **comprehensive integration.** This trend is quite timely, as the expansion of China to the markets of Kazakhstan, for instance, has acquired a very impressive scale and caused concerns for the Kazakh leadership.

According to the comments of the main participants of the process, **Eurasian integration** is contemplated not only as the means of economic cooperation, but as the development of a region with the common history and civilization. However, **the possibility of creating an active political union in the short term is still questionable, for a number of reasons.**

The key concern lies in the safeguarding of one's identity and sovereignty, while concurrently not abandoning the benefits of Western civilization.

The cult of consumption in Western society, which has spread to Asian countries, has caused an acute shortage of spirituality and resistance to destructive external influences, even in the most conservative countries. This crisis has provoked in the foreign markets **lackluster demand for the new edition of the "American dream"** – a dubious commodity that the United States has been trying to sell rather aggressively in recent times.

The population of the United States proudly touts its high level of consumption, while ignoring the exorbitant debt that has accumulated as a result of this *high consumption policy*.[143] In actuality, the other so-called "developed economies" in Europe and Asia also "live on credit".

Some experts are certain that the U.S. does not have enough resources to sustain such a level of consumption.[144] That is why the U.S.-led G7 countries are trying in various ways to establish and, if possible, maintain control over countries that supply the resources and industrial production.[145]

These efforts are completely genuine and, in principle, deserve respect, as they are aimed at protecting the interests of their own countries. Nevertheless, the efforts taken by politicians of such countries in the name

---

[143] According to official statistics, an average American produces about 25 kg of waste daily. In Russia, for comparison, this figure barely exceeds 1.5 kg per capita. According to the research of some American corporations and scientific centers, a consumption decrease by only 10% in the United States threatens its disintegration.

[144] Even during the "stagnation" times, the USSR's production GDP exceeded the U.S. GDP. The aggregate U.S. GDP exceeded the Soviet GDP, but only thanks to the service sector, primarily because of the extremely developed sphere of financial services, which converted virtual funds to cash, necessary to maintain and increase the consumption.

[145] In this context, the statement of former U.S. Secretary of State Condoleezza Rice, made once in 2009 and twice repeated in 2010, is very typical. She "was convinced" that all the natural resources of Siberia must serve the interests of all mankind, and not only of Russia. These resources must be managed by a "civilized international community."

of the United States can rightly be considered destructive, as they are not directed to the benefit of their own states.[146]

The problem is that the BRICS countries and some other developing countries no longer agree to follow the "American dream" and demand their own place in the global game.

This, however, is still very difficult to achieve, despite the "crisis of Western civilization" in general and the weakening of the US political influence on the global processes, in particular. With the help of manipulative technologies (e.g. downgrading a country's investment attractiveness rating, etc.), considerable funds are still being pumped out from the developing countries.

For instance, according to certain estimates, Russia received 3.5 trillion U.S. dollars for energy exports over the past 25 years (a large part of these funds was withdrawn from the country).[147] In return, the IMF allocates 15-20 billion U.S. dollars per year to maintain the existence of the ruling elites, which contribute to maintenance of these schemes in working order. Under the leadership of Vladimir Putin, Russia was one of the first states that tried to eliminate the "birth trauma" of the consumer society and dependence on the IMF aid.[148]

---

[146] Thus, the countries of the European Union actively participate in armed interventions in the interests of the United States only (Yugoslavia, Afghanistan, Iraq), in financing of military campaigns in the interests of the United States. For example, the "global war on terror", the creation of national armed and naval forces in the U.S. satellite developing countries (Yemen, Pakistan, etc.) are aimed to create a shield, a barrier to the Chinese expansion, which is the general task of the United States today.

[147] There are four flows of funds distribution: reinvestment in the oil and gas sector and export projects, reinvestment in the Russian economy, export of capital / investments, including subsidies to countries for political reasons (with uncertain effect), and export of capital to offshore zones (loss of sovereignty).

[148] The modern financial system of Russia plays against it: (a) The Central Bank is an institution, that does not depend on Russia and is practically a branch of the U.S. Federal Reserve; (b) cheaper and more readily available loans are obtained abroad, not in Russia; (c) there is no long-term money; (d) Russian banks are links in one chain for the export of capital; (e) the banks are the foremost speculators in the foreign exchange market and always turn an injection of liquidity by the Central Bank into speculation against the ruble, especially and primarily in difficult moments for Russia; (f) Russia does not have a sovereign payment card system; (g) Russian banks, financial and insurance companies are subject to the FATCA extraterritorial law of the U.S. Internal Revenue Service; (h) the tax and budget systems are built in such a way that the overwhelming majority of the regions are

Resume. *The Western establishment has waged an information war against Vladimir Putin personally ever since he delivered the "Munich speech" in February 2007, when the Russian president harshly expressed his thoughts on the "Western establishment", as well as since the conflict in Georgia (08.08.08).*

*Examples include the coverage of **Julian Assange**'s WikiLeaks and **Edward Snowden**, whom Putin called the "fighter for human rights" and whom he seems to really respect[149], the Sochi 2014 Olympics, the return of the Crimea to Russia, the situation in the Ukrainian Donbass, the crash of Boeing MH-17, as a special information operation for the initial introduction of the US-European sanctions, and the very "sanction war", which was supplemented by a doping scandal as a result of WADA's conclusions and McClaren's report. The "doping scandal" was specifically designed **as a blow to the Russian sports, the "weak point" of Putin's team**, as almost all of whom are involved in supporting the Russian sports.*

As for Snowden, Russias are well aware of his real role and contribution towards discrediting the NSA and other U.S. intelligence agencies, which created a global system of monitoring not only the opponents but also the allies of the USA. In Putin's view, Edward Snowden is an idealist who found the courage to "shake" the system. Any security schemes and technologies are powerless against such persons, since they act, so to speak, from their heart. However, the Russian president did not approve of what Snowden had done towards his country.

***Putin viewed** all these events and **attacks against himself very personally** and responded to each, "I do not forget anything," as he said during the "Direct Line" on June 15, 2017.*

The first truly hostile attack, which Mikhail Saakashvili undertook in August 2008, encouraged by Western countries, made a particularly strong impression on him. A mass killing of Russian peacekeepers in Tskhinval resulted in the break-out of the so-called five-day Russian-Georgian war.

---

subsidized, while the local authorities are powerless due to the lack of money. Now Russia has neither economic, nor financial, nor issuing sovereignty. See "To the Assessment of Russia in 2014" by I.A. Kozyreva.

[149] "Russia is not the country that extradites fighters for human rights," Putin said of Snowden at the plenary session of the St. Petersburg International Economic Forum (SPIEF). Putin about Snowden: Russia is not the country that extradites fighters for human rights. Vesti.Ru, 23.05.2014. https://www.vesti.ru/doc.html?id=1611339

Dmitry Medvedev held the post of President of Russia at that time, and Prime Minister Putin was at the Olympics in Beijing, along with George W. Bush. Perhaps, the Georgian president sought to serve his American patrons. The further fate of Saakashvili indirectly demonstrated that he was a real "agent of influence" of the United States, although in a somewhat caricature fashion.[150]

---

[150] The French magazine Nouvel Observateur published a dialogue between Putin and French President Nicolas Sarkozy, according to information provided by a diplomatic adviser of the Elysee Palace, Jean-David Levitte: "Putin: I am going to hang this Saakashvili by the balls. Sarkozy: Will you hang him? Vladimir Putin: Why not? The Americans hanged Saddam Hussein. Sarkozy: Yes, but do you really want to finish like Bush? Putin (after a moment's thought): Here you are right." The conversation between Putin and Sarkozy took place on August 12, 2008 in the Kremlin. The publication of the French magazine was cited by many Western media. According to Putin's press secretary Dmitry Peskov, the Nouvel Observateur article was "a complete insinuation of a provocative nature." "I am going to hang this Saakashvili by the balls" is an insinuation. Polit.ru, 14.11.2008. http://polit.ru/article/2008/11/14/nuts/

CHAPTER 6.
SYRIA: PUTIN'S IDEAL WAR

Readers should be aware that the intervention of the United States into Iraq and the intervention of NATO troops into Libya entailed the de facto pillaging of these countries. This involved the destruction and illegal export of historical artifacts into private collections, and the export of gold belonging to the former leadership of Iraq and Libya.

The city of Palmyra is an object of world heritage; and it was Palmyra that became the symbol of Syria's liberation from ISIS, because it was there that the world cultural treasures were "publicly destroyed" for the camera, as an explicit challenge to the world community.

The city of Deir Ez-Zor is famous, first of all, for its oil fields; the liberation of Deir-Ez-Zor from ISIS became a turning point in the financial strangulation of the so-called "khaliphate".

Getting involved in the events of the Syrian civil conflict, Vladimir Putin immediately determined the limits that Russia was going to maintain during its military operation. Thus, the day before the start of the Syrian campaign in 2015, Putin personally promised that there would be no land operation in the Syrian Arab Republic. He did not rule out Russia's participation in air strikes against "proven" terrorists in Syria, but, importantly, only within the framework of international law.[151]

Despite numerous fears expressed in Russian society that the country would get entrenched in the "new Afghanistan" of the Middle East, **for the two years since the launch of operations Russia has managed to maintain the initial strategy of a limited presence in Syria.** Moreover, the sequencing of actions, their public coverage (the Ministry of Defense organized the most open reporting on the actions of the Russian Aerospace

---

[151] Putin ruled out Russia's ground operation in Syria. Interfax, 29.09.2015. http://www.interfax.ru/world/469841

Forces in the region on a daily basis), and, of course, the *real* success of the Russian Aerospace Forces defined new vectors for Moscow's interaction with its Middle Eastern and world partners, having turned the Syrian campaign into Russia's **"ideal war"**.

The active intervention in the Syrian war was, of course, a thoughtful step by the Russian leadership, prepared well in advance. For Russia, it was not just another foreign policy project: the state worked from the thesis that it is fighting terrorism, preventing the supporters of ISIS from subsequent uninhibited return to Russia to continue their activities.[152] Explaining the launch of the military operation, Putin bluntly stated that **it was necessary to neutralize the terrorist threat "at distant approaches" to Russia.**[153]

Unlike the actions of the American coalition, Russia's intervention in the fight against ISIS was **legitimate.** The launch of military operations was preceded by an **official request** of the legitimate President of the Syrian Arab Republic Bashar al-Assad. By September 2015, when the Federation Council authorized the launch of the campaign, the civil war in Syria had been underway for three and a half years.

During this time, since the beginning of the so-called "Arab spring",[154] unprecedented events occurred in the whole Middle East. With the approval and active participation of NATO countries and their excessive use of force in the implementation of UN Security Council Resolution No 1973,[155] Libya ceased to exist as a state, turning into an arena for rivalry between clans and terrorist groups.

---

[152] As of September 2015, over 5,000 immigrants from Russia and Central Asia fought for ISIS. FSB: over 5,000 citizens from Russia and Central Asian countries are fighting on the side of IS. TASS, 18.09.2015. http://tass.ru/politika/2272750. Неофициальные данные говорили о 16 тысячах в 2016 году.

[153] Putin: terrorists must be destroyed at distant approaches to Russia, this is lawful. TASS, 03.12.2015. http://tass.ru/politika/2494776

[154] The term "Arab spring" stands for a wave of demonstrations, social protests and uprisings in the countries of the Arab world (Tunisia, Egypt, Libya, Bahrain, Syria, etc.) that swept since the end of 2010 and resulted in a change in the leadership of these countries or simply destabilized the situation.

[155] UN Security Council Resolution No 1973, adopted on March 17, 2011, became the legal basis for the operation of the international coalition in Libya, but the coalition greatly exceeded its authority, having gone beyond the mandate given by the UN Security Council.

That is why Russia's announcement of its initiation of the active phase in the fight against terrorism met with **a lively reaction and even certain approval of practically all interested states,** despite the fact that NATO countries, primarily the United States, sympathized with various groups opposing Assad in Syria. In turn, the leaders of the Middle East, who had had the opportunity to witness the sad fate of former Libyan President Muammar Gaddafi and Egyptian President Hosni Mubarak (both of them, albeit to varying degrees, cooperated with Western countries and therefore counted on their support) did not oppose Russia's participation in the Syrian affairs. After all, Putin was trying not only to eliminate the terrorist threat, but also **to build a working model to prevent the crippling of political regimes in the Middle East and North Africa.**

At the same time, despite the supportive or at least neutral attitude of the countries of the world to Russia's participation in the fight against ISIS, **the issue of the radical / moderate opposition** (uncontrolled radicals vs. coalition-controlled rebels) remained a stumbling block in Russia's relations with the so-called "broad coalition" for a long time.

The issue of the "moderate Syrian" opposition (fighting against President Bashar al-Assad, but not for ISIS) throughout the whole period of the conflict was mocked and often accompanied by the sarcastic "so-called" wording in the Russian press. The cause lay in the numerous cases of barbaric cruelty by the armed Syrian opposition towards the country's civilian population, which the Russian Defense Ministry repeatedly reported to the public.[156]

The Russian position, regularly sounded by Putin, was that **terrorism must be eradicated regardless of whether it was supported by someone or not.** As Putin said in one of his speeches: *"You should not play with words and divide terrorists into moderate and immoderate ones. Do the moderate terrorists decapitate people in a particularly gentle way? They even fight each other – for money, not for ideological reasons. Their essence and methods are the same – terror, murders, turning people into an oppressed, intimidated mass."*[157]

---

[156] For example, Syria: the Defense Ministry told about the atrocities of the "opposition" over the refugees from Aleppo. Federal news agency, 07.10.2016. https://riafan.ru/562073-siriya-mo-rf-rasskazalo-o-zverstvah-oppozicii-nad-bezhencami-iz-aleppo

[157] Vladimir Putin: Moderate terrorists are those who decapitate gently?

Instead, the Russian President suggested a different way to divide them into those fighting against Assad and those fighting against ISIS: *"There is only one ordinary legitimate army there. This is the army of Syrian President Assad. He is opposed, according to the interpretation of some of our international partners, by the opposition. In reality, the army of Assad is fighting against terrorist organizations."* Putin explained.[158]

The President's words did not mean that Russia was not ready to respect the opinion and interests of the U.S. and its partners on this matter. Russian diplomats repeatedly proposed to the Americans to compile the lists of terrorist groups in Syria and to define the configuration of the opposition, against which the Russian Aerospace Forces would not strike. The Russian Foreign Ministry and the Defense Ministry repeatedly drew the world community's attention to the fact that the American side delayed the process of such coordination.[159] As a result, various incidents periodically occurred, leading the U.S. partners to claim that the Russian side was striking at "erroneous targets".

The problem was partially solved by the creation of de-escalation zones, which were negotiated at the "Syrian problem" talks in Astana (Kazakhstan) by representatives of Russia, Turkey, Iran, and the moderate armed Syrian opposition, but this happened only in 2017. After that, Russia carried out much less "erroneous" air strikes, according to NATO.

Despite the acuteness of the question about the true aims of the Syrian opposition, **the main contradiction between Russia and the so-called "broad coalition" was the fate of the Syrian leadership in the person of Bashar al-Assad.** As is known, representatives of the United States, Europe and a number of Middle Eastern countries repeated the following phrase like a mantra: *"Assad must go."* Russia, in turn, proposed a counter-formula: *"The fate of Assad should be determined by the Syrian people."*[160]

Komsomolskaya Pravda, 22.10.2015. https://www.kp.ru/daily/26449.4/3319415/

[158] Vladimir Putin: Russia is not going to fight in Syria. BBC Russian Service, 28.09.2015.
http://www.bbc.com/russian/international/2015/09/150927_putin_cbs_interview

[159] The United States and Russia cannot agree on lists of terrorist groups in Syria. Kommersant.ru, 30.05.2016. https://www.kommersant.ru/doc/3000274

[160] For example, Putin: the future of Assad should be determined by the Syrian people. RIA Novosti, 08.07.2017. https://ria.ru/syria/20170708/1498130809.html

It is important to emphasize that Russian officials have never suggested that Assad should stay in power *forever*. Russian diplomats, just as Putin himself, only pointed out that Syria should not repeat the fate of Libya, and that President Assad should only leave his post on the basis of a democratic process. Moreover, a truly democratic vote would be possible only after the end of the war and the formation of a broad coalition government. As is known, before the civil war the leadership of Syria had been represented by the so-called Alawite minority[161], which caused the discontent of the Syrian Sunni majority.

To clearly understand this matter, it is necessary to cover the basis of claims by several countries against Bashar al-Assad. First of all, Assad's Syria had a clear pro-Iranian orientation. Earlier, in Soviet times, a considerable amount of money flowed from the USSR into the country. The Soviet Union also helped with military equipment. However, in the late 1980's, when the USSR, fascinated by "perestroika", began to withdraw from the Middle East arena, Syria, accustomed to living on subsidies, began to look for new rich allies and sponsors. This turned out to be Iran. It was then that the Syrians, so to say, "remembered" that Alawism is a brand of Shiism, and the ruling Assads ordered to build mosques in Alawite settlements (Alawites do not have temples and pray in prayer rooms).[162]

Syria even participated in Operation Desert Storm on the side of the coalition against the enemy of Iran – Iraq, then ruled by the Arab Socialist Ba'ath Party, just like in Syria. Syria thus turned on Iraq, despite the fact that merely a decade before the conflict the leadership of the two countries – Syria and Iraq – had considered unifying – not only the two wings of the Ba'ath Party, but even the two states into a single one.[163]

Thus, the relations between the West and Syria cannot be considered separately from the relations between the West and Iran (in this case, the West stands for the Western countries and their allies in the Middle East). Tehran has an exceptional influence on Damascus, and the latter is, in

---

[161] The Alawites are supporters of a religious trend in Islam, which some consider to be a kind of Shiism, while others consider it a mixture of Islam, Christianity and pre-Islamic Middle Eastern beliefs.

[162] From the peace to war. Essay on the political history of Syria in the twentieth and early twenty-first centuries. Analytical report. M.V. Khlyustov. Moscow, 2013. Center for Strategic Assessments and Forecasts. http://csef.ru

[163] Ibidem.

turn, the most important representative of Tehran's interests in the region. After having "blown up" the pro-Iranian leadership of Syria, Iran's opponents both in the region and in the world had planned to deal a powerful blow at the authorities of the Islamic Republic.

As the Western press repeatedly claimed, numerous acts of aggression by the Syrian government army against the peaceful population of the country were the formal reason for their anti-Assad rhetoric.[164] This rationale was similar to the charges that had been brought against Saddam Hussein and Muammar Gaddafi, which by this very notion looked extremely suspicious and unsettling for the Syrian authorities.

At first, the intensity of the accusations was much higher in Middle Eastern media than even in the European or American ones.[165] This is explained by the fact that the regional opponents of Syria, especially Qatar, Saudi Arabia, Turkey,[166] were most interested in a speedy regime change in the country.

In all fairness, it has to be noted that not all the accusations were groundless. In June 2011, the Syrian military carried out an operation in the city of Jisr ash-Shugur. According to Middle East media, hundreds of residents were killed, thousands were arrested, and thousands more fled to Turkey.[167] Even if the figures were overstated, it is impossible to deny the fact that the government army actually carried out arrests and forced some people to leave the country. However, on the other hand, 120 policemen were killed[168] during the same operation, which indicates that the government forces were not the sole aggressors.

---

[164] For example, Syria chemical attack: What we know. BBC, 24.09.2013. http://www.bbc.com/news/world-middle-east-23927399; Syrian regime and Isis carried out chemical attacks, say UN investigators. The Guardian, 25.08.2016. https://www.theguardian.com/world/2016/aug/25/assad-regime-isis-chemical-attacks-syria-un-investigators

[165] Middle East Poker. A new round of the Great Game. G.V. Mirzayan. Eksmo; Moscow; 2016.

[166] For Qatar, it was important to have a friendly regime in Syria in order to build a Qatar-Turkish gas pipeline through its territory; for Saudi Arabia - to weaken Iran; for Turkey – to squeeze Iran out of Palestinian affairs and replace the Alawite regime in Syria with an Islamist-Sunni regime, which is close to Turkey. Each of the countries supported their groupings on the territory of Syria.

[167] Thousands of Syrians flee to Turkey. Aljazeera, 12.06.2011. http://www.aljazeera.com/news/middleeast/2011/06/201161114504365900.html

[168] Militants killed 120 policemen in Syria. Rossiyskaya Gazeta, 07.06.2011.

The initiative to brutally suppress the demonstrations in 2011, which ran through the entire Middle East, belonged first of all to the Syrian security forces and the members of the close circle of Hafez al-Assad, the father of the current Syrian president (the president of Syria until 2000).[169] The old guard had retained their representation in power and feared for their positions.

The Syrian leader himself acknowledged the bloody actions, but not in the volumes that were attributed to him by the West: *"When a surgeon in the operating room … cuts, cleans, and amputates, and the wound of the patient bleeds, do we tell him: 'You have blood on your hands?'"*[170] Moreover, after the incident in Jisr ash-Shugur, Damascus learned its lesson, and the Syrian government troops began to conduct operations to "calm" the rebellious territories more scrupulously: large-scale operations were replaced by local cleanups and were no longer accompanied by extensive casualties among the population. **Nevertheless, it was already difficult to stop the whirl of the information war against Assad. Opponents of Damascus and Tehran saw their opportunity in the impending reformation of the Syrian political system.**

However, the image of Libya, self-destructed after the overthrow of Gaddafi, forced a number of forces in Syria (especially national minorities) to rally around President Assad. The war turned from a blitzkrieg of the motley opposition into a protracted civil war of "all against all".

There was only one thing that could reverse the course of events – a legitimate (UN-sanctioned) foreign intervention, similar to the one carried out earlier in Libya. In the meantime, foreign states, primarily the USA and the EU countries, did not rush to bring troops in or to "at least" organize a no-fly zone (i.e. shoot down Syrian aircrafts) without the approval of the UN. The United States feared possible reputational damage on the eve of the presidential election (Barack Obama had positioned himself as the president who brought the American boys back home from

---

https://rg.ru/2011/06/07/siria-site-anons.html

[169] Middle East Poker. A new round of the Great Game. G.V. Mirzayan. Eksmo; Moscow; 2016.

[170] Zeina Karam. Assad: the massacre in Syria is the doing of "monsters." The Associated Press. Translation InoSMI, 03.06.2012. http://www.inosmi.ru/asia/20120604/193056919.html

Iraq and Afghanistan). Based on the experience of the Libyan campaign, Europe realized that it was not yet ready to fight without the U.S. playing the leading role. The countries of the Middle East did not dare to interfere in the affairs of Syria one by one, whereas unification was out of the question. Although Saudi Arabia tried to create an antiterrorist coalition in 2015[171], it did not dare to launch a full-fledged intervention.

Any attempts to pass UN Security Council resolutions, similar to the one that initiated the military campaign in Libya, were vetoed by Russia and China (several such resolutions were proposed in 2012). The positions of Moscow and Beijing were conditioned by the Libyan precedent. Under the leadership of Dmitry Medvedev, Russia had earlier abstained from using its veto power in the voting on the "Libyan" resolution. It should be mentioned here that, despite the fact that the document had dealt only with the creation of a no-fly zone over Libya, Europeans and Americans **interpreted it as the right to strike at the troops loyal to Muammar Gaddafi.** As a result, not only was the political system destroyed, but the country was pushed to the brink of complete collapse.

Consequently, there was no intervention in Syria in 2012, and the belligerents in the country began to seek additional help: the opposition – from their partners abroad, the official Damascus – from Iran and Russia. The main support for Assad still came from Tehran, both financial and military (comprising both weapons and volunteers).[172]

Incidentally, **the expenses approved by the U.S. Congress for training and clothing the Syrian armed opposition amounted** to more than $567 million in 2015 and $416 million in 2016. The amount of assistance provided by Washington declined further in 2017 (the U.S. Congress approved $270 million).[173] The flow of manpower and Western-made weapons into the ISIS from the "moderate opposition" units became a serious problem, which had remained critical for a long time.

---

[171] Saudi Arabia announced creation of an Islamic anti-terrorist coalition. TV and radio company "Petersburg", 15.12.2015. https://www.5-tv.ru/news/102903/

[172] Middle East Poker. A new round of the Great Game. G.V. Mirzayan. Eksmo; Moscow; 2016

[173] Armed Conflict in Syria: Overview and U.S. Response. Congressional Research Service. 7-5700. http://www.crs.gov RL33487. August 10, 2017

It would seem that active military actions reached a positional phase, but the matter of intervention again appeared on the agenda in 2013. Its origin lay in the statement that Barack Obama sounded a year earlier that the United States would bring troops into Syria only if Assad crossed a certain "red line". (Incidentally, the U.S. president's propensity for "drawing" red lines on various foreign policy issues characteristically met with irony in Russia.) This time, Obama defined the use of **chemical weapons** by the Syrian President against his own population or their transfer to "the wrong people" (i.e. terrorists) as the "red line".[174]

It was in 2013 that the incidents of chemical weapons use began to be recorded in Syria. In particular, in August 2013, missiles with sarin struck at the outskirts of Damascus, in the town of East Gut, and killed more than 600 people. Since the region was controlled by militants, suspicions fell on the official Damascus.

The motives that would have prompted Assad to use chemical weapons immediately after a special investigative UN group completed its work in Syria, with the consent of Damascus, were never clarified. Representatives of the Russian Foreign Ministry, on the contrary, found the entire claim unfounded. They noted that the Syrian Army was at the time conducting multiple successful operations against militants in various directions (which rendered the use of chemical weapons needless), and was further attacked by militants with a homemade missile reportedly similar to the one *"used by terrorists on 19th March 2013 in Khan Al-Asal, with an unidentified chemical poisonous substance."*[175] A few months before the tragedy, the Turkish intelligence agencies had **detained a group of militants with sarin.**[176]

It may surprise that **every mention of the use of chemical weapons by Damascus coincided either with the military or political (and often both)**

---

[174] Obama threatens Syria with U.S. military action if Assad regime crosses 'RED LINE' by using chemical weapons. Dailymail.co.uk, 21.082012. http://www.dailymail.co.uk/news/article-2191303/Obama-threatens-Syria-U-S-military-action-Assad-regime-crosses-RED-LINE-using-chemical-weapons.html

[175] Syrian rebels claim death of more than one thousand people as a result of chemical attack near Damascus. News.ru. 21.08.2013. http://www.newsru.com/world/21aug2013/syria.html.

[176] Militants tried to transport the poison gas "sarin" into the territory of Syria. Rossiyskaya Gazeta, 30.05.2013. https://rg.ru/2013/05/30/zarin-anons.html

success of the Syrian leadership, and was advantageous to Assad's opponents, not to him.

The events in East Gut thrust Barack Obama into a very difficult situation. On the one hand, it was necessary to keep his word, on the other hand, intervention in Syria without UN authorization meant opening a personal "Vietnam" – with a classical war against Iran (and possibly with Russia) on the periphery. In the end, after a week's hesitation, the U.S. president finally expressed his readiness to enter the war with Assad and began to call on his allies to join.[177]

Syrian groups opposing Assad seemed to have expected this, and they showed maximum enthusiasm[178]. Panic ensued in the Middle East: the stock exchanges faced record-breaking falls in the ratings; the Israelis started buying gas masks.[179] Obama's European colleagues, on the contrary, behaved in a rather restrained manner. The United Kingdom was the first to refuse joining the potential coalition (the Parliament voted against the intervention);[180] the French President Francois Hollande announced support for the USA, with the reservation that it would be a *short-term* deterrent attack;[181] the rest of NATO allies similarly did not hurry to join the military operations.

Washington was sober in evaluating the situation. The Senate, which was supposed to pass a resolution on the intervention, hesitated. Polls showed that Americans were skeptical of even weapons deliveries to the militants (70% of respondents did not support this idea, only 27% were in favor).[182] Nevertheless, on September 1, 2013, Barack Obama sent a draft

---

[177] On the Verge of Appeasement in Syria. Michael Hirsh. 01.09.2013 http://www.nationaljournal.com/nationalsecurity/on-the-verge-of-appeasement-in-syria-20130901

[178] Syria nears a turning point. David Ignatius, The Washington Post, 05.09.2013 http://www.washingtonpost.com/opinions/david-ignatius-syria-nears-a-turning-point/2013/09/04/e259ba1e-15b4-11e3-a2ec-b47e45e6f8ef_story.html?hpid=z3

[179] Boom of gas masks sales in Israel begins against the backdrop of the war in Syria. NEWru.com, 27.08.2013. http://www.newsru.com/world/27aug2013/israel.html

[180] The British Parliament voted against intervention in Syria. Gazeta.ru, 30.08.2013. https://www.gazeta.ru/politics/video/britanskii_parlament_progolosoval_protiv_in terventsii_v_siriyu.shtml

[181] France will not fight in Syria until the mission of UN experts is completed. RIA Novosti, 30.08.2013. http://ria.ru/arab_sy/20130830/959690670.html

[182] Obama, ignore the polls on Syria. Rothkopf David. 04.09.2013

resolution authorizing the military operation against Syria to the Senate and the House of Representatives. U.S. lawmakers did not have an unequivocal opinion on the expedience of the military action.

It was obvious to the Russian leadership that **the Americans were not too eager to discuss the matter of intervention in Syria and therefore the Kremlin "came to the rescue".** In particular, Russia proposed something that the politicians in Washington initially did not believe: Damascus commits to eliminate the weapons of mass destruction (WMD) or to export them out from the Syrian territory and joins the Organization for the Prohibition of Chemical Weapons (OPCW)[183]. Damascus quickly responded with agreement, as the international situation around the "Syrian problem" grew rather tense.[184]

Barack Obama also seized on this opportunity and declared that the implementation of the plan could become a "breakthrough". A political dialogue was launched, and the U.S. was "saved" from the need to intervene in the Syrian territory. However, running a little forward, **the political dialogue between Russia and the United States never got off the ground, while the chemical weapons continued to supply a formal pretext for pressing the Assad regime,** despite the fact that Damascus consistently destroyed them under the control of the OPCW,[185] as was chronicled by the United States authorities themselves.

One of the latest high-profile cases of accusation of Damascus occurred in April 2017, when residents of the Syrian city of Khan-Shaykhun (the Idlib province) were poisoned with chemical weapons, allegedly as a result of air strikes. Just three days after the incident, by order of President Donald Trump the U.S. navy carried out a missile strike at the Ash-Shayrat air base in Syria,[186] provoking righteous indignation in Russia. The U.S.

---

http://edition.cnn.com/2013/09/04/opinion/rothkopf-obama-syria-polls/index.html.

[183] Russia proposes Syria chemical weapons deal to avert U.S. strike. Reuters. 09.09.2013. http://www.reuters.com/article/us-syria-crisis-russia-proposes-syria-chemical-weapons-deal-to-avert-u-s-strike-idUSBRE9880HY20130909

[184] Syria is ready to join the Convention on the Prohibition of Chemical Weapons. RIA Novosti, 10.092013. https://ria.ru/arab_riot/20130910/962300965.html

[185] Eliminating Chemical Weapons and Chemical Weapons Production Facilities. Opcw.org, March, 2016. https://www.opcw.org/fileadmin/OPCW/Fact_Sheets/English/Fact_Sheet_6_-_destruction.pdf

strike was interpreted by the Russian leadership as an "act of aggression."[187] Moscow argued that three days were clearly insufficient to make a balanced decision, especially in light of multiple ambiguities surrounding the chemical attack. Neither the Americans nor anyone else had any evidence that it was committed by Damascus.

Later, after scrutinizing the photo and video reports on the chemical attack, Russia presented the analysis showing that the attack was staged.[188] Russian political experts, in turn, noted that against the backdrop of the Syrian Army's breakthrough in the fight against terrorists, the use of chemical weapons would have been political suicide for Assad, which he was clearly not inclined to commit. However, these arguments were of little concern to the Western public – the perpetrators had already been indicted; strikes against Syria had already been carried out.

Regardless, the solitary and by no means most destructive nature of the American air strike allowed Russian experts to believe that the strike **was motivated much less by the desire to punish the "bad" Assad, but by the American internal political reasons.**

In general, the entire specter of U.S.-Russian cooperation during the short presidency of Donald Trump, including on Syria, is coupled with the domestic policy of the United States, in one way or another. The attack on the Ash-Shayrat base was delivered almost on the eve of U.S. Secretary of State's visit to Moscow. The incident made the talks between the heads of the foreign ministries of the two countries, Sergei Lavrov and Rex Tillerson, virtually useless. It was no secret that any overture by the U.S. toward Russia (which, of course, the visit of the U.S. Secretary of State could initiate) was strongly criticized in the United States. Trump's rigid response to the alleged chemical attack in Syria provided Tillerson with a less than "smooth" visit. Alas, this fact did not contribute to the Russian-American dialogue.

---

[186] What we know about Donald Trump's strike on a Syrian regime air base. Newsweek, 7.04.2017. http://www.newsweek.com/what-we-know-donald-trump-strike-regime-air-base-syria-assad-580353

[187] The Security Council of Russia about the U.S. missile attack against Syria: the act of aggression. Russia Today, 07.04.2017. https://russian.rt.com/world/article/375999-ssha-udar-tomagavk-siriya

[188] Russia provided evidence of a false flag chemical attack in Syria. RBC, 20.04.2017. http://www.rbc.ru/politics/20/04/2017/58f7d6f19a794731b1108423

Nevertheless, the episode with the strike at Ash-Shayrat did not prevent Putin and Trump from conducting successful negotiations at the G20 summit in Hamburg, which led to an agreement to create a de-escalation zone in south-west Syria.[189]

By September 2017, there were already four such zones in Syria (three of them were agreed upon without the participation of the USA). The position of the U.S. and Europe on the fate of Assad had softened noticeably, too. Thus, in one of the dialogues Tillerson declared Washington's readiness to give Russia the freedom to choose the fate of the Syrian President.[190] French President Emmanuel Macron also ceased to consider the removal of Assad an indispensable condition for achieving peace in Syria.[191] Indeed, **Bashar al-Assad's staying in power (at least for a while) in no way prevented clearance operations against terrorist groups in Syria.** The Syrian opposition, which previously had an intransigent attitude toward the official Damascus, is increasingly cooperating with it and even acts as a guarantor of one of the de-escalation zones (near the city of Homs).

Making the Syrian armed opposition sit down at the negotiating table became possible only after the army of Assad liberated the city of Aleppo with the support of Russia. The capture of this strategic point from the militants became a symbol of the changed course of the war, and the opposition realized that there was a strong player in the region – Russia – and, having estimated its chances, turned to the negotiating table.

The existence of agreements between Russia and the U.S. does not mean that the two countries actually cooperate on Syria (especially since the United States, through the State Department and its military, denies the relevance of this dialogue). Contrary to Trump's pre-election promises to organize a joint fight against terrorism, there are more problems than solutions at this stage. The Russian Defense Ministry expresses open concern that the peace process in Syria can be thwarted with U.S. efforts.[192]

---

[189] Territory of tranquility: the U.S. and Russia agreed on the establishment of the first de-escalation zone in Syria. Russia Today, 09.07.2017. https://russian.rt.com/world/article/407203-ssha-rossiya-siria

[190] The fate of Assad to be determined by Russia. Gazeta.ru, 03.07.2017. https://www.gazeta.ru/politics/2017/07/03_a_10760312.shtml

[191] Macron: France does not consider Assad's withdrawal a condition for peace in Syria. Radio Liberty, 22.07.2017. https://www.svoboda.org/a/28573729.html

[192] The Ministry of Defense of the Russian Federation reported about the

While Syria's government army is sweeping away terrorist cells, the U.S.-led coalition reduces the intensity of attacks against the militants in Iraq (presumably to allow them to move into Syrian territory), while U.S.-made weapons are increasingly more often found in the hands of Syrian militants.[193]

September 30, 2017 marked two years since the beginning of the Russian air operation in Syria. **Almost 90% of the territory of Syria has been liberated and 53 thousand militants were killed with the support of the Russian aviation. More than 2,000 settlements,** including the long-suffering city of Aleppo, **were liberated from the "Islamic state".**[194]

The fact that the Syrian war will not become Russia's "second Afghanistan" (where the Soviet Union got bogged down for 10 years) became clear as early as March 2016. Then Russia withdrew a significant part of the Aerospace Forces from Syria,[195] making it clear that it did not intend to intensify military campaigns abroad to the detriment of its domestic affairs.

Simultaneously, Russia continued to expand its infrastructure in Syria and even began to "break in" its new military equipment there. For instance, the launches of Calibre missiles at the terrorists from the submarines based in the *Russian* Caspian Sea were spectacular for potential customers of Russian military technology.[196] As a result, Putin managed to make the "Syrian campaign" a showcase of the new Russian weapons and had aroused strong interest among potential buyers. This, incidentally, compensated the ouster of Russia from various specialized exhibitions at

---

"selective blindness" of the USA in Syria. TASS, 11.10.2017. http://tass.ru/armiya-i-opk/4635550

[193] The Russian Defense Ministry told about a "strange" case with militants from the U.S.-controlled zone in Syria. Gazeta.ru, 11.10.2017. https://www.gazeta.ru/army/news/10677812.shtml

[194] 92 thousand air strikes: what results were achieved by the Aerospace Forces for the two-year operation in Syria. Russia Today, 28.092017. https://russian.rt.com/world/article/434447-rossiya-vks-siriya-operaciya-godovshchina

[195] Withdrawal with development. Gazeta.ru, 21.03.2016. https://www.gazeta.ru/army/2016/03/20/8133929.shtml

[196] Russian missiles 'hit IS in Syria from Caspian Sea'. BBC, 07.10.2015. http://www.bbc.com/news/world-middle-east-34465425

the initiative of its opponents acting within the format of the "anti-Russian sanctions".

It should be noted that the military campaign in Syria was funded from the federal budget resources allocated for the organization of military exercises of the Ministry of Defense. Therefore, the running-in of the new weapons, which took place in the military field, did not require additional funds from the budget; at least there was no official information on the allocation of additional funds.

The political outcome of the Russian military operation is much broader. This was the first war that Russia waged outside the territory of the CIS countries for the first time since the collapse of the Soviet Union. This fact made the Syrian campaign **a kind of a test of Vladimir Putin's ability to solve global problems,** and, consequently, Russia's right to claim the role of one of the world leaders.

Undoubtedly, the war in Syria had not been a "walk in the park" for Russia. Like any war, it was accompanied by human and financial losses[197]. However, the efforts of the Russian military and political leadership have made these losses, if not minimal, then certainly not destructive for the mentality of the country's population. On the contrary, Russia's actions in the Middle East helped to unite certain political groups and resulted in an additional rise in Putin's rating.[198] Interestingly, thanks to his active efforts to combat terrorism, the popularity of the Russian president grew not only in Russia. In Syria, Putin's image can be seen on a variety of objects,[199] and even in the United States, the rating of the Russian president has increased.[200]

---

[197] According to some reports, for the first year of the military operation in Syria, public spending amounted to at least 58 billion rubles. In addition, Russia officially recognized the death of 41 of its citizens in Syria. One year in Syria: how much did the military operation cost Russia? RBC, 30.09.2016. http://www.rbc.ru/politics/30/09/2016/57ebb7199a7947db5bb2b309; What is known about the Russian soldiers who died in Syria. Kommersant, 10.10.2017. https://www.kommersant.ru/doc/2946383

[198] Putin's rating hit a historic record due to the operation in Syria. News.Tut.by, 22.10.2015. https://news.tut.by/world/469624.html

[199] Putin is incredibly popular in the Syrian capital. El Pais. Translated by Inosmi.ru, 22.02.2016.
http://inosmi.ru/social/20160220/235493047.html

[200] Putin's Image Rises in US, Mostly Among Republicans. Gallup News, 21.02.2017. http://news.gallup.com/poll/204191/putin-image-rises-mostly-among-republicans.aspx

The demand for Russian military equipment is also growing, as was previously mentioned.[201] Turkey's order of the Russian S-400 surface-to-air missile systems caused discomfort among the NATO countries.[202] In October 2017, a similar order was discussed with the King of Saudi Arabia during his first visit to Russia. Both countries are very important conductors of U.S. interests.

Such a partial turn of the traditional partners of the U.S. towards Russia (Turkey, Qatar, Saudi Arabia) was the result, on the one hand, of inconsistent U.S. actions, and on the other hand, of Russia's stable foreign policy position. Thus, Washington – under both Obama and Trump – has repeatedly committed actions that spoke of the United States neglect for the interests of its allies.[203] On the contrary, Russia displays maximum diplomatic tact and remains the only country that maintains a dialogue with absolutely all participants of the Middle East process.

Russia's consistent defense of Bashar al-Assad demonstrated to the Middle East leaders, who do not want to repeat the fate of the same Mubarak (who completely relied on U.S. defense), that Moscow does not leave its "own" behind. This does not mean that tomorrow these leaders will withdraw U.S. bases from their territories and reorient their policies to Russia. Russia itself is not interested in this, mindful of the experience of "overstrain" in the wake of the USSR arms race. But, it was the Syrian war that demonstrated that Russia is ready to play an effective role in solving global problems: in two years, the Russian Aerospace Forces achieved those results, which the so-called "broad coalition" could not even approach for three and a half years, when the ISIS area of influence consistently expanded.

The further fate of Syria is still an equation with many variables, including the fate of Bashar al-Assad personally. The interests of large

---

[201]   Air-commercial   forces.   Kommersant.ru,   28.03.2016. https://www.kommersant.ru/doc/2932551

[202] NATO don't cry: how the U.S. urges Erdogan to abandon the purchase of S-400   from   Russia.   Russia   Today,   25.07.2017. https://russian.rt.com/world/article/412010-erdogan-rossiya-s-400

[203] Turkey is displeased with the fact that the U.S. refuses to extradite Fethullah Gulen, whom Ankara considers to be involved in the military coup; Qatar hardly thanked the United States for not joining the Doha side during the blockade; Saudi Arabia still cannot "forgive" the U.S. deal with Iran.

players are colliding in the region, and hence the future configuration of power will be determined over time.

Russia, taking a pragmatic, de-ideologized position, to a large extent successfully maintains a balance between the heterogeneous and conflicting forces of the Syrian war, and preserves equal and yet meaningful relations with both internal and external players in the conflict. At the same time, Russia remains completely within the legal framework, unlike Turkey and the United States, which have intervened in the territory of Syria illegally.

At the same time, the ongoing clashes between the forces loyal to Russia and the U.S. are part of the trend and are programmed to emerge in the future, as the struggle for spheres of influence and determination of the future of the post-war Syria will intensify.

Resume. *After Saddam Hussein (hanged by a court order) and Muammar Gaddafi (liquidated without trial and investigation), many leaders of sovereign countries ceased to feel safe, and Putin tried to create an effective model to prevent "managed crises" in the Middle East and in North Africa. Various special operations in the territory of Syria became a response to his efforts and the efforts of the Russian Aerospace Forces in the region.*

The cooperation between Russia and the Western countries represented by the so-called "broad coalition" within the Syrian campaign carried a rather specific character.[204] In part, it bore a resemblance to the struggle against Hitlerite Germany in 1944-1945, when it was no longer a question of suppressing the Nazi army, but of controlling Europe. Here lies the next game in the "battle for Syria" and the greater Middle Eastern geopolitical match, which is yet to be played and which, apparently, is already starting. The most important thing for Russia is that, despite all the difficulties, the country managed to withstand the "Syrian test".

*For Vladimir Putin personally, as for the Supreme Commander-in-Chief, **the "Syrian campaign" has become an ideal war** that will enter the annals of military art.*

---

[204] The coalition included the United States, Australia, Bahrain, Belgium, Great Britain, Denmark, Canada (ceased participation in the operation in October 2015), Jordan, Morocco, theNetherlands, the UAE, Saudi Arabia, Turkey and France. Members of the coalition led by the United States to combat IS in Syria and Iraq. RIA Novosti, 25.01.2016. https://ria.ru/infografika/20160125/1365036848.html

CHAPTER 7.
"INTERFERENCE" IN THE US ELECTION – "RUSSIAN HACKERS" AND GLOOMY PROSPECTS FOR INTERSTATE RELATIONS

In the modern era of "hybrid wars", superpowers no longer compete in overt military confrontations. The rivalry has moved into the virtual space, where it goes on constantly.

It is no wonder that the notorious "interference" of Russia in the 2016 U.S. election became an integral part of the electoral process. The extent of the hype even made Russia somewhat proud of itself, though it certainly carried a negative connotation. Russia was de facto accused of "unfair play" and of undermining the foundations of the political process of the United States, an attempt on the holy of holies of the U.S. democracy – the election of its president.

Although the connection of the hackers with Russian intelligence agencies or representatives of other government bodies has never been proven, it is worth assessing the scale of the deployed campaign.

On June 14, 2016, the Washington Post published an article titled "Russian government hackers penetrated DNC, stole opposition research on Trump".[205] This was the beginning of a large-scale campaign to

---

[205] Russian government hackers penetrated DNC, stole opposition research on Trump. The Washington Post, 14.06.2016. https://www.washingtonpost.com/world/national-security/russian-government-hackers-penetrated-dnc-stole-opposition-research-on-trump/2016/06/14/cf006cb4-316e-11e6-8ff7-7b6c1998b7a0_story.html

popularize the ideas of Russian interference in the election in the United States.

The starting point occurred in April 2016, when the server of the Democratic National Committee (DNC) of the United States Democratic Party was allegedly hacked. Emails, audio messages, and data of the participants of the election campaign became publicly available. In addition, the hackers received compromising evidence against Donald Trump, collected by the Democrats.[206]

On July 22, 2016, thousands of emails of the Democratic Party members were posted on the WikiLeaks portal (since then, the project of Assange is especially persistently referred to as "pro-Russian" by the American media). In addition, information that the Democratic National Committee favored Hillary Clinton over Bernie Sanders during the primaries,[207] which resulted in Mrs. Clinton's nomination as the party candidate, was released. Consequently, the Democratic Party officially accused Russia of hacking, and WikiLeaks and Julian Assange were named "Putin's surrogates".[208]

It is noteworthy that the Chairwoman of the Democratic National Committee Debbie Wasserman-Schultz resigned because of the scandal,[209] which, incidentally, can be regarded as a tacit acknowledgment of liability for the data leakage.

Someone under the pseudonym Guccifer 2.0 assumed responsibility for the attack. He positioned himself as a Romanian hacker acting alone. Nevertheless, his identity was disproved by the facts: he spoke poor Romanian, he used extremely sophisticated software, which is not available for "ordinary mortals", and his motives were unusual for a single hacker – he did not attempt to sell the information and did not post the data immediately, but bided time.[210] Hence, the Western media came to the

---

[206] Bears in the Midst: Intrusion into the Democratic National Committee. CrowdStrike Blog, 15.06.2016. https://www.crowdstrike.com/blog/bears-midst-intrusion-democratic-national-committee/

[207] Wikileaks posts nearly 20,000 hacked DNC emails online. The Washington Post, 22.07.2016. https://www.washingtonpost.com/news/the-switch/wp/2016/07/22/wikileaks-posts-nearly-20000-hacked-dnc-emails-online/

[208] Wikileaks Dismantling of DNC Is Clear Attack by Putin on Clinton. Observer, 25.07.2016. http://observer.com/2016/07/wikileaks-dismantling-of-dnc-is-clear-attack-by-putin-on-clinton/

[209] Dems open convention without Wasserman Schultz. CNN, 25.07.2016. http://edition.cnn.com/2016/07/22/politics/dnc-wikileaks-emails/

conclusion that he was a cover for the activities of the Russian organized *"hacker factories"*.

Consequently, an active media campaign was launched to inflate this situation. However, as the events unfolded, it seemed that the U.S. Democratic Party struggled to shift the public attention away from the incident with Bernie Sanders and his complicated relations with Hillary Clinton and, instead, began to create the image of a behind-the-scenes enemy – Russia and its "army of cyber-terrorists".

President Barack Obama became actively involved in the processes – he had already assumed an extremely tough position towards Putin personally; now he participated in the investigation of the *"Russian hacker attacks"*[211] whenever possible, and officially stated, on behalf of U.S. authorities, that it was Russia behind the hacker attacks.[212]

CrowdStrike came to the help of the Democratic Party to substantiate this position. This company, headed by Russian emigrant Dmitry Alperovich, focuses on cybersecurity. The choice fell on CrowdStrike for a good reason: Dmitry Alperovich managed to build up his business thanks to his participation as an informer in an FBI operation on liquidation of a forum Dark Market.[213] Companies such as FireEye, Eset, TrendMicro – all in some way related to the FBI – were also involved in the investigations.[214]

In their investigations, the American companies came to the conclusion that there were two independent teams of hackers, Fancy Bear and Cozy Bear. They both allegedly worked for the FSB and the GRU, did not know each other, but acted solely in the interests of almost Putin personally.[215]

---

[210] Shiny Object? Guccifer 2.0 and the DNC Breach. ThreatConnect, 29.06.2016. https://www.threatconnect.com/blog/guccifer-2-0-dnc-breach/

[211] Barack Obama orders 'full review' of possible Russian hacking in US election. The Guardian, 09.12.2016. https://www.theguardian.com/us-news/2016/dec/09/us-election-hacking-russia-barack-obama-review

[212] U.S. Publicly Blames Russian Government for Hacking. NBC News, 07.10.2016. https://www.nbcnews.com/news/us-news/u-s-publicly-blames-russian-government-hacking-n662066

[213] The Russian Expat Leading the Fight to Protect America. Esquire, 24.10.2016. http://www.esquire.com/news-politics/a49902/the-russian-emigre-leading-the-fight-to-protect-america/

[214] APT28 – is it a myth or a big mistake of Russia? Forbes, 15.05.2017. http://www.forbes.ru/tehnologii/344297-apt28-myth-i-bolshaya-oshibka-rossii

[215] Cozy Bear and Fancy Bear: did Russians hack Democratic party and if so, why? The Guardian, 29.07.2016.

Interestingly, in 2015 Root9B, one of the leading companies on the cybersecurity market, discovered signs that Fancy Bear hackers operated from Africa, not from Russia.[216] The company was eventually accused of bias, since the information it provided did not fit into the version of the "Russian trace".

Finally, on January 6, 2017, the CIA, the NSA and the FBI published an unclassified part of the report on Russia's meddling in the US election.[217] The following facts became the basis for the accusations: the IP-addresses were allegedly connected with Russia; Guccifer 2.0 so actively tried to represent himself as Romanian, that he definitely should be Russian; hacking activity was detected from Monday to Friday from 8 am to 6 pm Moscow time, which "certainly" indicates to the Russian origin of the attacks.

Needless to say, the report supported with such an evidentiary basis caused, at a minimum, a sense of disappointment[218] among technical specialists: when it came to the test, the "Russian" IP-addresses were output nodes of a Tor network, which can be used by anyone – from a hacker to an old lady, say, in Iceland. Guccifer 2.0, whose Romanian identity does raise big questions, does not have to be necessarily Russian. The hackers' work on schedule from 8 am to 6 pm Moscow time elicited ridicule: there are 21 more countries in the same time zone, and the working day in Russia, as a rule, does not start at 8 am, but rather at 9 am. Not to mention the fact that the report was based on the analysis of the behavior of *"politicians loyal to the Kremlin, state media and pro-Kremlin users of social networks"*[219] (quite likely, including the author of this book).

https://www.theguardian.com/technology/2016/jul/29/cozy-bear-fancy-bear-russia-hack-dnc

[216] root9B Uncovers Planned Sofacy Cyber Attack Targeting Several International and Domestic Financial Institutions. PR Newswire, 12.05.2015. https://www.prnewswire.com/news-releases/root9b-uncovers-planned-sofacy-cyber-attack-targeting-several-international-and-domestic-financial-institutions-300081634.html

[217] Intelligence Report on Russian Hacking. The New York Times, 06.01.2017. https://www.nytimes.com/interactive/2017/01/06/us/politics/document-russia-hacking-report-intelligence-agencies.html

[218] FBI and Homeland Security detail Russian hacking campaign in new report. The Guardian, 29.12.2016. https://www.theguardian.com/technology/2016/dec/29/fbi-dhs-russian-hacking-report

As a result, a lot of bold statements were made to the public, but not a single real technical proof of Russia's guilt was presented. Moreover, several companies reported that many attacks originated from the territory of the European Union, and their victims included the websites of Russian media.[220] In addition, for unexplained reasons, the U.S. agencies are apparently not even attempting to investigate the financial traces of the attacks, which to the Russians seems extremely suspicious.

According to Russian experts, the most important paradox lies in the fact that no one, absolutely no one in the world, wagered on the victory of Donald Trump. Even in Russia, which is considered as his "behind-the-scenes mentor", only the most flamboyant politicians believed in Trump's victory.[221] It seemed so unlikely, that any attempts to push Trump through via some outside interference would have seemed meaningless: why invest so much in a project doomed to failure, according to all the preliminary signs?

More and more new contradictory and fragmentary details of the "Russian intervention" emerge today. Thus, Facebook's CEO Mark Zuckerberg claimed that a Russian "troll factory" had operated in his social network, posted various political materials, thereby influencing the election in the United States.[222] There was information that hacker attacks were detected in 21 states of the USA; they were attributed again to Russian intelligence agencies.[223] Later it was reported that some of these states actually had not been attacked by the Russian hackers.[224] Russian IT

[219] WikiLeaks laughed at the report on hackers "drawn up based on Twitter posts". Vesti.RU, 07.01.2017. http://www.vesti.ru/doc.html?id=2840251

[220] Two Years of Pawn Storm. TrendMicro, 25.04.2017. https://documents.trendmicro.com/assets/wp/wp-two-years-of-pawn-storm.pdf

[221] Zhirinovsky believes that Trump will win the US presidency. RIA Novosti, 02.11.2016. https://ria.ru/us_elections2016/20161102/1480508402.html

[222] Facebook will tighten the rules for placing political ads because of the Russian "troll factory". Meduza, 22.09.2017. https://meduza.io/news/2017/09/22/facebook-uzhestochit-pravila-razmescheniya-politicheskoy-reklamy-iz-za-rossiyskoy-fabriki-trolley

[223] U.S. Informs 21 States They Were Targeted By Attempted Russian Hacking. The Wall Street Journal, 22.09.2017. https://www.wsj.com/articles/u-s-informs-21-states-they-were-targeted-by-attempted-russian-hacking-1506119620

[224] California, Wisconsin deny election systems targeted by Russian hackers. Reuters, 28.09.2017. https://www.reuters.com/article/us-usa-election/california-wisconsin-deny-election-systems-targeted-by-russian-hackers-idUSKCN1C32SQ

companies also came under fire. Thus, the U.S. Senate banned all public agencies from the use of software developed by the Moscow-based Kaspersky Lab – the world's leading producer of cybersecurity and antivirus software.[225] The company was accused of cyber espionage in favor of Russia.

In a word, the hackers' theme had not exhausted itself after the election and remains in the information mainstream.

The reaction of the Russian side to the accusations ranged from ironic to severely negative. Russia and Putin were accused not just of espionage and gross interference in the affairs of the sovereign state, but also of the use of absolutely illegal methods – the actions of the hacker organizations fall under article 273 of the Criminal Code of the Russian Federation (creation, use and distribution of malicious computer programs).[226] Anyway, Russia's motivation of these actions is clearly not justified.

On July 26, 2016, Russian Foreign Minister Sergei Lavrov reacted to the accusations of Russia's involvement in the hacking as follows: *"I would not like to use words of four letters."*[227] (The abundance of four-letter strong words in the Russian language puzzled the experts as to what the Minister exactly meant).

On December 23, 2016, during the annual end-of-the-year press conference, President Putin noted: *"The loser always looks for reasons outside. They should better look for problems inside. Who knows what these hackers are? Maybe they operated from another country, lying in bed or on the couch. Is this the main thing? Did they tamper with something or falsify information? Of course, not!"*[228] He also drew attention to the fact that *"the main thing is the essence*

---

[225] U.S. Senate votes to ban Kaspersky Lab software from government networks. Reuters, 19.09.2017. https://www.reuters.com/article/us-usa-cyber-kasperskylab/u-s-senate-votes-to-ban-kaspersky-lab-software-from-government-networks-idUSKCN1BT2PW

[226] The Criminal Code of the Russian Federation of 13.06.1996 N 63-FZ (as amended on 29.07.2017) (as amended and effective of 26.08.2017). ConsultantPlus.
http://www.consultant.ru/document/cons_doc_LAW_10699/a4d58c1af8677d94b4fc8987c71b131f10476a76/

[227] Lavrov responded to statements about Russia's trail in hacking of the emails of the United States Democratic Party. RBC, 26.07.2016. http://www.rbc.ru/politics/26/07/2016/5796ed239a7947d1ed353919

[228] Putin talked about the "evil Russian hackers": they told the truth. Vesti.RU, 23.12.2016. http://www.vesti.ru/doc.html?id=2836323&cid=9

of the information disclosed. Hackers showed the public opinion manipulation by the Democratic Party, which caused the Chairwoman of the Democratic National Committee to resign. That suggests that the disclosed information was true."[229]

On January 9, 2017, Russian President's Press Secretary Dmitry Peskov also commented on accusations against Russia: "*We are seriously fatigued by these accusations. From our point of view, they are absolutely unsubstantiated and ungrounded, their level is rather amateurish and emotional, which is hardly applicable to the highly professional work of really high-quality intelligence agencies. We understand that our American counterparts have gone through the times of "witch hunts" at different stages of their history. We remember such history periods, we know that later they are replaced by more sober specialists, more sober approaches, focused on a dialogue rather than emotional attacks.*"[230]

The "serious fatigue" was, apparently, the ultimate aim of all these information attacks against the leadership of Russia.

On June 1, 2017, during a meeting with the heads of international news agencies, which took place within the St.-Petersburg International Economic Forum, Putin slightly fueled tensions when he said: "*Hackers are free people, like artists: if they get up in the morning in a good mood, they paint. Hackers are the same: if they wake up and read that something is happening in interstate relations and if they are patriotic, then they start doing their part. We are not doing and not going to do this at the state level. On the contrary, we try in every possible way to fight this within the country.*"[231]

On June 3, 2017, Putin also pointed to the possibility that it was U.S. hackers who meddled in the U.S. election: "*By the way, these could be hackers in the United States, who very cleverly and professionally rolled over on Russia.*"[232] That is, it could well have been an operation under a false flag.

The facts that the companies, which reported the "investigations" about Russian hackers, are linked to the FBI, and that these investigations were actively promoted in the media testify to the likelihood of such a scenario.

---

[229] "Hackers told people the truth", Putin said. Regnum, 23.12.2016. https://regnum.ru/news/2221266.html

[230] Peskov complained of fatigue with accusations of hacker attacks against the Russian Federation. IA Interfax, 09.01.2017. http://www.interfax.ru/russia/544569

[231] Putin compared hackers with free-lance artists. Lenta.ru, 01.06.2017. https://lenta.ru/news/2017/06/01/hudohakeri/

[232] Putin stated possible impact of US hackers on the US election. RBC, 03.06.2017. http://www.rbc.ru/politics/03/06/2017/593207b69a7947d38353f3a8

Whose interests were represented by the FBI and the mass media is an entirely different issue. In any case, the fact that these manipulations put the U.S. president in a very weak position indicates that these actors did not play to the advantage of the United States.

It should be noted that **Vladimir Putin actually favors these kinds of understatement games, especially on the foreign policy track.** They give him a real opportunity to influence the emotional state of some particularly sensitive politicians.

Ultimately, Russia's response to these accusations was too lax. Perhaps, the reason was that unsubstantiated and precipitous statements usually do not cause any reaction from the Russian leadership: if there is no evidence, there is no field for discussion. In this vein, reports of outrage from the Russian oppositionist Alexei Navalny, though they attract public's attention, typically do not receive any sound feedback from the authorities, because, as a rule, they are not factually based. The same is true with respect to the accusations of hacker attacks: high-profile, but infertile "investigations" do not cause any counteraction. This approach of the Russian side is understandable – why react to bogus stories?

Nevertheless, such a passive behavior plays against Russia: it should have moved beyond the verbal response, resort to concrete measures. It is possible to file lawsuits, for example, against CrowdStrike, FireEye and TrendMicro for such accusations – the international law provides for this. In addition, it is possible to carry out an investigation under the above-mentioned Article 273 of the Criminal Code of the Russian Federation. Without doing anything, Russia seemed defenseless against the aggressive pressure of Western media and anti-Tramp politicians.

Certain measures were indeed taken by the Russian side. First of all, Russia continued to forcefully strengthen its cyberspace.[233] The United States had to launch a broad anti-Russian campaign – with no end in sight – mainly for internal reasons, because its security system proved to be vulnerable, and it is always difficult to recognize and acknowledge one's own mistakes. At least the United States fiasco has raised awareness

---

[233] Experts: Russia's cybersecurity depends on consolidation of the information community. TASS, 11.07.2017. http://tass.ru/politika/4406609

throughout the world, and all countries are now reexamining their cybersecurity measures.

In addition, Vladimir Putin went for broke, forcing high-level meetings with Trump – if the latter was accused of links with Russians, it was imperative to exploit this trend. The first official meeting of Putin and Trump took place in Hamburg on July 7, 2017 at the G20 summit. The issue of cracking, espionage and hacking was raised among others. It should be noted that the dialogue between the two presidents was carried on from the position of mutual respect and equality.

After the meeting, U.S. Secretary of State Rex Tillerson noted: "*They discussed this issue in great detail for a long time. The President has repeatedly asked President Putin about Russia's interference. President Putin denied this interference, as, I think, he has before.*"[234]

Sergei Lavrov said: "*Trump heard the clear statements of President Putin that it was not true. President Trump said that the campaign was already taking a strange form, because not a single proof had been produced for many months since these accusations had been sounded.*"[235]

Putin himself noted: "*Our position is well known, I have reproduced it: there are no grounds to believe that Russia interfered in the election process in the United States.*"[236]

Trump's impression about the meeting was quite interesting: "*I twice heavily pressed on President Putin about Russian interference in our election. He categorically denied that.*"[237] The statement is loud, but it is worthwhile that the parties finally came to discuss the problem face to face, as until that moment the Russian side could deal only with "fake news" and unfounded accusations.

Despite the mutual understanding, **an emotional connection between Putin and Trump has not yet established:** the U.S. President is still engaged

---

[234] Tillerson: Trump asked Putin about the hackers, he denied everything. BBC, 07.07.2017. http://www.bbc.com/russian/news-40538771

[235] Experts: the cybersecurity of the Russian Federation depends on the consolidation of the information community. TASS, 11.07.2017. http://tass.ru/politika/4406609

[236] Putin: it seems to me that Trump accepted assurances about the election in the United States. BBC, 08.07.2017. http://www.bbc.com/russian/news-40544330

[237] "I strongly pressed President Putin twice..." Twitter, 09.07.2017. https://twitter.com/realDonaldTrump/status/884012097805406208

in solving domestic political problems and rapprochement with his Russian counterpart is clearly outside his plans; it is too risky for his current status.

In the meantime, Russia is already negotiating with the U.S. to establish a cybersecurity working group.[238] The group is an important step in the settlement of the hacking issue, since it is not a question of unilateral strengthening of security, as in case of confrontation, but of cooperation aimed at combating the common threat. Talks on cooperation in the field of cybersecurity are also underway between China and Russia. The discussions with China are, naturally, more productive, since there is greater mutual understanding between the Russian Federation and the People's Republic of China at this stage.[239]

Although the statements of our American partners are not supported by concrete facts and are built on the speculations of a number of decision-makers (speculations, which only resonate with the help of mass media interested in maintaining the "anti-Tramp sentiments"), they have led to certain results:

First, regardless of one's attitude towards Trump the candidate, his reputation, which had not been crystal clear in the first place, was practically destroyed in connection with the "ties with Russia" attributed to him. Subsequently this tied the hands of Trump the president and put him in an extremely vulnerable position in relation to his opponents. From now on, his relations with Russia will always be in the cross hairs of not only relevant agencies, but also the media and the entire American society. This state of affairs cannot but affect the Russian–U.S. relations, since any progress of the new U.S. administration towards a dialogue with the Russian Federation will be deemed as connivance to the "Russian masters".

It is worth mentioning that there is the practice of employing such accusations during the election process is well–established: they add interest to the candidates' contest, while the media receive their ratings.

---

[238] Russia and the United States are negotiating the creation of a working group on cybersecurity. RIA Novosti, 20.07.2017. https://ria.ru/politics/20170720/1498833684.html

[239] "The goals of China and Russia in the field of cybersecurity are the same", Krutskikh said. RIA Novosti, 27.07.2017. https://ria.ru/world/20170727/1499248373.html

But it is quite doubtful the pursuit of this campaign after the inauguration of Donald Trump is worthwhile, since a president with weakened positions within his state cannot conduct a strong policy outside.

Second, the accusations have underscored the existence of clear Russophobic sentiments in the American mainstream. Russia, which until recently was a country that evoked not only fear, but also respect among Americans, now appears to be a treacherous aggressor, capable of doing anything out of self-interest. The world community has once again reached the verge of a pseudo-ideological confrontation, blended with the old fears of the Western elites over "Russian weapons".

Third, the status quo potentially provokes Trump to act more harshly against Russia, as only by conveying manifest power he will be able to overcome the reputation of the "puppet" of the Russian President. This is fraught with the possibility of the potential deterioration in the relations between Russia and the United States.

Accordingly, the activities of Trump's opponents are pushing towards an open conflict between the United States and Russia. **Basically, America has demonstrated that guesswork and speculations are enough for barefaced aggression.** This is what Putin regularly attributes to his American partners for both in public and in backstage discussions.

Resume. *The so-called "interference" of Russia has become an integral part of the history of the U.S. elections in 2016. As a result, the slogan of the twentieth century "The Russians are coming!" has been modified and now sounds almost like "The Russian hackers are coming!".*

Many in Russia, and even Putin himself, regarded accusations of this "interference" with notable irony, since the purported problem completely defied the theses that the presidents and representatives of the establishment had long defended in the United States: that Russia is a "gas-station country" so technologically backward that it hardly be treated even as a regional center of influence.

Putin only "added fuel to the fire" when publicly denied Russia's involvement in this scandal. In fact, the whole scandal was built on the associative feelings and private opinions of a number of officials, which repeatedly resonated with the help of the media, interested in maintaining the public in the "anti-Tramp" tone. This game proved to be effective: today Donald Trump's hands are bound, and he actually does what his opponents demand him to do.

Of course, theoretically one can assume that hackers really did their job in the U.S. information space and, of course, one can assume that they were of Russian origin. The fact that many countries are "probing" each other's cyberspace in such a manner cannot be ignored, while the influence of American companies Twitter and Facebook is difficult to overestimate. If desired, many traces of serious illegal intervention of the U.S. in Russia's internal affairs can be found, but nobody claims this as a global problem.

The outcome of the sandal around the "Russian hackers" in the U.S. was unfortunate: stimulated by the media resources, Russo-phobia as a phenomenon began to penetrate into the pores of the American and European societies. As a result, the world community found itself on the verge of a pseudo-ideological confrontation, blended with the old fears of the Western elites over "those Russians".

Exploitation of these stereotypes, unfortunately, leads to the creation of a pre-war situation in Europe, although the current armed conflicts are still localized and literally "scattered" around it.

CONCLUSION
PUTIN OF TOMORROW – WHO IS HE?

The question "Who is Mr. Putin?" still remains unanswered. And perhaps, it will go unanswered for at least 10-15 more years. Today, it is clear that Vladimir Putin is **a political idealist and pragmatist in one person. He is also a philosopher** who believes in his messianic mission to restore Russia's sovereignty, which was lost in the late 1990's. The plan is to restore it within the framework of **the Eurasian project,** which is turning into an analogue of the European Union in the post-Soviet space.

The Eurasian project is not about **rebuilding the USSR, which would be "expensive and senseless"** – **the world has changed.** But it is quite realistic to form fundamentally new political entities around an economic basis on the site of the former Soviet Union, as Putin has repeatedly said. Moreover, their emergence is not inhibited, but rather stimulated by the aggressive behavior of some Western leaders (and countries) in relation to Russia.

At the same time, the cult of "aggressive" Russia, implanted in Western countries certainly causes serious concerns for the Russians and the Kremlin. Russia perceives itself as a part of the world community, and "self-isolation" is not planned by either the society or the establishment. Putin regularly insists that "self-isolation" is absolutely off the question.

The defensive mechanisms of the Soviet period revived when Barack Obama uttered the words "cold war 2.0": the weapons buried in the Soviet land long ago were extracted from the depths of the citizens' post-Soviet consciousness and began to work as in good old Soviet days. It can be said that it was Western leaders who, with their rash behavior, in an effort to subordinate the Russian leadership at all costs, actually **forced the entire**

Russian society to switch into the mobilization mode, which back in its day helped Stalin and his team to place the USSR among the world leaders. At the present stage, this level of economic, social and political mobilization could not have been achieved by internal politics – the political system started getting "tired" of Putin. However, the attempt to discredit him personally in the eyes of Russians turned him into a real national leader on par with Joseph Stalin.

The Western community, in the person of Secretary of State Hillary Clinton and Chancellor of Germany Angela Merkel, reacted adversely to the attempts to organize integration processes on the territory of the former USSR in the form of the Customs Union, as well as other processes within the framework of the Eurasian project that are actively being developed by Putin's team. This, however, only instigated and supported the initiators of these processes. As is well-known, integration processes accelerate under external pressure.

As a result, the G8 turned into G7. Russia was expelled from the so-called G8 format, which actually *left the country with the latitude to* **form its own regional center of influence.** The USA, trying to reduce Russia's influence, ended up with a self-created problem without rhyme or reason.

Contrary to the prevailing view that Russia was "disciplined", it became obvious that the G7 countries limited their own influence on the economic and political processes in the Eurasian space, having encouraged the development of another format – the G20[240].

Attempts to exclude Russia from this format as well revealed the sustained resistance to the initiatives of the United States and its G7 partners. In self-defense, the other countries began to form their own financial transnational institutions as counterbalance to the IMF and the

---

[240] As the global crisis unfolded, it was the G-20 that became the leading official format for coordinating interstate relations, testing and smoothing emerging conflicts. These twenty countries account for 90% of world GDP, 80% of the world trade and two thirds of the world's population. Initially, it was established as a working group (officially called the Group of Twenty Finance Ministers and Central Bank Governors) to hold negotiations between the seven developed countries with the developing countries on economic and financial problems arising from the crisis.

World Bank and to duplicate the functions of the international UN institutions weakened because of the U.S. actions.

The international community began to regard Russia, among many things, as a country that can say "no" to the U.S., which is striving to maintain dominance over other countries. In fact, **Washington has achieved the opposite effect by its actions, having forged a rather strong counter-opposition** in the form of various regional alliances.

Putin's team believes that the idea of Eurasianism can contribute to **a systemic counteraction to the strategy of the so-called "color revolutions",** put into service by the U.S. in many countries across the world. The most recent examples include the actual overthrow of the government in Bulgaria with the aim of blocking the South Stream project and the attempt to overthrow the government in Macedonia to block the alternative option – the Turkish Stream. Ukraine is the most vivid example of the employment of the "color revolution" technology, ultimately resulting in a rapidly degenerating economy, social sphere, state institutions and declining intellectual potential in the target nation.

The crisis of ideas in the U.S. and its methods of interaction with the world community was especially evident in Yugoslavia, Afghanistan, Iraq, Libya and Syria. Attempts to control the situation merely led to the emergence of new "network enemies" – Al-Qaeda and, subsequently, ISIS.

Full-fledged cooperation within the framework of economic and political platforms is likely to exist in the future only on the basis of the restored sovereignty of national economies. And the signs of a split in the supranational elites provide a unique opportunity to realize this plan without military turmoil, but with a victory in the *"war of ideas"*.

The real challenge for the United States today is not Russia, but **radical nationalism in China, India, Japan, Europe, and Africa.** Nationalists there already reject not only the American way of life but, more importantly, the American way of thinking as a benchmark.

Nonetheless, the United States continues to behave as if it were alone in the world. Of course, if Russia wants to get out of the "sanctions war" with minimal losses, it should encourage this behavior, since the decisions taken under such a paradigm will be neither beneficial nor ultimately increase American influence in the world.

It should be clearly understood that **at some stage the United States establishment de facto declared Russia a "war of extermination".** The Kremlin, while hiding its true intentions, even somewhat encourages the United States and its ambitions, without going into open combat. Meanwhile, the USA prefers to act by proxy – the Baltic countries, Georgia, Ukraine – those countries that are ready "to work for food".

It seems that the American dream has been imperceptibly replaced: now it manifests as **a naked desire for world rule and domination,** which was clearly articulated in public speeches of Barack Obama, including those to the Congress in 2014-2015. Among those living today, Kim Jong-Un and Bashar al-Assad are labeled with the Washington's hostility. Supposedly that same fate was in store for Russia and Putin personally: the country and its leader have been demonized for a long time, and more and more resources are regularly allocated for this purpose. But, political strategists and organizers complain that these resources are absolutely inadequate, as there is no result: Russia won the Olympics in 2014, returned illegally annexed territories, won armed conflicts at its southern border, and dominated the information wars. In the process, Vladimir Putin is becoming more and more popular.

Nevertheless, the work done by the "Washington team" is also visible: Georgia, Ukraine, Moldova, Uzbekistan, Kyrgyzstan… The volume causes respect, the goals and the sense – the opposite. The adjustment of the position of the governments of Bulgaria and Macedonia, prompted by the "adjustment" of their governments, to disrupt the construction of the agreed upon South Stream and the emerging Turkish Stream, could serve as examples of textbook information wars, but, in fact, were only acts of unfair competition organized by one WTO member country against another WTO member country. The silence of this organization speaks volumes.

The hyperemotional policy, which had been pursued by the administrations of George W. Bush and Barack Obama, aimed to preserve the illusion of absolute domination by the United States over any other country in the world. This policy has inevitably been collapsing since the attack at the twin towers in New York. But, if the towers collapsed rather quickly, it takes a lot more to change the virtual reality, in which Washington irrevocably determines the fate of the world, woven in

Hollywood with the support of the Pentagon and about fifty U.S. intelligence agencies.

Ideas proved to be much more resistant than concrete and steel reinforcement.

Opponents of the incumbent President of Russia can be presented with a sole argument: before you "remove" Putin, you **need to find at least some worthy alternative.** Otherwise this demand (*"Putin must go away!"*) becomes *an empty shell.*

The Kremlin, in turn, must understand that the vulnerabilities that can really demotivate the pro-Putin groups are already "scattered" all over the political field.

The President's high popularity rating still causes a substantial degree of irritation among his opponents. Despite the serious economic problems associated not only with the notorious "anti-Russian sanctions" and the decline in energy prices, as well as the continuing consequences and manifestations of the 2008-2009 global financial crisis, the President's influence remains steadily considerable in many spheres of Russians' life.

It is true, Russia has lost several platforms of exerting its influence on the international situation (G8, PACE), and has gained a pool of overt and furious opponents in the face of the U.S. satellites – Canada, Australia, Poland, as well as Ukraine, which, in the words of its politicians, has literally declared war on Moscow.

Despite the fact that the situation is turned "upside down" and the true aggressor, who targeted the Russian population on its territory, has accused Russia of aggression, the so-called developed countries supported Ukraine. Today these "developed countries" look foolish, as they are forced to comply with the wishes and commands of the U.S., although this is contrary to their own economic interests.

The people of the countries that criticize Russia today, even being under the influence of anti-Russian propaganda, are very pragmatic about problems associated with the information confrontation with the Russian leader. That is why Putin regularly takes the top lines of various media ratings, based on independent polls.

Thereby, the population of the United States and Europe, comparing their own politicians with the Russian President, makes them understand that they have to try to rise to his level. Of course, **such a complimentary positioning of Putin causes jealousy among Western politicians**, which further spurs their anti-Russian sentiments.

The statement by U.S. Secretary of Defense Ashton Carter in 2015 that the USA and NATO were ready for a committed and long confrontation with Russia, regardless of who would hold the presidential post in the country (Putin or someone else), likewise speaks volumes.[241]

One of the reasons why the statement, so disappointing for the "doves of peace", was made is rather prosaic: the United States' satellite countries started feeling that the sanctions against Putin and his team "did not work", and Washington's political will was weakening. That is why it was necessary **to rouse the pro-American public with a decisive word.**

The calls to switch from the dollar to national currencies in mutual settlements in a number of countries were especially painful for the USA. These resulted in special statements by the Secretary of Defense, the Joint Chiefs of Staff and the Secretary of the Air Force of the United States, as well as the nuclear tests conducted by the USA during the BRICS and the SCO summits in Ufa, Russia (2015).[242]

In general, Russia has formed an impression that the U.S. is trying to solve its problems at the expense of other countries. To this end, the U.S. does not hesitate to use nuclear weapons; in fact, it is the only one, which has used them in the history of mankind. Those world leaders who say no to America are first discredited and then liquidated by the US.

It is no wonder that Vladimir Putin drew the attention of so many countries' population, when he said his decisive "no" to the United States back in 2007 at the Munich conference. Maintaining his policy, Putin is a living example of the fact that the USA is by no means "all-powerful".

The president of the Russian Federation is overburdened with functions and political significance; he bears too much authority and responsibility. This is the main "sore spot" of the current political configuration and an **obvious vulnerability of the system.** In the event the

---

[241] Pentagon: The US and NATO are getting ready for a long-term confrontation with Russia. RIA Novosti, 22.06.2015. https://ria.ru/world/20150622/1080182836.html

[242] The United States conducted the first tests of a new nuclear bomb in Nevada. NTV, 9.07.2015. http://www.ntv.ru/novosti/1439297/

"Putin factor" disappears, the country will most likely split into several camps, each of which will try to **"lustrate" its opponents following the "Ukrainian scenario"**: liberals against Putinistas, Putinistas against liberals and so on.

Regional separatism will most likely be multiplied by religious separatism. The threat that ISIS will shift the emphasis of its activity to Russia will become quite real.

The Kremlin understands that China poses an obvious threat to the Russian economy. **The United States gently pushes Russia to close cooperation with China, which pays for Russian energy resources with U.S. state obligations, thereby technically increasing the dependence of the Russian Federation on the U.S. in the economic sense.** In this regard, the increasing **technological dependence** of Russia on the PRC (under conditions of limited import substitution) can be offset by the supply of technology from South Korea and Japan.

The recent rapprochement with Turkey is also strategic. Further, judging by the sentiment in Europe, **Russia should get ready for a warming of relations with the European Union.** Further attempts to destabilize the Russian reality using coercive diplomacy and illegal sanctions will backfire on the Western economic and political systems, first European and then American, to produce strong destruction within them.

The problem is that, after the actual declaration of a new "Cold War", the world returned to a "bloc mentality": the parties gradually stopped speaking the same language and using the same discourse. **In these conditions, it will be extremely difficult to find consensus and avoid conflicts.**

The narrative of "a radioactive Russia" is used by the Western media for classical propaganda purposes. As a result, institutions cut financing for studies of economic processes in Russia, which leads to **a lack of understanding of what is happening here, and the West will inevitably incur investment losses in the future.**

Russians are accustomed to restrictions (thanks to the Soviet period), and the sanctions do not make much of an impression on the population (that is the mindset of the elites).

However, **the sanctions theme may well help Putin to distance himself from his business environment,** primarily from those top managers who discredit him with their love of the royal lifestyle, palaces and fur stores.

There is a good reason why the top managers of state-owned companies have recently driven up their salaries to an exorbitantly high level – such a practice is encountered in Russian companies just on the eve of a dismissal. In addition, there is a moral and psychological aspect to such dismissals: Putin's popularity will grow again. The dismissals are likely to be rationalized by unfavorable situations in the companies.

Quite likely, the population of Russia will witness the evolution of a new Putin. Then again, the game of numbers has evidently exhausted the guarantor of the Russian constitution. Among potential successors, the expert community considers Defense Minister Sergei Shoigu, Director of the Foreign Intelligence Service Sergei Naryshkin and Special Presidential Representative Sergei Ivanov. In this regard, when asked, *"Who will be the next president of Russia?"*, one can reply, "A man named Sergei".

It is probable that "damaged" people with personal drama appeal to Putin. Another problem lies in the fact that the representatives of the Russian president's entourage are all of similar age. Russia already has such an experience: before the very end of the USSR, the team of **gerontocrats from the Politburo** did not allow young politicians to the helm. Admittance of the relatively young Mikhail Gorbachev to power was recognized a mistake. However, Putin already played around with his version of "Gorbachev" in 2008-2012.

Given the obvious (manic) desire of the Western community to remove Putin from the post of president of the Russian Federation, he will not reformat the system under the external pressure to avoid its destruction.

Washington, London and Berlin thereby de facto "preserve" the political system of Russia. To Putin's credit, he keeps it mobile (modifiable) from within, keeping the operational apparatus "free-flowing". That is why the current political system can still successfully respond to external challenges and is prepared not only for the escalation of the information war (aka "sanctions war", "cold war", etc.), but also for a hot phase of competition, to the surprise of external observers.

The current team list of Vladimir Putin is formalized and fixed. This maintains loyalty, but, of course, also affects the effectiveness of the team's performance: the lack of challengers and a real competition generates relaxation and calmness, which can be used by the external opponents and which contributes to maintaining the destructive, albeit weak, opposition within the country.

This state of events affects the political system, preventing its renewal and development, making it unviable for the future. Information exchange between countries, however, can revitalize this structure. Nevertheless, any information exchange involves a mutual penetration that can be interpreted as hostile, which happened in 2016, when Russia was accused of trying to influence the presidential election in the United States.

The main challenge for Vladimir Putin to address over the period from 2018 to 2024 is the **search and institutionalization of his successor.** It is necessary to make sure that this person (or a group of people of whom Putin will choose) is not in his political shadow but is a relatively independent player with his own personal background.

This should be a person, who can deal with a difficult legacy, though Putin would try to make sure that this legacy is not as difficult as the one he inherited from Boris Yeltsin.

This person should not be "Putin 2.0", because he will always compare unfavorably to the original version of Putin. If image-makers will insist on a "duplicate" configuration, it will be a serious mistake.

The current Putin's team is already categorically thinking in terms of 2018-2024 and is preparing for his withdrawal after the presidential term ends. This does not involve a withdrawal from the political arena, where he will still have to represent the interests of Russia after 2024.

Russia still needs to compensate for the apparent "failure of the 1990's", when, as the consequence of the collapse of the USSR, the country lost its national sovereignty for a while and experienced severe shock from economic losses. This resulted in a kind of a "psychological breakdown" in Russian society, which **Vladimir Putin now seems to be trying to cure with injections of the nostalgic past of the Soviet Union and images of the country's great future.**

Putin reloaded. What is next?

The 2018 presidential campaign, in many respects, **resembled the 2004 campaign.** The difference was **a pronounced factor of "external influence"** by a number of Western countries, including the so-called "anti-Russian sanctions", pressure on the country's leadership, both direct and indirect, and pressure on the business community.

All these, of course, produced a depressing effect on the population of the country. Ideological mobilization was carried out very quickly in response; it became especially apparent during the scandal with the likely poisoning of the Scripal family in the UK, when the Russian leadership was directly accused of involvement in this case by the British top officials.

These accusations and the pressure, which was exerted immediately after the scandal in line with the so-called "diplomatic solidarity" principle (the UK even managed to form a kind of a coalition of a number of European states and the U.S. against Russia), as well as the expulsion of Russian diplomats from a number of countries, led only to the growth of Vladimir Putin's support among the population. The voter turnout for the election on March 18, 2018 was much higher than that at the previous election.

This trend continued for some time after the vote in March 2018, and then began to decline. The Russian Presidential Administration was accused of special selection of obviously weak candidates to rival with Putin in the campaign. However, it was obvious that the civil society (specifically its oppositional force) was unable to advance or even propose an alternative to Putin.

The long intrigue before the vote (whether Putin will run for president or not) made it clear that **the candidate number one was outside the box, beyond any competition, who actually managed his own election campaign.** Consolidation of his electoral groups, their mobilization not only for external but also for internal reasons (the seizure of the opposition agenda, the "Crimean consensus", the "ideal war" in Syria) led to the fact that the youth factor was involved.

As a result, **the opposition,** both systemic and non-systemic, **fought** not so much with the Kremlin but **amongst each other.** At some point, there was even an impression that Putin was some kind of a *divine being* for this part of the political spectrum, without whom their political life lost its meaning – the obsession with Putin's figure was quite clear.

The attitude towards the issue of the political status of the Crimea and the events in Syria turned out to be destructive for the pre-election reputation of the non-systemic opposition. The so-called **"wandering focus" of public attention** also emerged due to the presence of Putin's personal factor and lack of campaign coordination.

Nevertheless, a **post-election "windows of opportunity"** opened for the parliamentary parties – the Communist Party, the LDPR (which is expected to replace its leaders), the liberal camp (which obtained a *motor for economic reform* in the person of Alexei Kudrin), and the "siloviki".

The next stage of the country's political development will proceed **from 2018 to 2024** under the banner of the so-called **"transfer of power",** that is, to an actual transfer of power to a political heir / heirs.

Due to the upcoming two-stage economic reform (first, a wave of nationalization, which is ongoing already, and then, likely, a wave of privatization), the elites interested in privatization processes **will continue to be consolidated around Putin,** and it will not be possible to split them with the help of the sanctions.

The Russian president will have to seek consensus on the format of economic transformations needed for the announced "technological leap" between Alexei Kudrin - Maxim Oreshkin and Andrei Belousov, who embody the different directions of the economic reform. Incidentally, **Putin's economic platform was never presented to the public during the election campaign** as a result of their disagreements.

Discussions and formulations of the economic platform for Russia began back in May 2016, in anticipation of Putin's new presidential term. The Ministry of Economic Development (**first Alexei Ulyukaev and then Maxim Oreshkin**), the Center for Strategic Research (**Alexei Kudrin, head of the CSR and Deputy Chairman of the Economic Council under the**

President of the Russian Federation), and the Stolypin Club (**Boris Titov, supported by Presidential Aide Andrei Belousov and Presidential Advisor Sergei Glazyev**) entered into rivalry for the development of the country's main economic strategy and the favor of the President.

The main task that the President set for the developers was to ensure economic growth above the world average, that is, up to 4%. It is obvious now that **the Kudrin strategy, supplemented by useful proposals of the Stolypin Club, will be adopted as the basis for the economic reform program.** According to a source from among the developers of the program, its main distinguishing feature is that it was ordered by the President and is a full-fledged and finalized document.

Most of the proposals of the CSR and the Stolypin Club are remarkably similar. Both versions of the program recognize the need to move to an innovative digital economy, reform the institutions and public administration, and increase investment in the development of human capital.

Lobbying for the implementation of certain mechanisms of the program will depend on the configuration of the future government. As is known, **Putin favors maintaining a balance of power in the government bodies.**

Meanwhile, **most regions of Russia have been living under serious budget deficits for several years now.** According to some data, the amount of state debt for all constituent territories of the federation has increased almost five-fold, from 432.6 billion rubles to 2.3 trillion rubles, over the past ten years. Among other factors, this is due to the so-called 2012 "May Decrees" that fulfilled Putin's election promises to increase social expenditures from the regions' budgets, as well as the ignorant fiscal and monetary policy of the regional authorities.

Restrictions imposed on the budgets of the regions have little impact on the implementation of investment projects in them, as the budgets were drawn up to meet current needs, rather than to aim at the integrated regional development. When implementing investment projects and regional development projects, the regional authorities rely on federal development programs, investment programs of state-owned companies operating in the region, and the possibility of attracting private investments (including foreign ones).

The change of the government and the re-appointment of Dmitry Medvedev as the "new old" Prime Minister meant that Minister of Economic Development Maxim Oreshkin, Minister of Industry and Trade Denis Manturov, and Minister of Finance Anton Siluanov (who also became the First Deputy Prime Minister) would remain in their roles as key players in the economic branch.

The forthcoming administrative reform involves **strengthening of the institution of presidential power** and his participation in the current economic and social processes.

The largest personnel changes will occur on the regional track with the **active personnel rotation of the corps of regional governors.** Sources believe that the regional project "Young Technocrats" has been closed by Putin: *the Russian regions need politicians, not accountants.* Accordingly, **the search and formation of the means of social mobility will continue.** For instance, the official *"presidential talent pool"* will remain relevant.

If the West has a plan and desire for Putin to quit the presidency of the Russian Federation, they have to start negotiating with Russia immediately, since **the future political reality of 2024 is being formed right now.** In 2-3 years, it will be too late.

Particularly, given the current situation, Russia will not be able now to agree with the USA and the EU on "every little issue" (lifting of the sanctions, etc.), but will be able to agree "in large" (START III, for example, in the name of nuclear security). On the other hand, a new renaissance is expected in the development of trade and economic relations with China within the framework of the Eurasian Economic Community and the New Silk Road: almost **synchronous re-election of Vladimir Putin and Xi Jinping for long terms was very symptomatic.**

The weakness of our "Western partners" lies in their morbid obsession with the figure of the Russian president. The "sanctions for Putin" scheme does not work (the analogue of *"Assad Must Go!"* causes nothing but irony in Russia now). It is necessary to take into account the peculiarities of the Russian political culture: sharp decisions are taken at a turning point (elections, etc.), while evolutionary decisions are made during a political calm.

In parallel, the announcement of "Cold War 2.0", the "Atlantic solidarity", the "energy dependence of Europe on Russia", and etc., conceal the real and unfair rivalry between the USA and Russia – beyond the framework of the WTO and international law.

In this regard, the so-called sanctions and even the relentless regularity of their introduction no longer make an impression on the vast majority of the population of the country. **Today, the sanctions regime is one of the most radical tools for adjusting the market space "for oneself".**

It has been used by the United States for a steady time already, and not only against North Korea, Iran, and Russia, but also against the countries of the European Union. The USA has even become somewhat addicted to it, trying to compensate for an obvious sense of political inferiority rising out of the gradual loss of international authority and influence on world processes.

The aim of the sanctions confrontation with Russia, which the U.S. instituted under various pretexts, was to show a more serious player – the People's Republic of China – the threat to its own economy if China acts on its geopolitical ambitions. **The USA counted on a "blitzkrieg" in Russia.** However, in the end, the U.S. will have to fight on two economic fronts, with Russia and with China. The latter has just started deploying its regiments to conduct a full-fledged "defensive" trade war, as China puts it. There emerge evident outlines of yet another front of the "trade war" - with the European Union. But that is rather a different story.

Some countries have already started carrying out mutual settlements in their national currencies, bypassing the US dollar. Some countries are creating their own payment systems, physically separated from the SWIFT system. Some countries have already completed the modernization of their armed forces and, in aggregate, represent military power, quite comparable with the power of the Pentagon.

Furthermore, a **"successor"** (rather, several candidates), who will be nominated for president in 2022-2023, **has already appeared in Putin's entourage.**

The main trends on the external and internal tracks will be as follows:

– Russia has switched from "being defensive" to **working with ideas in the political and economic spheres** (i.e. an active position aimed to prevent threats and challenges posed by Western countries);

– Russia has staked on the **formation of regional centers of influence,** having completed the transition from a monocentric system to a polycentric one (with the active participation of China, India, Iran and the attention paid to these processes by the EU, Saudi Arabia and other countries) and will keep on taking actions in this direction;

– The process of formation of the "Eastern Alliance" (Russia and China) against NATO, a bipolar structure simulating the USSR and the United States, is an attempt to reset the institution of the United Nation;

– Russia intends to make **a technological leap in the economy and restructure its financial system** (making the ruble convertible).

The main goal of the renewed team under Putin for the period from 2018 to 2022, is to create a **high-quality social environment in Russia,** as a country comfortable for the majority of its population (the Putin's "core electorate"), with the help of the 2018 May Decree.

After these projects are implemented, Vladimir Putin will consider a transfer to a new post, not associated with a large number of protocol meetings and events. It is also envisaged that the "transfer of power" may occur before 2024.

In this case, Putin may withdraw to a special position prepared in advance, such as the State Council (an analogue of the position occupied by Xi Jinping) or in the restored State Security Committee.

☒

APPENDIX
THE USA'S RELATIONS
WITH OTHER COUNTRIES[243]

Open confrontation

Conflict / pre-conflict / traditional tensions

Tensions exist (temporal, so far)

Neutral relations / limited contacts

General friendship and active cooperation in at least one sphere (disagreements on other issues may exist)

An ally country / close interaction

1. Russia
Relationship status - Conflict / pre-conflict / traditional tensions

Relations between Russia and the United States are moving towards the phase of **open political confrontation, despite mutual sympathies and the desire of the leaders of the two countries to conduct a full-fledged dialogue.**

During the election campaign in the U.S. and after the election of Donald Trump as President, Russia took a wait-and-see stand. The words of presidential candidate Trump about the possibility of removing / easing the anti-Russian sanctions or changing the official position on the Crimea inspired the political elite in the Russian Federation. However, a number of public steps by the United States (the air strike against Syria, the criticism of Russia from the rostrum of the UN Security Council, etc.) put the Russian leadership on alert. Despite the successful meeting between Vladimir Putin and Donald Trump, they did not manage to solidify interaction between the two countries. The adoption by the U.S. Congress of a law on sanctions

---

[243] The list shows the key countries by parts of the globe.

against a number of countries (including Russia) actually deprived the U.S. president of a field for maneuver in relations with the Russian Federation. Russia, in turn, lost the incentive and "hope" to build constructive relations with the United States and is developing (or already applying) measures of responding to the anti-Russian actions (diplomatic, political and economic).

The acuteness of the "Russian issue" in American politics is due to internal political reasons. Opponents of Donald Trump use this issue to discredit the President. Trump, in turn, is interested in Russia as a means in the big anti-Chinese struggle.

At present, there are no significant prerequisites for improving the relations between the Russian Federation and the United States. Establishment of the dialogue is possible, paradoxically, if the United States is headed by a leader with a tough stance towards Russia (e.g. Richard Nixon, Ronald Reagan).

EUROPE

2. The European Union
Relationship status - Tensions exist (temporal, so far)

The United States and the European Union have recently **split on a number of key issues.**

During the 2000s, the total volume of the GDP of the EU member states steadily increased, having outstripped the U.S. GDP in the late 2000s. In 2016 the eurozone for the first time since 2008 outstripped the U.S. in terms of GDP growth (1.7% vs. 1.6%). Despite the growing competition from the EU, the United States has steadily encouraged the integration processes in the European Union. The peculiarity of the current stage of the U.S.-EU relations is that Donald Trump placed his country's economic interests above political ones and almost openly supported the processes of the EU's disintegration (for example, through the encouragement of the so-called Brexit). In the spring of 2017, the current U.S. administration planned to revive the negotiations on the Transatlantic Trade and Investment Partnership (TTIP), because it could not persuade the EU countries to conduct trade relations on a bilateral basis (that is, behind Brussels).

In general, there is a lack of coherence between the EU and the U.S. (e.g., the anti-Russian sanctions caused criticism of the EU), and relations between Washington and Brussels are going through the most difficult period in their history. However, this period may be temporary.

3. The United Kingdom
Relationship status - An ally country / close interaction

The UK is one of the main political allies of the USA in the world. In January 2017, Donald Trump and British Prime Minister Teresa May confirmed their intention to develop friendly relations.

Unlike the previous U.S. presidential administration, Trump has consistently expressed support for the UK's exit from the EU. As a result of Brexit, the economic relations between the United Kingdom and the United States will strengthen. In July 2017, the two countries entered into negotiations on a bilateral trade agreement that should compensate for the UK's costs of the withdrawal from the EU, and become an alternative to the multilateral Transatlantic partnership for the United States, against which Trump spoke. Both sides are currently interested in strengthening NATO.

The countries' positions on the sanctions against Iran and Russia generally coincide. The main stumbling block is the Chinese issue, since China is one of the key economic and geopolitical partners of the UK.

4. France
Relationship status - An ally country / close interaction

France maintains close partnership with the United States and focuses on the U.S. in economic and foreign policy.

The weakening of the trans-Atlantic trend and the cooling of relations between the U.S. and Germany provides an opportunity to strengthen the bilateral American-French relations.

The similarity of the political campaigns of Presidents Donald Trump and Emmanuel Macron serves as an argument in favor of establishing relations between the two countries: both were not the obvious favorites of the presidential race in their countries, did not have much political experience at the time of coming to power, both are well acquainted with the world of business. Macron is known for certain sympathies towards Trump. Thus, after the G20 summit in July 2017, at the photographing ceremony, Trump turned out to be last in a row, which symbolizes the "low status" of a politician. Makron stood to next to Trump, having relieved him from excessive attacks by the media.

At the same time, Emmanuel Macron is influenced by Germany and personally by Angela Merkel, who will probably induce France to confront the current political leadership of the United States.

Disagreements between the U.S. and France may arise because of the Syrian issue. Macron significantly softened the country's position on the issue of Bashar al-Assad's withdrawal from power and intends to invest in the restoration of the Syrian economy, while the U.S. still cannot articulate a clear position on this issue, sometimes exacerbating rhetoric about the Syrian leadership.

5. Germany
Relationship status - General friendship and active cooperation in at least one sphere (disagreements on other issues may exist)

Germany is still an ally of the United States, but their relations have recently shown a tendency to cool.

The United States and Germany have different visions of integration processes in Europe at this stage. Serious disagreements arose on the grounds of the USA's decision to withdraw from the Paris agreement on climate. Germany expresses cautious dissatisfaction with the U.S. attempts to influence the internal affairs of Europe, for example, implementation of gas projects (especially Nord Stream-2, in which Wintershall Holding GmbH is involved) and imposition of its own energy resources (American LNG).

The personal antipathies of the leaders of the two countries can affect the relations of the countries in the near future. Thus, the party of Angela Merkel CDU / CSU lowered the status of the U.S. in its perception from "friend" to "partner". According to the polls, the rating of the foreign policy of Trump among the Germans is 11%.

The United States and Germany continue to cooperate within NATO. The headquarters of the U.S. Air Force in Europe (underground), the Rammstein base with more than 50 thousand of U.S. military is located on the territory of Germany.

6. Austria

Relationship status - General friendship and active cooperation in at least one sphere (disagreements on other issues may exist)

Austria maintains neutral (with a plus sign) relations with the USA, focusing on the position of the EU.

The United States is one of the largest foreign investors in Austria, its share is about 15 percent of total investments. Austria's oil and gas company OMV AG participates in the project Nord Stream-2, which may entail disagreements between the United States and Austria.

To date, Austria is not a member of NATO.

7. Italy
Relationship status - General friendship and active cooperation in at least one sphere (disagreements on other issues may exist)

Italy is in good relations with the United States.

Italian company ENI has participated in a gas project Turkish Stream since 2017. In this regard, Italy has a restrained position on the anti-Russian sanctions.

Several military facilities of the USA are located on the territory of Italy: the Aviano Air Force Base of the USA, the Ederl Garrison of the U.S. Army, etc.

8. Portugal
Relationship status - General friendship and active cooperation in at least one sphere (disagreements on other issues may exist)

The USA is an important trade and economic partner of Portugal. Political interaction is limited, but Portugal has an important geopolitical significance for the United States. The Layes Air Force Base of the U.S. is located on the territory of the island of Terceira (Atlantic Ocean, the only major point in the trans-Atlantic space).

9. Ukraine
Relationship status - General friendship and active cooperation in at least one sphere (disagreements on other issues may exist)

Ukraine is experiencing difficulties in relations with the United States.

The political leadership of Ukraine is focused on the EU and the USA, and depends on their financial and political support. The new American administration significantly reduced interest in Ukraine, having focused on the issues of the Middle East and Asia.

Complications in the bilateral relations arose after the leakage of information that the launch of North Korean missiles became possible thanks to the technology received from the Yuzhmash Plant, Ukraine.

Nevertheless, at this stage Ukraine **maintains "friendship" with the United States**, albeit in a modified format. The U.S. confirmed the allocation of $175 million for the armament of the Ukrainian army. Moreover, the recent activity of the U.S. Department of State special representative for Ukraine **Kurt Volcker** has shown a **significant increase in interest and support from Washington**. Interaction with the Ukrainian leadership is mainly carried out by the environment of the U.S. President rather than himself, which indicates that it is the American establishment that is aimed at supporting Ukraine.

10. Belarus

Relationship status - Tensions exist (temporal, so far)

Belarus is focused on cooperation with the United States in foreign policy, despite the traditional tension in the relations.

The trend of improvement of the Belarusian–American relations has continued since 2016. In the past two years, the U.S. expanded the list of visa services for Belarusian citizens and partially suspended sanctions against a number of Belarusian enterprises. The release of political prisoners and the presidential election of 2015, which were held without violence, were called the official reasons.

The real reason for improving Belarusian relations with the United States was a number of political decisions of the Belarusian government that did not meet Russia's expectations. For instance, Belarus reacted to the return of the Crimea to Russia with restraint in 2014, and refused to place a Russian airbase on its territory at the end of 2015.

The new vector of cooperation with the United States is primarily of a political nature. However, despite the fact that Belarus is an important potential partner in the region, Donald Trump extended the U.S. sanctions against some representatives of the Belarusian establishment for a year in

July 2017. The need to strengthen credibility by the Belarusian side was called the condition for lifting the sanctions.

11. Poland

Relationship status - An ally country / close interaction

Poland is one of the key partners of the United States in Eastern Europe.

Poland is focused on the U.S. position in its economic decision-making. For example, Poland's refusal to lay the second line of the Yamal-Europe gas pipeline is due to this fact.

Poland is important for the United States as an anti-Russian force in the region and a representative of the U.S. interests in the EU. The administration of Donald Trump is making efforts to maintain the ties between the two countries (see Trump's visit and his speech in Warsaw, 2017).

The EuroPRO NATO complex is located on the territory of Poland.

12. Lithuania

Relationship status - An ally country / close interaction

Lithuania is focused on the United States in the conduct of internal and foreign policy. Lithuanian President Dalia Grybauskaitė is an advocate of Euro-Atlanticism; she openly declares the U.S. supremacy and the need to be among its allies. The Lithuanian president had been an employee of the IMF for a long time, during the period of domination of the U.S. there. An example of Lithuania's orientation to the U.S. political position is that it broke with Russia, having preferred LNG from the Norwegian company Statoil, which was 40 percent more expensive than that from Russia. In 2017, Lithuania will become one of the first European buyers of LNG from the USA.

13. Latvia

Relationship status – An ally country / close interaction

Latvia is an ally of the United States in the post-Soviet space.

They cooperate in the military sphere. The U.S. is trying to persuade Latvia to buy LNG instead of Russian gas.

14. Estonia

Relationship status – An ally country / close interaction

Estonia is an ally of the USA. The Emari air base of NATO / the USA is located on the territory of Estonia. The U.S. Air Force is using the base as the location for the operational deployment of military aircraft.

15. Sweden

Relationship status – General friendship and active cooperation in at least one sphere (disagreements on other issues may exist)

Sweden is in partnership with the United States, primarily on economic issues.

Many American investments come to the country due to the balanced financial system of Sweden and other indicators.

Sweden is not a member of NATO, but cooperates with the USA on defense issues on a bilateral basis.

16. Finland

Relationship status – General friendship and active cooperation in at least one sphere (disagreements on other issues may exist)

Finland is in quite neutral relations with the United States.

Finland mainly cooperates with the U.S. on security issues on the Russian-Finnish border. At the same time, Finland opposes the deployment of NATO troops on the border with Russia.

Another sphere of cooperation is development of Arctic projects in the energy sector.

17. Serbia
Relationship status - Conflict / pre-conflict / traditional tensions

Serbia is in tense relations with the United States, despite recent progress in sphere of cooperation.

The main problem issue in the relations is the unrecognized republic of Kosovo. A new level of cooperation between the U.S. and Serbia was reached after the extradition treaty was concluded many years later, which will improve cooperation on combating terrorism and attract U.S. investments to Serbia.

The United States supports Serbia's commitment to European integration. However, Serbia remains the weakest partner of the USA in the Balkan region.

18. Moldova
Relationship status - Neutral relations / limited contacts

Moldova is in relatively neutral relations with the United States.

The U.S. interests in Moldova mainly connected with expansion of anti-Russian influence in the post-Soviet space. There was information about the intention of the U.S. to build new facilities on the territory of Moldova, at a base in Bulboac located near the border with the unrecognized Pridnestrovian Moldavian Republic. In August 2017, the Dragoon Pioneer joint American-Moldovan exercises were held. Moldovan President Igor Dodon, who is considered pro-Russian, categorized this information as a provocation.

19. Greece
Relationship status - Tensions exist (temporal, so far)

Greece has contradictory relations with the United States, especially in the economic sphere.

Thus, Greece gets more than 35 percent of its oil from Iran (which causes the U.S. displeasure), having an unlimited credit for purchases. The option of supplies from Saudi Arabia is vulnerable because of the country's support for the activities of Islamic extremists, especially among almost 1.5 million illegal immigrants in Greece, who also contribute to explosive growth of unemployment with the knowledge of the EU and the U.S.

The leadership of Greece is dissatisfied with the U.S. intervention in the economic policy of the country (the Greek-Russian-Bulgarian project of Burgas–Alexandroupolis pipeline was suspended at the initiative of the U.S.).

20. Bulgaria
Relationship status - General friendship and active cooperation in at least one sphere (disagreements on other issues may exist)

Bulgaria is a longtime partner of the United States in the Balkan region.

In making economic and political decisions, Bulgaria traditionally focuses on the U.S. position. A good example is Bulgaria's refusal to implement the South Stream project with Russia in 2014. Shortly before that, Bulgaria had consistently opposed the third wave of sanctions against Russia at several summits of the EU leaders.

The United States has experience of cooperation with Bulgaria in operations to supply arms from Eastern Europe to the Middle East, Afghanistan and Iraq. In prospect, Bulgaria and the USA consider joint training of Libyan military at Bulgarian military bases and topical issues of development of the Balkan region. In Bulgaria, there are several NATO facilities: the Graf Ignatievo airbase, the U.S. Landfill Novo Selo and others.

MIDDLE EAST, CAUCASUS AND CENTRAL ASIA

21. Turkey
Relationship status - Tensions exist (temporal, so far)

Turkey is a traditional partner of the USA in Europe, however, there are a **number of significant differences** at the current stage.

Turkey is an important player in the Middle East region, exerting serious influence on the Trans-Caucasus, primarily Azerbaijan and Georgia. In recent years, Turkey has been moving away from the European course, focusing on the Middle East and post-Soviet space, including Russia.

The main disagreement in the Turkish-American relations is the U.S. policy of supporting the Kurds. The U.S. provides assistance to Kurds living in Turkey and categorically prohibits Ankara from full-fledged military operations against the Syrian Kurds.

Traditional (though tacit) areas of cooperation between Turkey and the United States include counteraction to Iran and ousting Russia from the Caucasus region. However, after a failed attempt of coup d'état in Turkey, organized by Fethullah Gülen allegedly living in the United States, the relations between Turkey and the USA entered a phase of uncertainty. The U.S. base Ingirlik located on the territory of Turkey was sealed.

22. Syria
Relationship status - Open confrontation

Syria is in a state of acute conflict with the U.S. (at the level of the official leadership of the countries).

The Administration of Donald Trump generally continued the course of Barack Obama on direct intervention in the conflict in the Syrian Arab Republic. The position of the current U.S. leadership can be considered not quite definite. The USA combines a tough policy towards the pro-government forces in Syria with periodic attempts to interact with the allies of the Syrian leadership (Russia) to resolve the situation in the country. In Syria itself, the U.S. is perceived as an aggressor country. The U.S. mediation services in the establishment of peace are not welcomed by the leadership of the SAR. Changes in the relations between the two countries are possible under new configuration of power in Syria (for example, expansion of representation of the so-called moderate opposition or Kurds, the U.S. allies). These prospects are also uncertain.

23. Israel
Relationship status - An ally country / close interaction

Israel is one of the main allies of the USA in the world, despite some difficulties at the present stage of relations.

The United States sees Israel as one of its key partners in the Middle East region. To maintain the relations the U.S. provides regular financial assistance to the country. For instance, in September 2016, Israel and the United States signed an agreement on military assistance for a period of ten years - from 2018 to 2028. The total amount of military financial support will reach $38 billion. The U.S. State Department reported that this is the largest military assistance program in the history of the United States.

Former U.S. President Barack Obama and Israeli Prime Minister Benjamin Netanyahu had difficult relations: after the arrival of the politicians to power in their countries, the process of negotiations with the

Palestinians about the possibility of creating two states was suspended. Even during the election, Obama strongly criticized the construction of new Jewish settlements on Palestinian lands, that is, what became an integral part of the policy of Netanyahu.

In addition, Obama supported the UN statement on the destruction of nuclear weapons in the Middle East, which involved control over the nuclear potential of Israel (officially, the country did not announce its availability).

There are also disagreements over Iran's nuclear program. Unlike the Israeli side, not ready for compromise, the United States considered the option of partial lifting of the sanctions from Iran in exchange for concessions on the transparency of their nuclear program.

With the coming of Donald Trump to power, the level of mutual understanding between Israel and the United States has grown significantly. Trump paid a visit to Israel in May 2017. Analysts note the growing influence of the pro-Israel lobby on the Middle East policy of the United States. The desire of the Trump Administration to review the nuclear deal with Iran proves this.

The U.S. missile defense radar is located on the territory of Israel.

24. Iraq
Relationship status - General friendship and active cooperation in at least one sphere (disagreements on other issues may exist)

The relations between Iraq and the United States **are uneasy**.

Fourteen years after the start of the American anti- terrorist campaign in Iraq, one-third of the country's residents now believe that Washington supports the terrorists of the ISIS. For the United States, Iraq is of strategic importance in terms of control over the Middle East region. Despite the withdrawal of the U.S. troops, the USA still has an impact on Iraqi internal political processes.

There are several American military facilities on the territory of Iraq: the Ramadi U.S. base, a U.S. airbase, etc.

25. Iran
Relationship status - Open confrontation

Today, **Iran is one of the most vociferous opponents of the U.S.** in the world.

With his criticism towards lifting of the sanctions from Iran, Donald Trump actually leveled the progress achieved by the agreements between Barack Obama and Hassan Rouhani. The position of the current U.S. administration is greatly influenced by the Israeli lobby in the United States.

26. Qatar
Relationship status - Tensions exist (temporal, so far)

Qatar has difficulties in relations with the U.S. but remains an important ally.

Qatar is one of the major footholds of the United States in the Middle East region. American multinationals ExxonMobil and Conoco Philips operate in Qatar. Former U.S. Secretary of State Rex Tillerson (until 2018) used to be president of ExxonMobil (2006-2016). El-Udeid, the largest air base of the U.S. Air Force in the Middle East, is located on the territory of Qatar.

The blockade of Qatar by a number of Middle Eastern countries and the USA's criticism (albeit indirect) of the Qatar's relations with terrorism, created tension between the two countries. The conflict is not permanent or acute. The United States is generally ready for mediation in resolving the dispute over Qatar. Transfer or liquidation of the U.S. air base from the territory of the country is not planned.

27. Saudi Arabia
Relationship status - An ally country / close interaction

For many years, **Saudi Arabia has been a strategic partner of the United States in the Middle East**, however a **number of difficulties** have recently arisen in their relations.

The seeming flexibility of the U.S. towards Iran reduces the confidence of Saudi Arabia. The Kingdom of Saudi Arabia wages an expensive war in Yemen and is subjected to presser from Iran, which is becoming stronger.

Stability in Saudi Arabia and the Persian Gulf continues to be of key interest to the United States. After the Trump's visit in May 2017, the states signed contracts worth about $ 350 billion dollars, of which $ 110 billion were to be spent on combating the Iranian threat.

There are several U.S. military facilities located on the territory of Saudi Arabia: the Escan U.S. base, the King Fahd airbase, etc.

28. Yemen
Relationship status – Tensions exist (temporal, so far)

Yemen is in a state of civil war and a military crisis. The U.S. is not formally involved in the conflict. Through the UN Security Council, the United States pursues a policy of sanctions (restrictions on the supply of arms). The U.S. tacitly favors one of the parties to the conflict (the one supported by Saudi Arabia).

29. United Arab Emirates
Relationship status – General friendship and active cooperation in at least one sphere (disagreements on other issues may exist)

United Arab Emirates is in partnership relations with the United States.

The United States provides financial support to the UAE in the development of the nuclear industry.

The Al-Dafra U.S. airbase is located on the territory of the UAE.

30. Georgia
Relationship status - General friendship and active cooperation in at least one sphere (disagreements on other issues may exist)

Georgia is in partnership relations with the United States.

It is important for the U.S. to control Georgia as one of the main representatives of its interests in the post-Soviet space. Georgia is also important and useful for advancing the U.S. interests in the Transcaucasus against Turkey.

31. Armenia
Relationship status - Neutral relations / limited contacts

Armenia is in quite neutral relations with the United States.

The main cause for tension in the relations is the U.S. position on Iran – one of Armenia's key economic partners. The Armenian lobby in the USA is extremely strong.

32. Azerbaijan
Relationship status - Neutral relations / limited contacts

Azerbaijan is in neutral (with a plus sign) relations with the United States.

The administration of Trump took, in fact, a neutral position on the key issue for Azerbaijan (Nagorno-Karabakh). The U.S. is interested in the stability of the region to ensure the operation of its oil and gas companies (the Baku-Tbilisi-Ceyhan oil pipeline). The U.S. is interested in Azerbaijan as a big oil player, Iran's rival in the Caspian region and Turkey's main trading partner.

33. Kyrgyzstan
Relationship status - Tensions exist (temporal, so far)

Kyrgyzstan is in neutral (with a minus sign) relations with the United States. These relations are important for the United States because of the access to Afghanistan and Central Asia, as well as to the southern borders of Russia. After a U.S. base was withdrawn from Kyrgyzstan, there is a certain tension.

34. Kazakhstan
Relationship status - Neutral relations / limited contacts

Kazakhstan is in neutral relations with the United States. Kazakhstan is part of the U.S. geopolitical plans for the creation of Great Central Asia - from Afghanistan to the Middle East. Today, a program of military cooperation between the countries for 2018-2022 is in force. The program implies the possibility of building a U.S. base in Kazakhstan.

35. Tajikistan
Relationship status - Neutral relations / limited contacts

Tajikistan is in neutral relations with the United States.
The USA is mainly interested in Tajikistan as a neighbor of Afghanistan. In 2010, Tajbat was formed with the financial support of the United States. Tajbat is a Tajik peacekeeping battalion, conducting exercises abroad under the patronage of Washington.

36. Uzbekistan
Relationship status - Neutral relations / limited contacts

Uzbekistan is gradually building cooperation with the United States. Interaction is limited for the time being.

After the change of leadership of Uzbekistan, the U.S. took an attempt to "come back" to Uzbekistan (for the first time after the Andijan events of 2005). Uzbekistan is the only country, for which the United States Agency for International Development (USAID) increased funding. Both sides, Shavkat Mirziyoyev and Donald Tramp, express sympathy for each other and their intention to cooperate in the future.

Cooperation with Uzbekistan is based on the operation of the Northern Distribution Network (NDN), a land route for the delivery of military cargo to the Coalition and NATO forces through the north of Afghanistan, since the southern routes through Pakistan are too dangerous.

37. Turkmenistan
Relationship status - Tensions exist (temporal, so far)

Turkmenistan has disagreements with the U.S. in the gas sector.

The Turkmenistan–Afghanistan–Pakistan–India gas pipeline project (TAPI) runs counter to the interests of the U.S. in the Asian region. China is one of the main consumers of Turkmen gas.

38. Afghanistan
Relationship status - General friendship and active cooperation in at least one sphere (disagreements on other issues may exist)

The leadership of Afghanistan **is directly influenced by the United States.** However, this balance cannot be considered sustainable, since the allied relations are determined solely by the presence of the U.S. military contingent on the territory of the country. Afghanistan **can be conditionally called an ally of the United States,** but the country does not have a full-fledged independent policy. The increase of the U.S. presence in

Afghanistan, announced by Trump, ensured preservation of the current balance in the relations between the two countries.

ASIA (SOUTH, EAST, SOUTH-EAST ASIA)

39. Pakistan
Relationship status - Tensions exist (temporal, so far)

Pakistan's relations with the United States are gradually worsening.

The United States increasingly criticizes Pakistan (for supporting terrorism and "chaos") and establishes cooperation with India. At the same time, the U.S. hints Pakistan at the possibility of financing, thereby forcing Islamabad to opt for the U.S. (as opposed to China). The current trend is deterioration.

40. India
Relationship status - General friendship and active cooperation in at least one sphere (disagreements on other issues may exist)

India actively develops cooperation with the United States.

At the meeting of Donald Trump and Indian Prime Minister Narendra Modi on June 26, 2017, the American leader noted that the relations between the two countries had never been as good as they were at that moment. At the meeting it was agreed to sell India 22 unmanned reconnaissance aircrafts worth $2 billion, so that New Delhi could monitor Chinese activities in the Indian Ocean.

Provision of economic assistance to Afghanistan is another area of the U.S.-Indian relations.

41. People's Republic of China
Relationship status - Conflict / pre-conflict / traditional tensions

China is the most important trade and economic partner and, simultaneously, the main geopolitical rival of the United States. However, if earlier the confrontation between the two countries had been more cautious, then, with the Trump's coming to power, there emerged a threat of a full-scale political, economic, and even military confrontation, according to some estimates. The controversy is aggravating, mainly through the efforts of Washington.

The U.S.-China trade relations come to the forefront. Donald Trump apparently intends to fulfill his pre-election promises to resolve the issue of the so-called "unbalanced trade between China and the United States" and bring production facilities back to their homeland. The United States has already taken steps in this direction; for example, investigations were launched against China on violation of technology transfer rights. Under the pretext of assistance to the North Korean regime, the U.S. imposed sanctions against some Chinese companies. According to some experts and representatives of the White House, the "trade war" between China and the USA is gradually unfolding.

There is a tense situation around the disputed islands in the South China Sea, with minor incidents, so far; but the U.S. military have resorted to provocative rhetoric about the use of nuclear weapons. Besides, the U.S. has recently begun to resolutely strengthen traditional alliances with the countries of the region opposing the PRC (Japan, the Republic of Korea,

India, Vietnam, etc.). The tests of ballistic missiles by North Korea did not lead the U.S. and China to a closer dialogue on the problem, and even on the contrary, Trump began using the "North Korean tests" to exert pressure on China. The tension in the U.S.-China relations is also caused by the issue of deployment of the American missile defense system on the territory of South Korea (as a potential threat to China).

42. Japan
Relationship status – An ally country / close interaction

Japan has close ties with the U.S. in the field of politics, economy and security.

Japan restrains China in Northeast Asia (including in the interests of the United States). The bilateral treaty since the Cold War suited both sides: Japan economized on defense and concentrated on economic development, while the U.S. could use Japanese territory as an "unsinkable aircraft carrier" to maintain its military and political presence in East Asia.

Donald Tramp and Shinzo Abe openly expressed the desire for further cooperation. Controversy over the U.S. military presence on the Okinawa Island did not disrupt the balance between the two countries. At the current stage, the USA returned Japan a part of the territory occupied by the U.S. Marine Corps air base.

There are several U.S. military bases located in Japan, including the Misawa Air Force base and the Kamiseya Naval base.

43. The Republic of Korea
Relationship status – An ally country / close interaction

The Republic of Korea maintains friendly relations with the USA.

South Korea is a zone of strategic interests for the United States. Maintenance of partnership relations with South Korea is beneficial for the

United States for geopolitical reasons, as an opportunity to gain a foothold in the immediate vicinity of the Russian maritime borders in the Pacific.

The alliance South Korea – the USA is also a link in the coalition South Korea – the USA – Japan. A well-established alliance between Japan and the United States increases the security of South Korea.

For the United States, such an alliance is useful in the fight against China for domination in Northeast Asia.

South Korea depends on the ability of the U.S. to resist in a full-scale war with the DPRK. There are a large number of American bases on the territory of South Korea: Red Cloud, Kunsan, etc.

44. Democratic People's Republic of Korea
Relationship status - Open confrontation

The DPRK is in confrontational relations with the United States.

The last round of the conflict between the U.S. and the DPRK was provoked by the rigid rhetoric of Trump towards North Korea (the goal was to press on China through the DPRK and force the former to assist the U.S. in resolving (at least partial) the North Korean problem).

The fact revealed during the confrontation that North Korea is capable of delivering warheads to U.S. territory (Guam) and potentially to the shores of the United States, limited room for maneuver for the United States and neared the possibility of a military conflict on the Korean peninsula.

As of today, the U.S. – North Korean relations have been put on the pause again (probably temporarily).

45. Thailand
Relationship status - Neutral relations / limited contacts

Thailand is in neutral relations with the United States.

Regular coups d'états make Bangkok an unreliable partner for the United States in the South Asian region. The presence of the military in the government of Thailand restricts the relations between the two countries (it is disadvantageous for the United States' reputation).

The U.S. Marines are serving on the territory of Thailand.

46. Vietnam
Relationship status - General friendship and active cooperation in at least one sphere (disagreements on other issues may exist)

Vietnam is in partnership with the United States, despite historical contradictions. The main reason for the cooperation is the strengthening of China's positions in the Asia–Pacific Region, which is disadvantageous for both sides.

47. Myanmar
Relationship status - Neutral relations / limited contacts

In recent years, **the relations between Myanmar and the United States have partially improved.** The United States intends to turn Myanmar into a model for all the authoritarian countries (developing ones). There are many minerals in Myanmar: oil, gas, gold, silver, uranium, etc. However, U.S. companies are not yet adapted to work there.

48. Malaysia
Relationship status - Neutral relations / limited contacts

Malaysia is in neutral relations with the United States. Malaysia was seen as one of the allies in the APR.

49. Indonesia
Relationship status - Neutral relations / limited contacts

Indonesia strives to establish partnership relations with the United States. With the coming to power of Barack Obama, who spent his childhood in Jakarta, the U.S.–Indonesian relations became warmer. The United States and Indonesia are also planning cooperation in the anti-terrorist area.

50. Philippines
Relationship status - General friendship and active cooperation in at least one sphere (disagreements on other issues may exist)

The Republic of Philippines is in friendly relations with the USA., despite the harsh statements by new Philippine President Rodrigo Duterte against Barack Obama and the U.S. as a whole. Dutterte congratulated Trump on the victory in the election and stated on the prospects for cooperation. In turn, Trump expressed respect to the leadership of the Philippines. At the same time, part of the U.S. establishment and general public criticize the current leadership of the country for too harsh measures of combating drug trafficking.

A division of the U.S. Army is stationed on the territory of the Philippines. In April 2014, the countries signed a military agreement, under which the U.S. aviation and ships can be stationed in the Philippines.

AUSTRALIA AND OCEANIA

51. Australia
Relationship status - General friendship and active cooperation in at least one sphere (disagreements on other issues may exist)

Australia is a traditional ally of the United States. However, at present, the leaderships of the two countries do not find mutual understanding (the migration issue).

NORTH AND LATIN AMERICA

52. Canada
Relationship status - An ally country / close interaction

Canada is in partnership with the United States. Canada is one of the main importers of American products. One of the topical issues in the relations between the countries is the United States' withdrawal from the North American Free Trade Agreement (NAFTA) and the subsequent review of the agreement. The U.S. withdrawal from the agreement will not affect the relations of the countries that concluded bilateral trade agreements.

A military unit of the U.S. Armed Forces is located on the territory of Canada.

53. Mexico
Relationship status - Tensions exist (temporal, so far)

Mexico is in strong economic relations with the U.S., but there is a trend of their deterioration in the political sphere. If the U.S. withdraws from NAFTA, the Mexican economy may suffer greatly, since most of its exports are U.S.-oriented. The issue of labor migration from Mexico, sharply raised by Donald Trump, adds tension to the relations. The leaders of the two countries feel mutual dislike.

54. Nicaragua
Relationship status - Conflict / pre-conflict / traditional tensions

Historically, **Nicaragua is in difficult relations with the United States.** Nicaragua cooperates with Russia in economic and military spheres.

55. Cuba
Relationship status - Conflict / pre-conflict / traditional tensions

Cuba is still in rather strained diplomatic relations with the U.S., despite the changes in the sphere of economic cooperation in recent years.

The so-called "Cuban thaw" began in late 2014, when U.S. President Barack Obama and Cuba's leader Raul Castro announced resumption of the bilateral relations between. In the summer of 2015, the operation of the embassies of both countries was resumed. In 2016, Barack Obama paid a two-day visit to Cuba, which was the first official visit of the U.S. President since 1928. American business received the opportunity to invest in Cuba, subject to special permission from the U.S. Treasury. Certain bans on money transfers from the U.S. to Cuba were removed, and a number of restrictions on the work of the Cubans in the United States were lifted. The fact that the United States has the opportunity to regain control through Cuba over a significant part of the Latin American region, which is experiencing the "crisis of the left-wing ideology", is the main profit from these reforms for the U.S.

However, despite all the innovations, the relations between the U.S. and Cuba continue to be tense. Thus, Trump introduced new restrictive measures into the Cuban-American relations, for example, a ban on visiting Cuba alone. The U.S. is cutting the diplomatic mission in Cuba against the background of the scandal with "acoustic attacks" on American diplomats in Havana.

56. Venezuela
Relationship status - Conflict / pre-conflict / traditional tensions

Venezuela is in the conflict phase of relations with the United States.

During the period of Hugo Chavez's presidency, the U.S. maintained economic ties with Venezuela, but could not exert political influence on the processes in the country and the region. After the death of Chavez and the onset of the crisis of world oil prices, it became more difficult for Venezuela to support financially the allied "left" regimes in the region. The leave of the bright leader in the person of Chavez also influenced the "crisis of the left-wing ideology" in the region. In turn, the U.S. saw the opportunity to regain its influence in Latin America. They chose the way of confronting the current leadership of Venezuela and supporting the opposition.

57. Colombia
Relationship status - Neutral relations / limited contacts

Colombia is in quite neutral relations with the United States. For a long time Colombia enjoyed financial support from Venezuela. The main topics of the dialogue with the United States are the fight against drug trafficking (an extremely active role of the United States) and terrorism.

58. Brazil
Relationship status - Neutral relations / limited contacts

Brazil is in neutral relations with the U.S., despite a period of tension or political "incidents". For example, the fact of espionage by U.S. intelligence agencies against the former president of Brazil, Dilma Russef, was revealed, which complicated the process of reaching a new level of bilateral relations. Brazil is focused on the BRICS partner countries and cooperation with Iran in the oil sector, which also does not suit the U.S. side.

59. Argentina
Relationship status - Neutral relations / limited contacts

Argentina is in neutral relations with the United States. Until recently, Argentina adhered to the left-wing political course, but the 2016 presidential election was won by an advocate of market economy Mauricio Macri, who is ready for close cooperation with the U.S. in the economic sphere.

60. Ecuador
Relationship status - Neutral relations / limited contacts

Ecuador is in neutral relations with the United States. Ecuador cooperates with the U.S. in the sphere of trade, at the same time developing economic relations with Russia, in particular, in the field of medicine.

61. Peru
Relationship status - General friendship and active cooperation in at least one sphere (disagreements on other issues may exist)

Peru is in partner political relations with the United States, which are expressed in the joint pressure on the government of Venezuela.

AFRICA

62. Egypt
Relationship status - Tensions exist (temporal, so far)

In recent decades, Egypt was one of the traditional U.S. allies in the region, enjoying solid financial support. After the coming of Abdul-Fattah As-Sisi to power in Egypt, the relations became more strained (e.g., the United States refused to allocate almost $300 million to Egypt due to non-compliance with human rights by its authorities).

The dissatisfaction of Egypt is due to the overactive role of the U.S. in supporting the so-called "Arab spring" and the "betrayal" of Hosni Mubarak, who was a faithful representative of the U.S. interests.

The Israeli lobby of the United States is interested in Egypt's active role in the settlement of the Arab-Israeli conflict.

The U.S. relations with Egypt are somewhat tense now, but without an open confrontation.

63. Libya
Relationship status - Tensions exist (temporal, so far)

Libya's relations with the United States are difficult to characterize because of the lack of statehood in Libya. The United States supported a coup in Libya and murder of Muammar Gaddafi. At the same time, the role of the United States was not the most active. The incident with the murder of the U.S. ambassador to Libya showed the inability of the current "recognized" government of Libya to ensure security in the country, and, of course, damaged the relations between the two countries. There are Special Operations Forces of the U.S. Army (SOF) in Libya.

64. Algeria
Relationship status - Conflict / pre-conflict / traditional tensions

Algeria is in difficult relations with the United States. In recent years, Algeria has opposed the implementation of the plans of Qatar, Saudi Arabia and other traditional partners of the United States in the region. For example, in 2015, the Algerian leadership declined the proposal of Riyadh to send the "joint Sunni army" in Yemen against the pro-Iranian Huthis acting there.

Disagreements are also present in the field of countering terrorist organizations. Thus, in 2015 Algeria rejected the American proposal of cooperation in the fight against ISIL in Libya.

65. Ethiopia
Relationship status - General friendship and active cooperation in at least one sphere (disagreements on other issues may exist)

Ethiopia cooperates with the United States in the military sphere. There is an American military base on the territory of Ethiopia, near Arba Myncz.

66. Morocco
Relationship status - General friendship and active cooperation in at least one sphere (disagreements on other issues may exist)

Morocco cooperates with the United States in the military sphere. Since 2004, the country has had the status of an important U.S. ally outside NATO.

67. Kenya
Relationship status - Neutral relations / limited contacts

Since gaining independence Kenya has been focused on cooperation with Western countries, including the United States. The population of Kenya (large cities) speaks fluent English (a state language). The Kenyan origin of Barack Obama **strengthened the political relations between Kenya and the United States. However, the USA's relations with the African country are not close.** In parallel, China's interests are represented in Kenya more and more widely.

68. Republic of South Africa
Relationship status - Neutral relations / limited contacts

In the 2000's, South Africa's relations with the United States were unstable. In 2007, South Africa protested against the deployment of the African Command (AFRICOM) of the U.S. on the continent. In recent years, South Africa and the United States led a low-grade trade war, which ended in 2016. South Africa eventually opened access to its market for American beef, pork and poultry. Despite tense situations, the country periodically expresses interest in cooperation. The USA and the RSA have a number of contracts in the financial and economic spheres. In general, as of today, **the relations have been established, and they are developing in a positive way**.

A small U.S. Marine Corps is stationed in South Africa.

ABOUT AUTHOR
ALEXEI MUKHIN

Alexei Mukhin was born in 1971 in Moscow into a family of doctors.

In 1995 he graduated from the Moscow State Institute for History and Archives (known as the Russian State University for the Humanities since 1991) as a historian and archivist specializing in Russian History of different periods.

Alexei Mukhin embarked upon his career in 1988 as a librarian in the library of the Trade Union Committee of the Central Aerohydrodynamic Institute (TsAGI) in the City of Zhukovsky, Moscow Region. After completing his service in the Armed Forces of the USSR in 1989-1991, Mr. Mukhin worked as a research assistant at the information and research center «Panorama» while simultaneously working towards his degree in Russian History.

In January 1996 Alexei Mukhin organized the Service for Political Information and Consultation - Center (SPIC-Center), an independent research organization and information agency, in which he held the position of Executive Director (later – Director).

Since 1997, Alexei Mukhin has served as the General Director of the Center for Political Information. The Center is an independent consulting company in the field of risk management, providing its clients with solutions in the sphere of political analysis and consulting, tools for reducing commercial risks and information support of their businesses, as well as a package of services in the field of corporate and personal reputation management. Clients of the Center include foreign and Russian oil and gas companies, financial and industrial holdings, as well as foreign embassies and consulates in Russia. In 2015 Alexei Mukhin co-founded the Center for Political Information – IT Ltd. Since 2017, he has served as President of the CENTRUM Foundation.

In 2002, Alexei Mukhin established and served as Editor-in-Chief of the Internet-based magazine FEC (Facts, Events, Comments). In 2004-2005 Alexei Mukhin led a special course "Information wars" at the Russian State Social University. In 2012, he became an Associate Professor at the Russian State University for the Humanities. In 2016-2017, he served as a Member of the Board of Trustees of the University and Consultant to the Rector.

Alexei Mukhin is an author of over 100 scientific papers, including monographs in the field of political science and the history of Russia. He is a member of the Association of Historians of intelligence services and participant in the "Social Environment" project by the Russian Ministry of Defense. He participates in the Valdai Club and has been a member of the Valdai Club Academy since 2016. He has also participated in the annual International Economic Forum in Krynica (Poland).

Alexei Mukhin serves on the Expert Council for the Chairman of the State Duma of the Russian Federation. Since 2012 he has been an active participant of "Open Tribune" round-tables at the State Duma. He is also a member of the Expert Council for the Government of the Tatarstan Republic.

Mr. Mukhin is a columnist of Echo of Moscow, Slon.ru, RBC-daily, Nezavisimaya Gazeta, Argumenti Nedeli. Alexei Mukhin's comments on current political and economic developments are regularly cited by the leading national and international media, such as Spiegel, The New York Times, Le Figaro, France 24, Deutsche Welle, Kommersant, Vedomosti, RBC-daily, Nezavisimaya Gazeta, Expert, Profile, Izvestia, Channel One, Russia today, Channel 5, Business FM, Finam FM, Kommersant FM, Echo of Moscow and many others.

Spheres of Alexei Mukhin's professional interests include:

- political analysis (analysis of political processes);
- formation, behavior, and psychology of elites;
- military reform and the reform of the Russian intelligence services;
- state agencies and the administrative reform in the Russian Federation;
- national security;
- economic risks;
- organized crime;
- fighting corruption;
- Russian regional political processes.

Alexei Mukhin's hobbies include Oriental philosophy, psychology, world religions. He is the President of the Federation of Development of Aikido Ren Wa Kai, which in 2016 won the National Award «Tornado» in the category «Commitment to the traditions of Aikido». Alexei holds the Fourth Dan of Aikido. Since 2015 he has also been a Member of the Presidium of the Russian Aikido Aikikai Federation.

Made in USA

219

www.ingramcontent.com/pod-product-compliance
Lightning Source LLC
Chambersburg PA
CBHW022357280326
41935CB00007B/214